Budgeting

Budgeting

1st Edition

Athena Valentine Lent

Budgeting For Dummies®

Published by: **John Wiley & Sons, Inc.**, 111 River Street, Hoboken, NJ 07030-5774, www.wiley.com

Copyright © 2023 by John Wiley & Sons, Inc., Hoboken, New Jersey

Published simultaneously in Canada

For general information on our other products and services, please contact our Customer Care Department within the U.S. at 877-762-2974, outside the U.S. at 317-572-3993, or fax 317-572-4002. For technical support, please visit www.wiley.com/techsupport.

Wiley publishes in a variety of print and electronic formats and by print-on-demand. Some material included with standard print versions of this book may not be included in e-books or in print-on-demand. If this book refers to media such as a CD or DVD that is not included in the version you purchased, you may download this material at http://booksupport.wiley.com. For more information about Wiley products, visit www.wiley.com.

Library of Congress Control Number: 2023934393

ISBN 978-1-119-98514-3 (pbk); ISBN 978-1-119-98515-0 (ebk); ISBN 978-1-119-98516-7 (ebk)

SKY10059676_111023

Contents at a Glance

Table of Contents

Introduction

For most people, personal finance wasn't offered in high school until recently. Even now, it's usually not a required course to graduate. Millions of people are in debt, behind in retirement, or don't have any space in their finances to cover a minor emergency, such as a needed car repair. Many live paycheck to paycheck and don't see a clear way out. If you're one of the many who are overwhelmed by financial stress, a key strategy to help you finally gain control of your finances is to adopt a budgeting method that works for you.

TIP

One way to think of your finances is like a house, with budgeting as the foundation. You need a solid foundation before you place your walls (financial goals) and roof (your overall financially healthy self).

But budgeting itself can feel overwhelming or pointless for various reasons. A fluctuating income makes planning harder and raises inflation costs. Random emergencies, including changes in life circumstances, pop up when you least expect them. People are managing work lives, running households, and attending to their relationships and even personal goals. No wonder they can have difficulty sticking to a budget!

Traditional financial advice doesn't stress the importance of a budget enough. A budget can help you make your money work for you by showing you how much you have coming in and going out at all times. After you're fully aware of your income and expenses, you can plan for your future while living in the present.

To get started, you need a budgeting method that works for you. Along with tracking your income and spending, finding out what your pain point is so that you can make your budget stick is important. That's where *Budgeting For Dummies* comes in. The information in this book can help you figure all that out, as well as pay off debt, save for a rainy day, prepare for a change in life circumstances, and live life on your terms so no matter what life throws your way, you'll be ready without blinking an eye.

About This Book

Here are some things you can expect to find in this book and not necessarily others:

>> The budgeting method that some are surprised to find out is one.

>> Why you automatically spend less when using cash envelopes.

>> The importance of fun money and how it actually helps when saving for the future.

>> How to invest on a budget. You read that right: You can invest on a budget because investing shouldn't be a pipe dream. I also share ways that you can make money from saving your money.

>> Budgeting apps for teens, college students, singles, couples, and more. I'm talking budgeting in the 21st century, baby!

>> How a budget can help you save over $100,000 when purchasing a house.

Other experts may be hesitant to share their financial bloopers, but I put my financial mistakes in print for you and all the world to see. I share my experiences with you, even if they're embarrassing, because I hope you can get something from them the same way I did.

As a nationally certified trauma support specialist, I also know that money can be emotional. Everyone has their own hang-ups, which can prevent them from using a budget correctly. That's why I feel sharing all the resources I can is essential. Throughout this book, I recommend financial tools and budgeting methods, share financial resources, and provide strategies to talk to bill collectors when times are tough. I prioritized ensuring the websites and apps I recommend are unbiased so you can make your money work for you.

The number one thing I loved about writing a *For Dummies* book was knowing that you don't have to read it from front to back to get something out of it. Each chapter explains concepts in depth and lets you know where you can find out additional information in other chapters. I also loved the ability to bring you real-life examples throughout the book to help show how the information may pertain to you.

Foolish Assumptions

I'm not going to lie. My cat and I made some assumptions about who may read this book. We assumed the following:

>> You appreciate humor and feel absorbing information is easier when you can relate to an expert.

>> You've never made a budget before, or you have but didn't follow through or it just didn't work out.

>> You love your money so much you want to take care of it.

>> You know you should budget but don't know how.

>> You're budgeting for the first time on your own, as a single parent, or as a couple.

>> You have financial goals.

>> You want a shame-free space to figure out budgeting at your own pace.

Money is personal, which includes your budget. I want you to know that I acknowledge this fact and do my best to help you feel comfortable along the way.

Icons Used in This Book

I sprinkle the following icons throughout this book to help you find the information you may need in your budgeting journey.

This icon shares tidbits that can help you succeed at budgeting.

Consider this icon as my gentle reminder for you to file away certain important aspects of budgeting.

Make sure you pay attention to these icons to avoid budgeting blunders.

This icon designates info that's interesting but ultimately not crucial to understanding the topic. If you're short on time, you can skip these paragraphs.

Beyond the Book

In addition to the information in this book, you also have access to other free resources. I created a budgeting Cheat Sheet to help you put together a successful budget. You can find it, along with other personal finance–related information, by going to www.dummies.com and entering "Budgeting For Dummies Cheat Sheet" in the search bar.

Where to Go from Here

You don't have to read *For Dummies* books from start to finish, so feel free to look through the book in any order to read about different topics related to budgeting. I suggest starting with the budgeting methods in Part 2. If you're interested in a particular type of budget, you can also flip to the Index or Table of Contents to find the corresponding page numbers. I also recommend making sure you know the importance of saving for an emergency by reading Chapter 8.

Have fun!

1

All about Budgeting

Review what a budget is, figure out why you can't seem to make one work, and assess your overall financial picture.

Examine the parts of a budget to successfully align your spending with your income.

IN THIS CHAPTER

» **Breaking down the benefits of budgeting**

» **Checking out common budget pitfalls**

» **Getting a quick snapshot of your financial situation**

Chapter **1**

Beginning with Budgeting Basics

Raise your hand if you know where your money went last month. According to a survey published by Mint.com on December 11, 2020, 65 percent of Americans have no clue where they spent their money in the previous month. Basically, millions of people are saying that their money disappeared without their knowing its whereabouts. No wonder money is considered the number one stressor in today's society! (It's also one of the leading reasons people cite when filing for a divorce.)

I've been in the personal finance industry for over ten years, starting with blogs like Money Smart Latina and now as a contributor on *Slate* magazine and BuzzFeed. I've seen and heard many people talk about money. But one thing I don't hear enough of is how accepting financial responsibility has helped them reach their personal goals.

If assuming responsibility isn't an issue, or even if it is, you're not alone. Millions of people are in debt, behind in retirement, or just don't have any space in their finances to cover a minor emergency, such as a needed car repair. Many live paycheck to paycheck and don't see a clear way out.

Because you've picked up this book, I'm going to assume you don't want to be one of those people. One of the key strategies to your newfound success? Finding a budgeting system that works for you. Budgeting is a basic financial concept that doesn't get enough credit for being one of the major parts of financial success.

Having a successful budget helps you accomplish whatever financial goals you may have, whether that's saving money, paying off debt, or something else. You can see in Figure 1-1 how much debt is costing people just like you. Knowing where your money goes and how much you have coming in is key to getting you where you need to be.

REMEMBER

Budgeting tells your money where to go and not the other way around. By properly utilizing a budget, you aren't clueless and wondering where your money goes every month like everyone else.

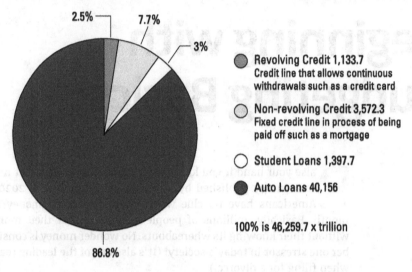

2.5%   7.7%

3%

● Revolving Credit 1,133.7
Credit line that allows continuous
withdrawals such as a credit card

○ Non-revolving Credit 3,572.3
Fixed credit line in process of being
paid off such as a mortgage

○ Student Loans 1,397.7

● Auto Loans 40,156

100% is 46,259.7 x trillion

86.8%

FIGURE 1-1:
Debt load
carried by the
United States of
America as of
October 2022.

Source: The Federal Reserve Consumer Credit G. 19, (www.federalreserve.gov/releases/g19/current/default.htm)

Knowing What a Budget Is and Why You Should Use One

A *budget* is a plan that tracks where you'll spend your money. Think of your budget as a monthly money to-do list. A budget helps you make sure your finances are in order so you can save for a rainy day (an emergency fund), spend your money on things that matter, and make sure all your bills are taken care of. Budgeting helps you take charge of your finances to ensure your current and future financial needs are met.

MY PATH TO BUDGETING

I didn't have the best financial role models growing up. My earliest memories of money involve my parents bouncing checks and frequenting the local pawnshop. Though I earned an allowance, I spent it as fast as I could, usually on a CD (remember those?) or a book. I lacked so much financial common sense that I got turned into Chex Systems when I was 18 years old.

Chex Systems is a national database that financial institutions report to with information about any checking or savings account you may have open, along with a history of your activity with these accounts. Based on this history, financial institutions can also check to see whether you're a risky customer since this database also stores any negative account history that resulted in closing one of your accounts due to abuse. Abuse can look like using your account to purchase items or goods you don't have money for, leaving your account in the red.

Since I didn't understand how a checking account worked, it was constantly negative. I always assumed I could just pay it back like a credit card without any consequences. I quickly learned this was not how a debit card worked when my account was closed and no other bank would allow me to open a new one.

Living in a small town right after high school was frustrating enough, but what made matters even worse was that I no longer had access to a traditional checking account or a debit card. So it was strictly cash spending only for me, baby. As much as I go on in Chapter 5 about cash envelopes, it's different when you don't have a say in the matter. I was able to squeak by because online pay wasn't a thing yet, but it was tough.

When I turned 22 and had a second chance at having a bank account, I realized more than ever that I needed help managing my money. I was only working part-time while going to school and needed to ensure I had enough funds to cover everything. I'd be remiss if I got turned over to Chex Systems again. Fool me once, shame on you; fool me twice, shame on my finances.

One thing I used to find terrifying was creating a personal budget — never mind the basic idea of sticking to one. I started reading everything the Internet offered about personal finance. Some concepts at the time were way over my head, and others didn't apply to me or my situation. But one thing a lot of the articles I read had in common was advocating for the importance of a budget.

Budgeting can be challenging, but it can also impact your life more than you realize. Here are several reasons why you should be budgeting:

>> **You can control your spending.** When you have more cash going out than coming in, you find yourself in a *deficit*. A deficit means you end up short on money for your bills. You can have a deficit if you don't have enough income to cover your general expenses. This scenario is one of the main ways people find themselves in credit card debt. If you know where your money is going, you can manage your spending and keep your account with a positive balance.

>> **You're less likely to waste time and money.** It's okay to be disorganized sometimes. You live a busy life and, in the words of the living meme Kimberly "Sweet Brown" Wilkins, "Ain't nobody got time for that." But disorganized finances can hurt you in the long run. You lose time looking for bills. You lose money by paying an occasional (or frequent) late fee because you forget when your bills are due. Utilizing a budget helps get you back on track to ensure your bills are in order so you're making payments on time. Time and money are two of the most powerful resources you don't want to waste.

Another way you can fritter away time and money is unnecessary shopping. Getting sucked into reading a list of items you need to buy from a major retailer while you're just trying to browse your social media is so easy. One minute you're buying cool pillowcases from Amazon, and the next, you receive an insufficient funds text from your bank. When you know exactly how much cash you can spend in a particular area, you're less likely to spend time scrolling for items to buy.

>> **It helps you make progress on your short- and long-term goals.** I'm going to assume that you have goals (if not, make some!). A budget helps free up money for accomplishing them. Budgets can also help you track your progress to see whether you're moving that needle closer to the finish line.

If you're like me, you've had times when you could've benefited from having extra cash. When you practice budgeting, you become more aware of when your money is coming in and where it's going, making you think about your finances differently. This knowledge will likely lead you to putting more money toward any savings goals you may have or allow you to pay off your debt faster. The faster you pay off your debt, the less money you pay toward interest and finance charges.

>> **It helps you flex your "be resourceful" muscle.** When people first start budgeting, they often realize that they may not have enough money to cover all their wants and needs and still have some to stash away for a rainy day.

When trying to make your money stretch further, you may find yourself trying to be more resourceful than usual. For example, instead of buying new shorts last year, I made a pair of jeans into cutoffs. They looked cute, and I was able to put that $25 away for my friend's wedding.

>> **It can save your physical, emotional, and mental health.** In 2016, the Mayo Clinic published a study saying that stress is one the number one causes of insomnia. Stress comes in all shapes and forms, but money problems definitely have a habit of keeping you up at night. Budgeting can keep you from wondering where your money is and how you'll pay your bills.

>> **Gaining financial stability is a game-changer.** Utilizing a budget that works for you is key to financial stability, which is a huge part of financial wellness. Besides feeling a sense of pride, you have the comfort of knowing your life is financially covered no matter what. When you're financially stable, you can leave toxic employer situations and unsafe relationships or cover emergency expenses, all on your own.

One of the ways a budget can help you gain financial stability is by allowing you to save for emergencies adequately. An emergency fund (which I discuss more in the later section "You don't have an emergency fund" and in Chapter 8) is a type of savings account that helps you when unexpected expenses crop up from time to time. It can keep these issues from turning into bigger ones because you're able to cover them without thinking twice.

>> **It helps you think about retirement before it's too late.** Setting aside money for a rainy day isn't the only reason you should be budgeting. Your retirement is also essential and can be an overlooked category. Many employers match retirement contributions, but when money doesn't flow like wine, taking them up on the offer can be hard. To start saving as early as possible to take advantage of compound interest (as shown in Figure 1-2) is important, but it can also be more complicated when your cash flow is strapped.

REMEMBER

Compound interest is commonly referred to as "interest earned on interest." When you save or invest, your money has the opportunity to make money grow, which is usually referred to as a dividend or gain. So say you saved $200 and earned 10 percent on it annually. This leaves you with a new total of $220. So now, you'll earn 10 percent on $220, not just the additional $200 you originally saved. This is how you earn interest on interest. With compound investing, you can invest any amount and still earn money without having to invest another cent.

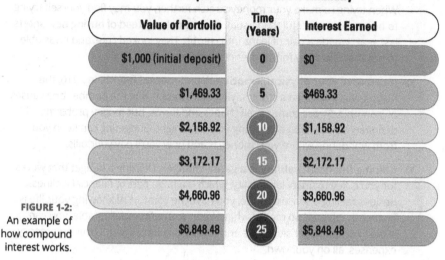

Compound Interest at 8% Annually

Value of Portfolio	Time (Years)	Interest Earned
$1,000 (initial deposit)	0	$0
$1,469.33	5	$469.33
$2,158.92	10	$1,158.92
$3,172.17	15	$2,172.17
$4,660.96	20	$3,660.96
$6,848.48	25	$5,848.48

FIGURE 1-2: An example of how compound interest works.

Living a happy and fulfilled life is hard to do when your cash flow isn't meeting your needs. I believe everyone has the right to live a life they love. You should get up every day and have something to look forward to. Money can't buy happiness, but it can help you accomplish your life's dreams. It can help you travel to that country you've always wanted to visit but have never been able to make time for. It can also help you treat your loved ones or help someone you care about out of a bind. It can even buy you a delicious coffee at the store while you smell the nice candles.

Understanding Why People Think Budgets Fail

Budgets get a bad rap, and many people hate them. They can feel too restrictive; isn't life supposed to be enjoyed? Maybe you've tried a budget and it just didn't work, or tracking down all your bills was too stressful.

I may lose my personal finance street cred, but I've agreed with these statements. A budget can be time-consuming, frustrating, and exhausting for a few reasons, as I explain in the following sections.

You forget to adjust it

One of the first steps of creating a budget is figuring out the different expense categories and then assigning an amount of money to each one. As time goes on, however, and your life and needs change, those original assignments may not work anymore. That's why adjusting your categories is essential to utilizing a budget after you create one. You can learn more about the different types of categories in Part 2.

For example, one of the categories in my budget is for my pet expenses. When I first adopted my cat from a foster family in 2015, he was relatively low maintenance. He was content living in his new digs except for litter and food. After a year of coexisting, he randomly became severely ill, which led to a diagnosis of FIV (feline immunodeficiency virus). After saving up an emergency fund for any future vet visits, I went back to putting aside $25 a month for his other expenses.

My budget remained untouched until 2019, when he had a bladder blockage that was so severe his only chance was to undergo an experimental procedure. It was successful, and to this day, I'm incredibly grateful. But one thing I hadn't planned for was the havoc it would wreak on my ability to manage my budget.

I now had to account for so many expenses I hadn't before, like medications and prescription cat food. After one month of these new expenses, I found myself scrambling to pay my rent. I reran my numbers, and that's when I realized I was still acting like I had a healthy cat. I'd forgotten to allocate additional funds to that category and kept spending as I had been.

You may find allocating a certain amount of money to a category, only to overspend, frustrating. This situation is one-way budgeting can make you feel bad. It can also have you feeling hopeless if you keep overspending and don't see a way out. But doing the work and adjusting your allocations to bring them in line with your current reality can help eliminate this stress.

When starting your new budgeting situation, you may realize you have emotions tied to your money that you weren't aware of before. If you're feeling stressed, take a ten-minute break and then come back. Going for a walk, doing some quick yoga, taking deep breaths for a few minutes, or drinking a glass of water can all be ways to refocus your mind before returning to the task at hand.

You don't have an emergency fund

An *emergency fund* is money you set aside for unexpected expenses or emergencies; car repairs, medical bills, trips to take your furry friend to the veterinarian, catching a flight to see a sick family member, or dealing with a burst water heater are all excellent examples. If you're lucky, these types of costs aren't the kind that happen every day. But if you aren't lucky, one emergency can be enough to derail your finances.

When unexpected calamities happen, you want a stack of cash sitting nice and neat for you, whether in a high-yield savings account or a cookie tin that's usually reserved for the sewing supplies.

However, if you don't have that stack of cash, something has to give. Sure, you have categories set up to pay for your gas and clothing, but you may not have a few hundred dollars put aside to take your car to the mechanic because it's making a funny noise. Because the money has to come from somewhere, you most likely have to take it from another category (or multiple categories), which is why your budget may not be working.

REMEMBER

Every time you're ill-equipped for an emergency, you'll most likely take on debt to cover it. Even when you have some cash to go toward an emergency, you may still need to look at alternative payment options, like putting it on a credit card or getting a personal loan. You're not a bad person for taking on debt, but when you do so, you also take on interest fees and finance charges. This arrangement means you're paying more money in the long run. Interest fees can add up to hundreds and sometimes thousands of dollars you're paying that could go elsewhere.

Even if you're not going into debt to cover an emergency, you're still ruining your budget. Budgeting helps you plan where your money is supposed to go in order to help you meet your goals. When you're too busy covering other expenses you didn't plan for, you don't accomplish your budgeting goals, and you eventually get frustrated because your budget isn't working.

WARNING

You have to be able to determine what is and isn't an emergency. Car repairs and vet bills are great examples of things you need to deal with immediately to prevent further problems. Getting a new phone because the latest version came out or tagging along on your friend's last-minute vacation? Not so much.

Your budget exceeds your income

The reason you can't seem to budget may be that your budget exceeds your income. This situation crops up in a couple of ways: spending excesses and living expenses, which I cover in the following sections.

Spending excesses exceed your income

If you're like me in my shopaholic days, your paycheck is spent the minute it hits your checking account. You don't even have to have a yen for shopping to have a spending problem. These days, everything is available at your fingertips right on your phone. Getting food delivered every night adds up. Adding stuff you don't need to your shopping cart just so you can get free home delivery is wasteful and can negatively impact your bank account. And don't forget all those streaming subscription services that you "need" to watch the latest shows.

WARNING

Having a shopping addiction can be a severe issue that budgeting may not be able to fix. I encourage you to seek professional help by meeting with a licensed therapist. You can also check out a support group like Debtors Anonymous (debtorsanonymous.org) or the group, Stopping Overshopping, created by Dr. April Lane Benson (behavioralcents.com/stopping-overshopping).

Living expenses exceed your income

Sometimes people know they make enough to get by and seem to be doing okay, so when an additional ongoing cost pops up, they don't overthink it. I mean, what's an additional $30 here and there?

Although that $30 here and there may not derail your overall financial picture, when you're consistently adding these expenses, you soon start to come up short. Even small amounts can come through your checking account at the worst time, causing insufficient fund fees when you least expect it.

Irregular pay schedules can also affect how well you're able to budget for living expenses. Many contractors and freelancers get paid huge sums after a project is due instead of receiving a steady paycheck, only to wonder where their funds went after paying all their bills. It can cause a nasty cycle of credit card debt or having to take on another part-time job to get by rather than focusing on their craft.

REMEMBER

Budgeting can relieve the heartache of having your bills exceed your income. When you sit down and realize where your money is going, assess your cash flow, and come up with a plan is when you find a light at the end of the tunnel.

Taking Inventory of Your Finances: A Spending Analysis

The first part of a new financial you is taking inventory of your finances. You're going to want to know where you're coming from so you can track your progress and pat yourself on the back when you start making actual financial moves.

By taking inventory of your finances, you can clarify where you stand financially — both good and bad. Here are just a few of the benefits:

>> **You have financial data to review anytime.** When you have actual numbers in front of you, you can assess where you're in good standing and where your finances may need a little work. Maybe you've been a rock star with that employer-matched 401(k) but have done little to pay down your student loans.

>> **You can set realistic monetary goals.** When you know your income and expenses, you know how much is left for things like debt repayment or saving for a vacation. It makes it possible to set a timeline for reaching those milestones.

>> **You notice when accounts don't serve your current needs.** You may discover you're paying credit card fees for a card you don't use. An account like a 529 Savings Plan may no longer be necessary because your child has changed their career goals. Maybe you're not earning enough in an investment vehicle, and that money can better serve you elsewhere. All these small things can add up to money lost.

>> **You can try to pay off debt faster, which can save you money.** By looking over your current liabilities, you may find that you can cut years off your payment timeline by making an additional payment or two. You may also realize that you can consolidate a current loan for a better interest rate.

>> **You can save time with organized finances.** Having all your accounts in one general place you can see, such as a spreadsheet or an online tool, can save you time and stress from having to always track them down individually. You can monitor due dates for debt repayments and check balances in accounts before any significant financial purchases are made. You also know which financial institution is in charge of what. You may uncover a forgotten bill or two that can still be saved from going into collections. And when any new accounts or bills come in, you can plug them in with the rest. I cover ways to organize your records in the later section, "Record-keeping systems."

I provide more in-depth instructions on how to make a list of your assets and liabilities later in this book. More specifically, I discuss how to track your expenses and income in Part 2. Below is an overview of the first steps of creating your budget. Think of it as an appetizer before the main meal.

Make a list of your financial assets and liabilities

Spoiler alert: This step may take a bit longer if you don't already have some kind of net-worth tracker or don't currently have all your financial accounts in one place. In the following sections, I give you an overview of assets and liabilities and your options for corralling your financial info in one place.

Assets

Financial assets are anything with a positive financial value. Lots of things can qualify as shown in Figure 1-3:

>> Checking and savings accounts, the cash you have under the mattress, and any checks you've been meaning to cash.

>> Money market accounts, your retirement fund at work, pensions, brokerage accounts, company stock shares, treasury bills, and bonds.

>> Some life insurance policies.

>> Physical items you can *liquidate* (convert into cash), such as your home; your car or other vehicles like ATVs, motorcycles, or boats; jewelry; collectibles; and anything else that you can sell for a profit. (That fancy purse you keep in a dust jacket that you can sell tomorrow for a few hundred dollars? Put that on the list, too.)

TIP

Make sure accounts such as financial assets have a beneficiary listed so your heirs have easy access. Having a will or trust is highly recommended because you never know what tomorrow will bring. Still, these can go to probate and can make your assets inaccessible to your beneficiaries for an extended period of time. You also want to ensure that will is detailed so there's no question of who inherits what. A clear and precise estate plan helps your loved ones focus on healing instead. See Chapter 14 for more information about estate planning.

Liabilities

Your *financial liabilities* are anything you owe money on. Your home is considered a positive financial asset (see the preceding section), but the mortgage you owe isn't. Other types of housing debt can include a second mortgage, a rental agreement, or property taxes.

Financial Asset Checklist

Traditional Banking

- [ ] Checking account
- [ ] Premium checking account
- [ ] Business checking account
- [ ] Rewards checking account
- [ ] Savings account
- [ ] High-yield savings accounts
- [ ] Money market account
- [ ] Certificates of deposit (CD)
- [ ] Prepaid cards
- [ ] Cash on hand

Retirement

- [ ] Traditional IRA
- [ ] Roth IRA
- [ ] 401(k)
- [ ] SIMPLE 401(k)
- [ ] 403(b)
- [ ] SIMPLE IRA plans
- [ ] SEP Plans (employee pensions)
- [ ] SARSEP Plans
- [ ] Federal government pension
- [ ] 457 plans

Brokerage

- [ ] Stocks
- [ ] Mutual funds
- [ ] Index funds
- [ ] Exchange-traded funds (ETFs)
- [ ] Government-issued bonds
- [ ] Corporate bonds
- [ ] Commodities
- [ ] Real Estate Investment Trusts (REITs)

College

- [ ] 529 Savings Plan
- [ ] Coverdell account
- [ ] Uniform Gift to Minor Accounts (UGMA)

Physical

- [ ] Real estate (primary residence)
- [ ] Real estate (rental properties)
- [ ] Vehicles (both primary and other)
- [ ] Jewelry
- [ ] Art and collectibles
- [ ] Life insurance policies
- [ ] Gold and other precious metals

FIGURE 1-3: A few suggestions of what can be considered a financial asset.

Other financial liabilities include the following:

>> Loans on other items you've financed, such as your car or education

>> Personal loans from a financial institution or family friend

>> Credit cards that currently have a balance

>> Other outstanding debt like medical bills

Even unpaid taxes, fines you owe a court, or child support can be considered financial liabilities.

Record-keeping systems

After you've made a list of all assets and liabilities off the top of your head (see the two preceding sections), track down any paperwork and/or information necessary to create an online account so that you can log into the accounts. Next, you need to decide how you want to keep all your financial documentation where it's not only safe but also accessible in case of an emergency.

You may choose to save your information in a spreadsheet program such as Microsoft Excel or enter all your information into an online tool like Personal Capital (www.personalcapital.com). Personal Capital is a net-worth tracking tool that takes your liabilities and subtracts them from your assets to determine your net worth. You aren't determining your net worth quite yet for this exercise, but this resource can be a neat tool to help get you started.

Another part of your record-keeping system should involve taking care of your physical paperwork. Having stacks of paper everywhere isn't helpful. You can store your paperwork in folders within a file box or filing cabinet; if you prefer a more minimalist approach, you can purchase a scanner, upload your paperwork to your computer, and discard the documents in a safe and secure manner.

Review your spending for the past three months

Anytime you're attempting a new goal, doing some research is a great idea. So for the second step to creating a budget, you need to review (research) the past three months of your spending habits. Where do you even start? Easy: your bank statements. Your bank has a lot of helpful information, including the option to see where your money is coming from and where it's flowing out.

TIP

Check whether your bank has a spending analysis tool. My bank has a "plan and learn" section that offers a spending report. It automatically breaks my spending into categories, shows me what I spend, and then gives me an overall percentage of where my money went for the month. This kind of resource can be a great place to start to see your spending in action.

Open a new spreadsheet on your computer or grab a pen and a piece of paper. Start to look over every expense you have. First, write down any expenses that are the same amount every month, such as your rent, Internet bill, car payment and insurance, streaming services, and any other expenses that rarely change unless you make a specific change to your service, such as upgrading a tier.

Next, look over your spending that can vary from month to month. Items under this type of spending can be groceries, dining out, gas for your car, and any entertainment expenses while having fun with your friends or family. You can list them individually by category. If this approach seems too overwhelming, or you buy different types of items in one general place, group the transactions by store (see Figure 1-4).

	A	B	C	D	E
1	**Expense**	**Category**	**Amount**		
2	Rent	Living Expenses	1200		
3	Target	Groceries	57.43		
4	Netflix	Entertainment	14.99		
5	Gas	Transportation	20		
6	Target	Household Items	14.87		
7	Amazon	Clothing	35.78		
8	Chewy	Pet Items	40.99		
9	Uber Eats	Dining Out	25		
10					

FIGURE 1-4:
A spreadsheet that displays how you track your spending.

TIP

When looking over your spending, don't forget to look at where you're using your credit cards and any apps you use to transfer money, like Venmo or PayPal. You can easily see these transactions while reviewing your bank statements, but they often don't list the retailer or item. For example, I use my PayPal account when I buy anything through my favorite food delivery service. My checking account then has a lot of PayPal transactions but doesn't categorize them automatically into "dining out." I have to review the transaction in my actual PayPal account.

After you've gone over the past three months of your spending habits, you notice trends. You may see that you've spent more money than you imagined on dining out or mindlessly shopping online. You see how those $5 transactions here and there add up over time, and probably to an amount you didn't realize. You may also be pleasantly surprised at how little you've spent and be able to congratulate yourself on keeping your expenses down.

REMEMBER

Money can be emotional, and when you realize you've wasted some of it, you can quickly feel like crap. But guess what? Money flows in and out. It's not gone forever and can find its way back to you. It's up to you where it goes next.

Chapter **2**

Breaking Down the Parts of a Budget

'm always in awe of my best friends because some kick-butt people surround me. They do amazing things like play roller derby, hike the Grand Canyon, volunteer at the drop of a hat to help others, and take up random new hobbies I'd never have thought of. Many are also money savvy and can tell you if they can't afford a random idea you come up with. I'm pretty sure they can tell someone no, not only because they're organized but also because they're *financially aware*. They know how much is in their checking accounts, whether they're on track to meet their goals, and whether they can afford to go eat sushi with you.

Anytime you become aware of an area of your life, it benefits you and those around you. People often don't realize that what's happening inside them affects what's happening outside them. Like my friends, when you become financially aware, your life can change in ways you haven't even begun to imagine. You can make room for things that matter so you're living life on your terms. But before becoming financially aware in all areas of your life, including your budget, you must recognize the different types of income, expenses, and financial goals. These items are all critical parts of your budget. Understanding the difference is key to budgeting correctly.

TIP

Grab a notebook and write out what your life would look like if you were financially aware. Maybe you'd be more generous with your time or pursue a new hobby you've always wanted to try. Perhaps you'd sleep better at night because you'd know where you financially stood at any time. When you see what financial awareness looks like, you can become it.

Seeing Where Your Money Goes: Your Expenses

Your money goes to various places, and hopefully, you've done a spending analysis (which I discuss in Chapter 1) to show you where. You've most likely discovered spending patterns. Some of the patterns may have surprised you, while other patterns didn't. If you're anything like me, you've realized you've spent way too much in a category, like takeout coffee. (Mmm, lattes.) That's okay.

TIP

If you haven't already completed the spending analysis I lay out in Chapter 1, I highly recommend you hit pause on this section and go do that. The info from your analysis will make breaking down your personal expenses so much easier.

Just know that your new budget has three components:

>> Expenses (how much money you're spending)

>> Income (how much money you have coming in)

>> Financial goals (things you want to accomplish, such as paying down debt or saving for something in the future)

All three are imperative to how your new future budget will affect your financial life. In fact, they're equally important to be financially aware of. Your expenses can affect how much income you need to bring in, which determines whether you can accomplish your goals by working one regular full-time job or you also need to get a part-time job or a side gig. Your income determines how much money you can spend on your lifestyle or put toward your future, like retirement. It's all related, so the sooner you figure out what you need to pay and what you want to accomplish, the faster a budget will work for you.

REMEMBER

Like anything in life, you're trying to improve; things may get worse before they get better. Finding where you are in life can be discouraging. Who in their right mind wants to feel discouraged? Not I, and I can imagine the feeling is mutual. But remember this: You're taking positive steps to change your finances. These steps will have a cascading effect and change all areas of your life for the better. I want you to live a good life, and I hope you want that too.

Identifying fixed expenses

Fixed expenses are expenses that are the same amount of money every billing period, such as paying your rent or mortgage. Most fixed expenses are paid monthly, but some are weekly, quarterly, or annually. For example, I pay for my car registration every year, but I pay monthly for my car insurance. Weekly fixed expenses may include things like a parking pass. Figure 2-1 shows various examples of fixed expenses.

Fixed Expenses

Household
- ☐ Rent
- ☐ Mortgage
- ☐ Property taxes
- ☐ HOA fees
- ☐ Rental or Homeowners insurance
- ☐ Internet
- ☐ Electricity
- ☐ Water
- ☐ Cellphone
- ☐ Gas

Debt
- ☐ Auto loan
- ☐ Student loans
- ☐ Personal loans
- ☐ Debt settlements
- ☐ Medical bills
- ☐ Government agencies
- ☐ Court-ordered debt

Financial
- ☐ Automobile Insurance
- ☐ Life Insurance
- ☐ Disability Insurance
- ☐ Retirement contributions
- ☐ Banking fees

Medical
- ☐ Health insurance premiums
- ☐ Insurance co-pays
- ☐ Flexible Spending Account
- ☐ Health Saving Account
- ☐ Therapy
- ☐ Prescriptions

Work
- ☐ Public transportation
- ☐ Parking
- ☐ Professional association fees
- ☐ Professional development classes
- ☐ Conferences/networking events

Personal
- ☐ Gym
- ☐ Subscriptions
- ☐ Memberships
- ☐ Streaming services

Children
- ☐ Childcare
- ☐ Tuition
- ☐ 529 and Coverdell savings accounts
- ☐ After school activities

FIGURE 2-1: Spending categories that are considered fixed expenses.

When you understand what a fixed expense is, you're ready to evaluate what you need to spend money on every month.

1. **Complete a spending analysis (see Chapter 1).**

   Because you divide your spending into categories, you should see a recurring theme with how much you spend each month on certain items or necessary expenses.

2. **Make a list of your fixed expenses.**

   Examples can include your rent, utilities, gym memberships, or fun things like subscription boxes or streaming services.

3. **Add up the total costs for these fixed expenses each month over the previous three months.**

   You now clearly see how much you spend every month on your fixed expenses. You can even divide this amount per paycheck if you feel like getting creative. (That may hurt your feelings, so be careful how far you want to dig.)

4. **Evaluate whether you need those fixed expenses.**

   Now's the time to see whether all your fixed expenses are necessary. Do you need to be spending money on a gym membership every month, or can you find a cheaper way to work out, such as utilizing local running trails? If you've signed up to get monthly items or deliveries, do you have the option to pause them and work through your current supply instead?

REMEMBER

Make sure you ask questions about your larger fixed expenses, too — not just the minor ones. Rent may be costing you more of your take-home pay than you realize you're comfortable with. Moving can be expensive, so I'm not suggesting you randomly decide to change apartments, but do make a note to research other living arrangements when you get closer to the end of your lease.

TIP

Just because an expense is fixed doesn't mean you can't find a way to lower the costs.

>> See whether you can save money by switching to purchasing items quarterly rather than monthly. Although I re-up my car registration yearly, I have the option through the state of Arizona to pay for two years at once to save on costs.

>> Call your providers, such as cellphone or Internet, to see whether you qualify for any discounts or loyalty rates.

>> Research competitors for insurance policies: healthcare, automobile, renters or homeowners, and life.

>> Consider switching to different tiers of subscription services, such as home streaming networks.

>> Take advantage of apps that provide coupons, cash back on your purchases, and price match for the best deal.

>> Install web browser extensions that help you shop a bit more savvily and save you some extra cash.

>> Check to see whether your bank offers you cash back for using your *debit card*. I have a few streaming services, and by paying for them with my debit card I was able to get 30 percent off.

TIP

Call your service providers to see whether they offer a loyalty rate or discount you may qualify for. Companies want to keep their customers, and if they know you're looking to jump ship, they'll be happy to assist. Some companies and service providers even offer discounts for students, public servants, or those in the military. If your current provider doesn't have anything for you, look to see whether another provider can better fit your needs. A switch may be a way to free up some additional room in your budget so you can breathe. It doesn't hurt to ask. The worst they can do is say no and have you keep paying what you already are.

You can even discuss options with your landlord or mortgage company. Nothing is off the table; the more money you can free up, the more you have to save for your goals or spend on things that bring value to your life.

Allowing for variable expense

Variable expenses, or *variable costs*, are different from fixed expenses (see the preceding section). Variable expenses are different from month to month and may be items you regularly purchase or ones you buy only occasionally (see Figure 2-2). Common variable expenses include the following:

>> Groceries

>> Gas for your car

>> Food for your pets

>> Items for any hobbies

>> Personal care items like hygiene products or makeup

These types of expenses can be more challenging for you to track. Depending on the time of year or stage of your life, your spending in these categories can fluctuate. You may spend nearly nothing in a category like household items one month and then easily spend a few hundred dollars there the next month. You may spend a lot more money during the holiday season between purchasing gifts and travel-associated costs.

Variable Expenses

Food
- ☐ Groceries
- ☐ Dining Out
- ☐ Lunch (work and school)
- ☐ Coffee

Transportation
- ☐ Gas
- ☐ Tolls
- ☐ Oil changes and other car maintenance
- ☐ Car repairs
- ☐ Registration and other fees
- ☐ Rideshares

Entertainment
- ☐ Concerts
- ☐ Alcohol
- ☐ Books
- ☐ Hobbies
- ☐ Games for family
- ☐ Admission to movies or museums

Household
- ☐ Pet food
- ☐ Other pet expenses
- ☐ Cleaning supplies
- ☐ Decor
- ☐ Clothing
- ☐ Personal grooming
- ☐ Child expenses such as diapers or formula
- ☐ School field trips and other extracurricular activities

FIGURE 2-2:
Spending categories that are variable expenses.

REMEMBER

Because variable expenses are less predictable, assigning a monetary value of what you should spend per month can be frustrating and challenging. You may have control over some of them but not for others, and that's okay. I get easily flustered when a category spikes for me and initially throws everything I had planned off course. You're going to figure this all out, too, and I'm here to help every step of the way.

Needs and wants

Variable expenses include both needs and wants. You can't just opt out of a lot of your variable spending. You have to purchase things like medicine, and you have to eat.

Generally speaking, *needs* include food, gas to get to and from work if you commute, clothing, and so on. *Wants* are things like getting the newest cellphone when your current one is perfectly usable or spending money on experiences like concerts or dining out.

REMEMBER

Just because you can't avoid purchasing some items doesn't mean you can't still save money. One of the ways you can cut your variable expenses is to consider lower-priced alternatives to your usual purchases.

Say you're in the market for foundation because your old bottle is empty. Instead of going to an expensive makeup counter to purchase your usual foundation, try to find a similar product from a different brand that's a lower price. In this example, the high-end foundation is considered a want because you can find less-expensive brands of foundation. But regardless of what some may say, foundation can be a need based on your own comfort and personal preference.

The difference between needs and wants can get murky quickly, especially because one person's want may genuinely be another person's need (see Figure 2-3). Spending money on your wants is perfectly okay; you just need to figure out how to budget for them properly. The 50/30/20 budgeting method, discussed in Chapter 4, allows you to categorize most of your expenses based on your needs (50 percent of your income) and wants (30 percent of your income); the remaining 20 percent goes toward savings and debt.

REMEMBER

Voluntarily spending money on nonessential items or items that are categorized as wants rather than needs is called *discretionary spending*.

REMEMBER

Be realistic when determining your wants and needs. Suppose you have a specific life situation that requires you to spend a bit more on your variable expenses. I have several chronic health conditions. Some things help me manage my quality of life on days when I can't get out of bed, like ordering takeout so I don't have to spend energy preparing a meal. I hate sometimes admitting that I need to pay more in a specific budget category, like dining out, than people say I should. But guess what? I'm realistic, and that's what keeps me under budget every month.

Needs versus Wants

Needs

- [ ] Rent
- [ ] Mortgage
- [ ] HOA/property taxes
- [ ] Homeowner/rental insurance
- [ ] Internet
- [ ] Electricity
- [ ] Water
- [ ] Gas for work
- [ ] Public transportation for work
- [ ] Health insurance

- [ ] Prescriptions
- [ ] Therapy
- [ ] Groceries (essentials to feed you and your family)
- [ ] Auto insurance
- [ ] Car payment
- [ ] Other debt with current payment arrangement
- [ ] Pet food and other essentials
- [ ] Child expenses such as diapers or formula
- [ ] Childcare

Wants

- [ ] Dining Out
- [ ] Alcohol
- [ ] Travel
- [ ] Home décor
- [ ] Nonessential clothing
- [ ] Subscriptions
- [ ] Streaming services

- [ ] Admission to museums, concerts, or other events
- [ ] Personal grooming services
- [ ] Travel
- [ ] Nonessential electronics

FIGURE 2-3:
A list of what expenses are needs and wants.

Value-based spending

One more idea to help save you money and curb your expenses is to evaluate whether your current spending is *value-based* (rooted in the things you value in life) or a result of trying to keep up with your friends and family. Maybe you didn't want to be the only one left out of a vacation, but you really don't want to visit that destination. Or maybe you've convinced yourself that life will be infinitely better if you just buy whatever product your favorite influencer recommends. (I'm guilty of this myself; I almost bought cool containers for my bathroom before I realized what I really needed was just to do a massive purge.)

TECHNICAL STUFF

If you don't know what your values are, that's okay. A lot of free surveys online can help you figure it out. The Barrett Values Centre provides a free Personal Values Assessment quiz online, found at www.valuescentre.com/tools-assessments/pva.

Knowing Where Your Money Comes From: Your Income

When I was younger, my family moved from Phoenix, Arizona, to Bullhead City, Arizona. It's such a small town that my graduating class was close to 175, give or take the few kids that didn't pass our finals. The point is I was bored, and there was nothing to do. Until we got a Hastings. Hastings was the coolest book/record/movie store in the whole wide world to a 9-year-old Athena. I only wanted to buy a Michael Jackson cassette and a *Baby-Sitters Club* book. The problem was that I didn't have any money flowing into my piggy-bank. Come to think of it, I don't even think I had a piggy-bank.

My parents got the best deal in the entire world when I agreed to do my chores for the cool price of a dollar a day. If I finished all my chores every day, I got a bonus that added up to ten dollars. I felt so rich and didn't even know that my little kid self soon developed hustling skills that many rappers would admire. What I didn't realize at the time was that my parents were teaching me how to earn an income — sneaky parentals.

Your *income* is an essential component of your budget. Knowing how much money you have coming in can ensure your expenses (which are probably now more of the electric-bill variety than my Hastings habit) don't exceed your income. It can also help you set realistic goals for all areas of your life that relate to your finances and perhaps even quality of life. You may realize you have more income than you initially thought you had, or a spending deficit that means you need to find ways to either cut back or earn more.

REMEMBER

When discussing your income, one dollar amount you need to keep in mind is your *net pay*, also referred to as *disposable income*. Net pay is the amount of money left over after any withholdings you may be subjected to, such as taxes (federal and state if your residence requires it), Social Security, Medicare, and any wage garnishments you may be paying off. It's important to consider because it's the amount of money you use to budget every month. It's the money you have to put toward your goals, pay your bills, and cover your variable expenses.

Depending on a monthly income

The first type of income you should consider is what you earn monthly to cover all your expenses. *Monthly income* can come from various sources. While it can be consistent dependent on your income type, it can also be different from month to month. Here's a list of different types of monthly income you can earn:

>> **Income from full-time and/or part-time employment:** This income you receive from an employer that has you on its payroll and that you regularly trade your time to for money. Some jobs pay a flat amount of money per paycheck, known as a *salary,* and others may pay an hourly *wage.* Hourly income can fluctuate because the hours you work may vary, while a salary doesn't.

>> **Income as a self-employed freelancer or consultant:** Freelancers and contractors make variable income depending on what's on their roster. Both are considered self-employed, but the main difference is the number of clients and the type of projects they're currently working on. *Freelancers* balance more than one client and work on projects with a short timeline. *Contractors* take on more significant projects with one main client and do smaller work for several. Although I consider myself a freelancer, I do have two contract gigs. I use the contract gigs to ensure my fixed expenses are covered, while my freelancing projects go toward my variable spending expenses and goals I'm working on.

TIP

For the longest time, I loved working in a salaried position because that situation made my budgeting much easier. As I got older, I realized I disliked the salary arrangement because I wasn't adequately compensated for my time in my nonprofit career. At different times in your life, you may prefer different compensation structures, and no one approach is right or wrong.

>> **Pensions and other paid retirement plans:** A *pension* is a type of retirement program that an employee, an employer, or both pay into. The plan pays a fixed sum to the employee at regular intervals on retirement. Each employer decides on a compensation formula approved by the U.S. Department of Labor (See Figure 2-4). Some pensions require you to work for the company for a certain number of years before you're eligible (or *vested*). Federal, state, and local government or other public sectors also allow for paid retirement plans.

>> **Retirement plans:** Outside of traditional pensions or government-paid retirement plans, you can still receive payments from your retirement accounts if you've previously planned. These types of retirement accounts allow you to save for retirement by investing. The most popular ones are 401(k), 403(b), and Roth IRAs, but you can find a complete list on the IRS website (www.irs.gov/retirement-plans/plan-sponsor/types-of-retirement-plans).

Pension Formula

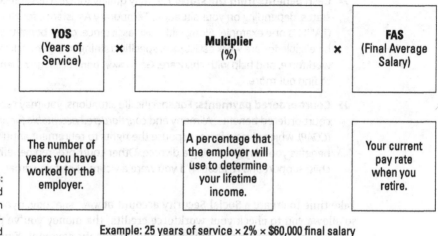

| YOS (Years of Service) | × | Multiplier (%) | × | FAS (Final Average Salary) |

| The number of years you have worked for the employer. | A percentage that the employer will use to determine your lifetime income. | Your current pay rate when you retire. |

FIGURE 2-4:
The formula used to determine an employer-sponsored pension.

Example: 25 years of service × 2% × $60,000 final salary
25 × 2% × $60,000 = $30,000 lifetime yearly pension payment

» **Social Security retirement benefits:** When people talk about receiving Social Security, they're usually referring to retirement benefits. Every year you remain in the workforce, you can receive up to four work credits. As of this writing, you must earn $1,640 to earn a work credit. This means that you must make at least $560 per year to earn all 4 credits you're eligible for. After you've earned 40 credits (which you could do over the course of 10 years), you're eligible to collect partial benefits at age 62 and full benefits at age 67. For up-to-date information, please visit www.ssa.gov/retirement.

» **Social Security Disability Benefits, Supplemental Security Income, and survivors benefits:** Social Security has three other benefits. If you're disabled, you can receive two different types of benefits.

- *Social Security Disability Insurance (SSDI)* benefits are granted when you match the Social Security Administration's definition of having a disability and have earned enough workforce credits, depending on the age you become disabled.

- If you've never worked due to a disability, you can qualify for *Supplemental Security Income (SSI)*.

Last but not least, if you're a child, a spouse, or a parent who relies on someone in the workforce to support you and they die, you can get *survivors benefits*. When I was younger, I received these benefits after my mom passed unexpectedly at age 38.

>> **Cash benefits from the state:** You may qualify for cash assistance in some states, depending on your situation. Temporary Assistance for Needy Families (TANF) is one example. Along with cash assistance, other benefits you may be eligible for are work assistance, specific training to enter back into the workforce, and help with childcare. Go to www.benefits.gov/benefit/613 to find out more.

>> **Court-ordered payments:** For specific life situations, you may receive court-ordered benefits. Alimony and *court-ordered acceptable for processing (COAP)*, which gives a former spouse the rights to retirement annuities, are benefits you may get during a divorce. Other court-ordered benefits include child support and restitution if you were a victim of certain crimes.

Take time to create a Social Security account at www.ssa.gov/myaccount/. Doing so allows you to check your workforce credits, the money you've paid into Social Security, and an estimate of your retirement benefit payment. You can also check to see what other benefits may be available to you, such as disability or survivor, along with the amount you or a loved one would qualify for. This information can help you budget better for life circumstances and save for retirement.

Identifying additional sources of income

Just like your variable expenses (check out the earlier section "Allowing for variable expense"), *variable* or *irregular income* means that your wages fluctuate every month. You can make this type of income yearly, monthly, weekly, or even daily. Variable income, for example from a side gig, is an excellent way to catch up on financial goals or supplement your income. *Side gigs* or *side hustles* are usually jobs that are dependent on task completion. You can freelance for a client or clients, using the skills you've learned from current or previous jobs.

REMEMBER

After you start budgeting, you may find that your net pay doesn't cover all your monthly expenses or the goals you've set for yourself. In this case, you have to either cut your spending or earn more money. I prefer to earn more money because it's easier for me than cutting my expenses.

I feel everyone should have additional income streams. The economy can be downright volatile sometimes. A job may be here one day and outsourced the next. Things happen, which is why being able to budget with the best of them is more important than ever. Chapter 8 provides several options for securing additional sources of income, but the following is a short list common side gigs.

>> Become a *ride sharer*, a person who drives others in their vehicle for a fee

>> Doing/delivering grocery shopping or delivering food purchased through a restaurant

>> Selling items you have lying around or buying items for a lower price and then selling them for a profit on sites like eBay and Amazon

>> Creating content online as a writer

>> Making and selling crafts on a site like Etsy or on social media

REMEMBER

Variable income from a side gig can still be considered earned income depending on the source, so check with the IRS to see whether you need to put money aside for taxes. Try to put 25 to 30 percent of any income earned from side gigs aside in a checking account. Pay your estimated taxes quarterly and save anything additional for business expenses. Even better, double-check to ensure you aren't missing expenses that you can use for tax deductions. Software fees, utilities such as Internet, and inventory are all expenses that may be potential tax write-offs. For more information on self-employment taxes, go to the IRS official website at www.irs.gov.

You Gotta Have Dreams: Financial Goals

Setting goals allows you to work toward something you want in your life with the end goal of eventually achieving it. I *love* goals. I'm a frequent goal-setter, but I can easily struggle with accomplishing them. Sometimes I don't come up with my dreams in the best state of mind, which leads them to be too audacious or even irrelevant to my overall lifestyle (a.k.a. my ADHD). Despite my struggles with staying consistent and overbooking myself, I'm pretty good at accomplishing at least half of my goals, so if you also have trouble staying on track, never fear.

Note: Chapter 16 has more information about planning for your financial goals. However, you should consider your financial goals when you choose your preferred budgeting method, which I discuss in Part 2.

Goals can be simple, like brushing your teeth at night. They can be moderate, like learning a new language or losing some weight. They can also seem unattainable, like climbing Mount Everest. After you're clear on where you want to go, figuring out the steps to get you there is easier. (If Mount Everest is your goal, please send me lots of pictures.)

Having a financial goal can help ensure your budget tells your money where to go. It causes you to look at your spending and evaluate your current lifestyle. It helps you not eat cat food in retirement. It can help you live a life you love and are proud of.

GOAL SETTING: A STEP IN THE RIGHT DIRECTION

I often compare goal setting to relying on directions to get where you're going rather than trying to wing it. Without being told where to go, you may not be able to reach your destination because you don't know the directions yourself. If you're semi-familiar with where you're driving, you may get there eventually, but directions make it so much easier. After you enter the address into your map app, your phone quickly starts to boss you around and has you taking U-turns in a hurry to get to where you want to be much more efficiently.

TIP

Setting financial goals can help you live a better quality of life, which can mean the difference in where you can afford to retire or whether you can take a leave of absence from an employer or have a life-changing emergency that causes you to pivot, such as an unexpected death. A budget can be flexible to meet the stage of life you're in, but having a bucket of money can shake things up. Oh, and make your overall life easier.

Saving for your future

As a personal finance columnist, I regularly get questions from people who want me to guide them through a financial situation. Sometimes it's easy, like directing them to a budgeting app. But often, they're more serious than that. One of the more common recurring themes: not saving for the future, mainly retirement (see Chapter 9). Letter writers are asking questions not only about their personal retirement plans but also their parents'. Life is short, and every day you don't put money aside for your future is a day you're setting yourself up for risk and, even worse, failure.

You're also better off saving for things you know will eventually happen. My fiancé decided that he liked it, so he put a ring on it. In my head, I was like, "okay, we'll eventually get married." Do you think I'd been saving for this eventual expense? Spoiler alert: No, I hadn't been.

Even if you have no plans to get married anytime soon, you know stuff will eventually happen. You may need a new car for transportation to and from work. The perfect bungalow of your dreams may hit the housing market, and you see yourself establishing some roots! You may even have kids heading off to college — or, better yet, you may want to go back to school yourself to make more money so you can have an even better budget than before. "Someday" can turn into your current day, so you may as well plan for it.

Saving for the future isn't just about retirement or replacing things that break. It can also include fabulous trips you want to experience, like going to Europe or wine tasting in Napa. Maybe it's establishing a scholarship fund in someone's name at a local nonprofit, redecorating your house in whatever the cool new style is, or buying a muscle car to restore. Your future needs to include fun, and your budget helps you do just that. In chapters to follow, I provide more information to help you save for your financial goals and life events.

REMEMBER

Make sure your goal is actually yours. One of the everyday things I see in the personal finance world is people telling others to become their own bosses. Do you know how hard it is to be your own boss?! I'm not saying you can't do it, but it's not as easy as many claim. I know many people who quit their jobs to make money but didn't have a clear plan or realized they didn't want self-employment at all. They let someone's goal become theirs instead of listening to their intuition. Make sure whatever financial goal you choose is one that you want to achieve, so you'll put in the hard work to make it your reality.

Paying down your debt

Another financial goal you can set is paying down your debt. I won't say debt is evil because if not for debt, I wouldn't be the first person in my family to have graduated from college. Student loans helped me fund my education. So although I hate writing a check to the U.S. Department of Education every month, I know I wouldn't be talking to you right now, dear reader, if it wasn't for the DOE. I will say that debt isn't evil if you use it strategically.

But having even strategic debt can still be problematic. Who wants to pay thousands of dollars in interest and financing fees? Setting a financial goal to pay your debt down can help in the long run when budgeting. Because as soon as you pay that debt off, you have more cash flow to do things with, like saving for retirement or adopting a dog from a shelter. Chapter 10 will give you some tips to help you eliminate your debt.

Putting your financial goals in place

TIP

Setting financial goals doesn't have to be complicated.

1. **Establish what your goals are.**

   For example, maybe you want to buy a house.

2. **Make the goal as clear as can be.**

   Decide precisely how much money you'll need to buy that house and when you want to be able to make the purchase.

3. **Take actionable steps toward completing it.**

Examples of actionable steps may be paying extra on your credit card so that eventual payment can go toward opening a high-yield savings account for the house you want. Every little bit adds up, so don't be discouraged if you have to start small. With every action, you move the needle closer to your goal.

Celebrate the small wins, and make sure you know you have your own back. I have it, too.

2

Finding a Budget That Works for You

Assess the zero-based budgeting method to nail down your spending to the penny.

Document your expenses to decide whether the 50/30/20 budget is for you.

Know why the cash envelope method drastically cuts back on your spending.

Discover a seemingly anti-budgeting method called the pay-yourself-first budget.

Check out categories, the right tools, and strategies to create your new spending plan.

IN THIS CHAPTER

» **Establishing a zero-based budget**

» **Exploring the advantages and disadvantages of zero-based budgeting**

» **Determining whether a zero-based budget can work for you**

Chapter **3**

Zero-Based Budgeting

A zero-based budgeting system is when you assign a job to every single dollar that comes your way. The overall goal of a zero-based budget is to leave no dollar unaccounted for. With this budgeting method, you should have a zero balance after you allocate funds to each category of your fixed and variable expenses. But that doesn't mean that you should spend *all* your money. That's not a wise move for anyone, ever. It just means that, in general, your income aligns with all your spending and doesn't leave you in a deficit.

I love that using a zero-based budget requires you to plan. It's a positive way to start being proactive with your money rather than reactive. When you're reactive, you can lose considerable progress in a short amount of time, leaving you discouraged. When you train yourself to think ahead, you find the process getting more manageable as you go.

WARNING

Never allow your checking account to have a zero balance. You can't plan for every single expense you have in life, no matter how hard you try. But overdraft fees can add up and leave you with a negative balance. Who wants that? Make sure you keep a buffer, or additional cash, in your checking account for unexpected expenses. I suggest starting small with $100 and then working your way up to $500 and then to $1,000. You don't need to allocate the $100 in one swoop, either. Save $5 here and there if needed.

Zero-based budgeting can apply no matter your income, whether it's $500 a month or upward of $5,000. Whatever amount you bring home, you need to assign it to a category. Budgeting is much easier if you have a higher income because you want to cover all your budget categories, including those that help you save toward your goals. But at the end of the day, how much you make doesn't matter if you aren't in control of your spending.

This control is why tracking your spending over the past few months is so important — so that your categories are realistic and accurately reflect your finances (refer to Chapter 2 for more information). You want to know precisely what each of your categories looks like for this budgeting method to work. If you're just guessing, you're not going to know exactly where every dollar goes, and you may end up overspending and coming up short at the end of the month. No one wants that.

It's also why I tell you in Chapter 2 to add up all sources of income you have coming in. Your categories need realistic amounts for this type of budget to work. And if you have a surplus, that's a great problem to have! It means you have extra cash to put toward that future trip you want to take.

Setting Up Your Zero-Based Budget

Your zero-based budget should include your fixed income and expenses, your variable income and expenses, and your financial goals. When you budget this way, you're proactive and not reactive with your finances. This way of budgeting also helps you make sure you're putting an adequate amount toward your savings as well. Remember, the objective is to ensure every dollar is accounted for so you can make every penny work for you. The following sections break down the steps for creating a zero-based budget.

If you haven't tackled the spending analysis I describe in Chapter 1, I suggest doing that before building your zero-based budget. The info you turn up in that exercise will inform your budget here.

List all expenses and subtract them from your income

Go over your spending analysis for the past three months and determine your expenses — that is, where your money has been going — for the past month. Figure 3-1 shows an example of what that can look like.

	A	B	C	D
1	**Date**	**Expense**	**Category**	**Amount Spent**
2	11-1	Rent	Housing	1200
3	11-1	Electric	Housing	50
4	11-1	Water	Housing	25
5	11-1	Internet	Housing	60
6	11-3	Groceries	Food	175.14
7	11-3	McDonald's	Food	11.03
8	11-4	Starbucks	Food	6.49
9	11-5	Spotify	Entertainment	9.99
10	11-8	Drinks with friends	Entertainment	40
11	11-8	Dinner with friends	Food	50
12	11-9	Cellphone	Housing	80
13	11-12	Starbucks	Food	6.49
14	11-12	Lunch with coworker	Food	15
15	11-15	Amazon	Clothing	55.6
16	11-17	Haircut	Personal Grooming	45
17	11-18	Sports league fees	Entertainment	75
18	11-19	Bank Fee	Financial	15
19	11-20	Subway pass	Transportation	120
20	11-20	Netflix	Entertainment	14.99
21	11-22	Starbucks	Food	6.49
22	11-25	Gift for friend	Gifts	25
23	11-26	Food with friends	Food	20
24	11-29	Amazon	Gifts for Holidays	87.54
25	11-30	Target	Household Items	25.97
26				
27			**Total**	**2219.73**

FIGURE 3-1:
An example of what tracking your spending can look like in a spreadsheet.

List all your spending individually. Doing so helps you better categorize your spending later (in the following section, in fact). Write down every single thing you've spent your money on.

Along with your *fixed expenses* (that occur on schedule and are the same amount every time you pay them), be sure to account for your *variable expenses,* such as gas and groceries. Debt repayment also counts as an expense, so be sure to include any payments you may have, such as student and/or auto loans and credit card payments. You can read more about fixed and variable expenses in Chapter 2.

REMEMBER

The most important part of using a zero-based budget is to be honest with yourself, even if it leaves you feeling some kind of way. Everyone has emotions tied to money, both good and bad. That's okay. If you need a break before moving forward, take one, and then come back.

TIP

If you realize that your emotions toward money may be too much for you to handle on your own, please reach out to someone who can help. The Financial Therapy Association (financialtherapyassociation.org/) is a great place to start. This website is loaded with resources and can help you decide what your next step should be. You aren't alone in your new money journey, I promise.

After you've listed your fixed and variable expenses, subtract your total expenses from your income, including both monthly and variable income. As I explain in Chapter 2, *monthly income* is regular income you can count on to be there every month, come rain or come shine. Examples include a job through an employer where you receive a regular paycheck, retirement benefits such as pensions or Social Security, and child support. *Variable income* is income you receive irregularly, such as income earned from side gigs, freelancing, or simply selling items from around your home. Figure 3-2 is an example of how total income is calculated, while Figure 3-3 shows a budget tracking income and expenses.

	A	B
1	**Regular Income**	
2	Day Job	$2,400
3	Roommate	$400
4		
5	**Variable Income**	
6	Amazon	$254
7	Uber	$125
8		
9	**Total**	**$3,179**

FIGURE 3-2:
How to add your total income.

	A	B	C	D	E	F
1	**Date**	**Expense**	**Category**	**Amount Spent**	**Income (starting balance $3,179)**	**Amount Left Over**
2	11-1	Rent	Housing	1,200	3,179	1,979
3	11-1	Electric	Housing	50	1,979	1,929
4	11-1	Water	Housing	25	1,929	1,904
5	11-1	Internet	Housing	60	1,904	1,844
6	11-3	Groceries	Food	175.14	1,844	1,668.86
7	11-3	McDonald's	Food	11.03	1,668.86	1,657.83
8	11-4	Starbucks	Food	6.49	1,657.83	1,651.34
9						

FIGURE 3-3:
An example of what subtracting your expenses could look like.

In a perfect world, your income minus your expenses would be as close to zero as possible. In an even better world, you'd have a surplus of income, which means you're well on the right track to growing your savings account. If your balance is negative, that means you have a deficit that you need to fix. I explain how to do that in the following section, so don't panic. You just need to know what you're working with here.

Assign your total income to budget categories

After you subtract your expenses from your income (see the preceding section), you can see not only where your money goes but also how it matches up to the income you're bringing in. The next step is to look at your spending and group similar expenses ino a mutual category. Some examples of main expenses placed into budgeting categories include the following:

- >> **Living expenses:** Things you can include for living expenses are rent or a mortgage, electricity, Internet, your cellphone bill, and water. You may also have fees related to your living situation, such as a homeowners association fee (HOA) that you pay regularly.

- >> **Children:** Clothes, school lunches, education fees, before- and after-school care, summer programs, sports equipment, club fees, school supplies, allowance, and other child-related expenses fit here. Even I know kids are expensive, and I don't even have one!

- >> **Food:** Dining out, groceries, meals you pay for while at work, and coffee are all expenses you can list here. If dining out and alcohol are often on the same receipt, pick between entertainment or food and then list them in that specific category only. I'd also include any treats you pick up for the office or items from the vending machine and gas station in this bucket.

- >> **Pets:** Food, vet checkups, medicine, medical supplies, grooming appointments, cat litter, animal bedding, treats, toys, and hygiene products are all items that can go in this category.

- >> **Transportation:** Any costs associated with how you get around town go here. Regular expenses may be gas, car insurance, a pass to ride on public transportation, or parking you regularly pay for. I'd also include any necessary travel you may have to take, such as buying a plane ticket to see a family member who may need you. But if I'm traveling for vacation, I put that under entertainment.

>> **Medical:** Feel free to put anything health-related here. I recommend including health insurance if you're paying for that out of pocket, as well as listing prescriptions, doctor co-pays, supplements, over-the-counter drugs, and items for everyday colds and pain relief. I also suggest sticking any therapy (physical or mental health) under this category if you pay for that outright and not through your insurance plan.

>> **Personal:** For this category, I list anything related to me personally that doesn't benefit anyone but me, such as clothing, makeup, and hygiene products. I also include my gym membership or anything toward self-development here. For example, I have a subscription box I love that sends self-care items like journals and fun personal things that aren't necessarily needed, like bath oils. Because it makes me take time to focus on myself and my well-being, I include it under this category.

>> **Entertainment:** You can drop subscriptions such as streaming services, gaming apps, supplies or fees related to a hobby, events like concerts with friends, and any bar tabs in this category. *Remember:* Entertainment is subjective to everyone. Your category may seem high compared to others, but you're the boss, not them.

>> **Debt repayment:** Put any financial obligations you have in this category. Include an amount you want to pay toward any debt you want to eliminate.

>> **Financial goals:** List any special events or items you want to start saving for, such as a house or that beautiful European vacation that you've been dreaming about.

REMEMBER

These options are simply a few categories and examples to get you started. You probably won't assign all your expenses to the categories listed here because it's your budget.

After you've decided what categories you want to use to group your expenses, add up your costs to see how much you've spent in that separate area. You now know the amount of money you need to assign to that category. Figure 3-4 shows an example of what it could look like.

If you still have money left over after assigning it to each category (including your financial goals), start brainstorming what you want to do with it. Should you be putting more money toward a specific category or adding more to debt repayment? Think about your financial goals and what makes sense for you. Remember, your overall goal when using this budgeting method should be to get to zero.

	A	B
1	**Category**	**Amount**
2	Housing and Utilities	$1,000
3	Transportation	$300
4	Groceries and Household Items	$300
5	Dining Out	$300
6	Entertainment	$300
7	Clothing	$100
8	Student Loans	$300
9	Credit Cards	$200
10	Emergency Fund	$200
11		
12	**Total**	**$3,000**

FIGURE 3-4:
Categories in a zero-based budget for an income of $3,000.

Having enough money to pay for your monthly expenses

If you don't have enough money to assign to all of your categories, you have some work to do, but I walk you through it.

First, go through your spending again to see where exactly your money is going. Here are a couple of particular pitfalls to look out for:

>> **Online shopping:** Shopping online is one of the most significant ways to overspend, especially with money you don't have. Retailers like Amazon have made at-home shopping so easy! They work hard to keep their ordering processes smooth to keep you wanting to go back for more. The other day I was looking at an ice maker when I started out looking for a book — a book I could check out of the public library and read *for free*. (I'm still unsure what I was going to do with the ice maker.)

>> **Dining out:** Another major budget killer is dining out. Lack of time is a big reason people eat out as often as they do. Are you grabbing a coffee daily on your way to work, catching up with co-workers over a quick lunch at the nearest fast-food place, and then ordering meal delivery when you get home? Unless you have a huge number of Benjamins in the bank, take a step back.

AVOID "BUY NOW, PAY LATER" FINANCING

Beware of financing your online purchases. Say you're online buying your favorite hiking gear and realize that the total amount in your cart is getting higher than you had initially decided to spend. You notice a colorful button on the cart screen that says "buy now, pay later."

Buy now, pay later (BNPL) companies have partnered with retailers to help provide their customers with alternative payment arrangements. With BNPL, you can divide your payment over a certain amount of time, usually something like four payments spread out over several weeks. You're also not subject to an interest fee like you'd be with a credit card. With this type of financing, spending more than you can afford to realistically pay back is easy. Before you realize it, you can get caught up in a cycle of making multiple payments to multiple BNPL companies. Failure to make payments can result in your being turned into collections and therefore damage your credit. Rule of thumb? Unless it's a significant purchase like a car, don't finance it. Take time to use your new budget to save for it instead.

If your spending isn't out of control, you need to do one of two things:

TIP

>> **Cut your expenses:** I offer lots of ideas for cutting your expenses in Chapter 2, but a few options include negotiating everything you can, evaluating whether you can make do with a lower tier of a subscription, and making sure you take advantage of loyalty programs at places like grocery stores and gas stations. Some grocery stores, for example, allow you to earn points to use as a discount for gas at a later date.

Don't look at changing tiers as "downgrading." Instead, look at it as making positive financial changes for you and your future.

>> **Earn more income:** Look for additional income streams that you aren't tapping into. For instance, you may be able to rent a room or start a side gig. I discuss a variety of income streams in Chapter 2 as well.

Depending on the season of your life, one of these options may be much easier to manage than the other.

REMEMBER

Cutting back your expenses when you don't know where to start can be draining. It can also be exhausting if you don't have enough money to meet your expenses. In times like these, make sure to cover what you need daily: items such as food, transportation, utilities, and some type of shelter. You need to ensure that your physiological needs are covered before you can make any more progress in your finances and, in general, your life.

TIP

Be sure to check out the experts at 211, a national service that provides information about resources available to you at a local, state, and national level. They can help you get assistance with resources such as food, utilities, clothing, shelter, and medical services. You can access 211 by dialing the number for free on any phone or online at www.211.org.

Accounting for periodic or unexpected expenses: a sinking fund

What about those expenses that you know exist but only remember when you receive a bill or a payment is magically taken out of our checking account? Things like car insurance (if you don't pay it monthly), car registration, estimated quarterly taxes, and holiday gifts. May I present to you the idea of a sinking fund?

A *sinking fund* is an account you have to help offset the cost of irregular or one-time expenses. It's a strategic way to set aside money every month and prevent your finances from becoming overextended on bills or purchases that might not always be on your radar. Here's how it works:

1. **Grab your calendar and make a list of periodic payments you made over the course of that year that weren't regular occurrences.**

   I'd also list any events you have coming up if they require you to spend any additional money that you usually wouldn't. For example, I already know that I have to purchase a few gifts for college graduations and plan my fiancé's birthday party.

2. **Group the items into categories like you do your other expenses and add up the total.**

3. **Divide the total from Step 2 by 12.**

   That's the number you should put aside as a monthly budget category. For example, if I plan on spending $1,200 for gifts over the year, I need to be setting aside $100 every month in a sinking fund designated for gifts — a sinking fund I allocate in my monthly zero-based budget. With this newly created sinking fund, I don't have to scramble to pay for gifts as they pop up. Instead, I use the money I've already allocated for this exact purpose.

TIP

Don't keep your sinking funds in your checking account. To prevent spending money you're trying to put aside, consider moving the funds to an online high-yield savings account (HYSA). HYSAs are a better idea than a traditional savings account for this purpose because you collect interest on the money you were going to put aside anyway. The interest rate on the types of these accounts varies, but it's usually anywhere between 1 and 2 percent. Some banks let you open multiple HYSAs for each goal you have. I'm a visual person, so seeing all my progress divided into different categories helps me determine where I am financially rather than where I want to be.

Sinking funds are a great example of how you can make the categories in your budget work for you and not against you. If you're going to go the sinking-fund route, I highly suggest making room for the following categories:

>> **Medical-related expenses:** You may have a clean bill of health now, but as you age, you'll have different medical needs. Being proactive is one way to ensure you stay ahead of the game for your health and your wallet. Doctor co-pays, yearly exams, medication refills, and visits to the dentist are all medical-related expenses you can put cash aside for. Also consider putting money aside for things such as supplements and random trips to urgent care during flu season.

>> **Gifts and holidays:** You know gift-giving holidays roll around yearly, so you may as well start saving for them. You can also use this fund for life celebrations such as weddings, baby showers, and housewarming gifts. One of the best things I do for my budget is to put money aside for gifts. My love language is gift giving, so when I find the perfect gift for someone dear to me, I can snag it without dipping it into a different category.

>> **Maintenance and replacement:** When you use something repeatedly, it may be subject to wearing out over time. If you own a car, you'll eventually need tires, brakes, oil changes, and battery replacements. Appliances and electronics need to be repaired or replaced from time to time. Putting money aside for these types of purchases or repairs helps relieve the pinch to your budget.

>> **Emergencies:** In Chapter 8, I talk more in-depth about having a separate emergency fund as a budget category. However, you can start by saving a small amount of money for an emergency using a sinking-fund category. You use this fund to cover an unexpected expense like a car repair after a breakdown or a new water heater to replace the one that stopped working while you were in the shower (been there!).

TIP

Make sure you know which sinking-fund categories are most critical to you. In my case, the one sinking-fund category that I always make sure I put money aside for is my medical fund. As much as I fly through life at hyperspeed, I have several chronic illnesses that I deal with daily. Some days I forget I'm sick, and then others are rough. Either way, after years of being a chronic illness warrior, I know that having extra cash at the ready is always a good idea. I never know when I may need to go to the doctor, which requires a co-pay, or whether I'll be too sick to work, which may affect my income for the next month. Having this sinking fund stashed away gives me an extra level of security, and that helps me manage my budget overall.

If sinking funds are too much for you to think about right now, that's fine, too. You can plan for unexpected expenses that aren't emergencies in other ways. Consider a *cash buffer*. Decide on an amount you feel would cover these unexpected, one-time expenses if you needed it to and then dedicate yourself to saving this amount and leaving it alone in your checking account. Even having an extra $20 in your checking account may save you an overdraft fee. See Chapter 7 for more information on creating a cash buffer.

TIP

Many banks now offer notifications by both texts and email when your balance is getting low. A bank app also offers these features so make sure you download it. If your bank doesn't have an app or these features, try a budgeting app instead. Budgeting apps can do the same thing when linked to your checking account and can also let you know when you've spent too much in a certain category.

I frequently press that every little amount adds up, because it's true. Five dollars here and ten dollars there eventually add up to a few hundred dollars, which snowballs into a thousand dollars. It's why you keep change on your dresser or in your car — because one day, you'll need just one dollar, and it'll be there.

Track your spending

After you've set up your categories for the month and have included the total amount of money allowed (more on that in the earlier section "Assign your total income to budget categories"), you're ready for the tracking stage of the zero-based budgeting system.

For the next 30 days, track every penny you spend. Write your spending and label it with the category it belongs to. You can write your spending out in any way that works for you. You just need to write it down to track your spending and keep yourself accountable. I'm a paper-and-pen person, but you can keep track of your new budget in an online spreadsheet or even an app on your phone if you prefer (see Figure 3-5). Just find a method that you'll stick with.

TECHNICAL STUFF

If manually configuring a spreadsheet isn't your thing but you always seem to lose paper, consider using a budgeting app on your phone. A ton are available to choose from, both free and paid. After you assign categories in your app, you can link your checking account so that the app calculates your expenses in real time and then shows you how much you have left to spend in your categories. Your app can alert you when you overspend so that you know to stop. If you don't want to enter your checking account information, you don't have to, but that means you're responsible for entering your expenses. One of the most popular apps for zero-based budgeting is You Need A Budget (YNAB), while Mint is excellent for just about any budgeting method you choose. You can find YNAB at www.youneedabudget.com and Mint at mint.intuit.com.

	A	B
1	**Category**	**Assigned Amount**
2	Housing	$900
3	Utilities	$150
4	Internet	$70
5	Groceries	$300
6	Coffee	$70
7	Dining Out	$200
8	Gas	$60
9	Beauty and Hygiene	$150
10	Travel	$300
11	Gifts	$100
12	Entertainment	$200
13	Student Loans	$250
14	Auto Loan	$300
15	Auto Insurance	$150
16	Rainy Day Savings	$300
17		
18	**Total**	**$3,500**

FIGURE 3-5:
A zero-based budget with an income of $3,500.

Making sure you track as you spend

After you spend money into a category, subtract it from the budgeted amount you decided on when creating this month's budget. For example, if you've budgeted $150 for takeout and then spend $24.35, you have exactly $125.65 left to spend for the rest of the month. *Remember:* Accurately documenting your expenses to subtract them from their category is essential. By entering your expenses, you're able to monitor your spending to keep yourself on track. Overspending is easier when you're not paying attention than when you're regularly tracking your spending.

TIP

Because the zero-based budget method can take up a lot of your time at first, and then later on as you routinely check in, figure out a way to make it stick. Like any new habit, you want to figure out a routine that works for you as you work with your new budget. Consider putting time aside each day to catch up on your spending so that you're not scrambling to remember later exactly what you've spent your money on. If daily seems like too much, consider weekly check-ins, but don't put it off any longer than that. Keeping an eye on where your money goes so you don't overspend makes you accountable.

Evaluating your success at the end of the month

At the end of the month, sit down and check to see how much you were able to stick to the amount you assigned to your specific categories. First of all, congratulations on sticking with it, regardless of whether you came out in the green or the red. If you ended up at zero (or with a surplus) with your budget, you're doing it right. When you aim for zero, extra money is always a pleasant surprise. You can put those additional funds toward different financial goals or any sinking fund(s) you've decided to start working on. I cover sinking funds in "Accounting for periodic or unexpected expenses" earlier in the chapter.

If you ended up with a deficit, never fear; you're still doing it right. I say that because even if you had a deficit, you tracked your spending for an entire month and stuck with it. A deficit in your first month of budgeting isn't the end of the world. Any type of budgeting method you use is going to require you to be flexible. Like many other things in your life, it will not be perfect on the first try. It gets easier over time and with practice.

That doesn't mean you should give up. Look over the expenses in the categories in which you went over budget and see whether anything sticks out to you, like multiple lunches at work or online shopping purchases. Now ask yourself a serious question: Are these overages a result of a lack of planning, or do I need to adjust the amount of money required for this category?

I think a lot of the expenses that drive people over their budgets stem from not properly planning. When my evenings get hectic, I'm less likely to pack my lunch or set up coffee for the next day. I'm also more likely to spend money on takeout if I don't make time to do grocery shopping or at least place an order for online delivery. I could avoid both of these additional budget killers if I just took time, even if it's ten minutes, to plan for the next day.

However, if planning isn't the issue, consider adjusting your budget category. You may have assigned too little without realizing how much you needed. Maybe you forgot an expense or a purchase you regularly need to take care of. If that's true, adjust it. Also, look at ways you can save on costs to make your budget go even further; I talk about cost-cutting options in Chapter 2.

Explore real-life examples

The example in Figure 3-6 shows a zero-based budget in action. In three columns, you can see the categories of the zero-based budget, the amount assigned and the actual amount spent.

	A	B	C	D
1	**Category**	**Assigned Amount**	**Actual Amount Spent**	
2	Housing	$900	$900	
3	Utilities	$150	$127.90	
4	Internet	$70	$70	
5	Groceries	$300	$259.67	$1,357.57
6	Coffee	$70	$63.45	
7	Dining Out	$200	$205.80	
8	Gas	$60	$54.33	
9	Beauty and Hygiene	$150	$160	$1,841.15
10	Travel	$300	$258.44	
11	Gifts	$100	$99.78	
12	Entertainment	$200	$247.22	
13	Student Loans	$250	$250	
14	Auto Loan	$300	$300	
15	Auto Insurance	$150	$150	$3,146.56
16	Rainy Day Savings	$300	$326.41	
17				
18	**Total**	**$3,500**		

FIGURE 3-6: Tracking spending against how much is assigned in a budget.

Figure 3-7 shows how your expenses may look different when splitting the expenses to correspond with paychecks rather than monthly. Instead of paying your expenses all at once, you can divide them by your number of monthly paydays and assign them to each paycheck.

Here's another zero-based budget example for a family with additional expenses for their children. I talk more in-depth about budgeting with kids in Chapter 12, but Figure 3-8 gives you an overall look at what that can look like when using a zero-based budget.

	A	B
1	**Paycheck 1**	**$1,400**
2		
3	Category	Budgeted Amount
4	Rent	$900
5	Groceries	$150
6	Subscriptions	$20
7	Gas	$60
8	Electric	$100
9	Water	$30
10	Fun	$140
11		
12	**Paycheck 2**	**$1,400**
13		
14	Category	Budgeted Amount
15	Student Loans	$300
16	Car Insurance	$100
17	Sinking Funds	$300
18	Groceries	$150
19	Gas	$60
20	Household Items	$200
21	Miscellaneous	$90
22	Gym	$50
23	Therapy	$150

FIGURE 3-7: Zero-based budgeting per paycheck.

	A	B
1	**Category**	**Amount**
2	Housing and Utilities	$1,800
3	Childcare	$500
4	Transportation	$500
5	Groceries and Household Items	$700
6	Dining Out	$300
7	Kids Allowance and Lunch Money	$100
8	Medical Expenses	$100
9	Date Night	$100
10	Personal Discretionary Spending Adult	$200
11	Personal Discretionary Spending Adult	$200
12	Student Loans	$300
13	Miscellaneous	$200
14		
15	**Total**	**$5,000**

FIGURE 3-8: An example of a zero-based budget for a family.

These examples aren't the only ones for zero-based budgeting, but they can give you a feel of how it looks in action.

Perusing the Pros of Using a Zero-Based Budget

Every single budgeting method has its advantages, and zero-based budgeting is no different. The following sections lay out some of the pros of using a zero-based budget.

Lets you see where every single dollar goes

You're not leaving anything to chance when you use the zero-based budgeting method. You know exactly where every dollar comes from and where every dollar goes off to. You've assigned a job to every cent you're bringing into your life, making it work for you and not against you.

Being in the driver's seat and telling your money where to go is exhilarating. You can customize your spending to fit your needs and ensure that all your expenses are covered. And if you're skidding off the track, you can quickly get back on thanks to the guardrails you have in place.

TIP

When you're creating a new zero-based (or any) budget for the first time, and especially one that works for you, you're going to feel so accomplished and financially stable. "Feeling accomplished" looks different for everybody, but to me it means having so much pride that you can barely keep it to yourself. When you feel proud of yourself in any area of your life, you'll be radiating confidence. It's okay to take a moment and whoop for joy, because look how cool you are. I firmly believe that if you don't toot your own horn, no one else will, so be the first person to celebrate your new ways and accomplishments.

Aligns your expenses with your income

Budgeting in general helps you stop spending more money than you're bringing in, but the zero-based budgeting method takes an additional extra step in preventing overspending. When you account for everything and preplan as much as humanly possible, you leave less to chance.

Putting aside money for sinking funds or your cash buffer is a good example. No longer will simple car repairs stress you out or have you scrambling to put them on a credit card. Car registration won't be another annoying forgotten-about expense. You'll even realize that you can afford your kid's birthday party without going broke for a paycheck. (Head to the earlier section "Accounting for periodic or unexpected expenses" for more on sinking funds and buffers.)

You're also more aware of your cash flow. When you're paying attention, you start to notice if things look off when you get paid. You aren't second-guessing whether you need to earn more to pay your bills because you already know where you are.

TIP

Zero-based budgeting also helps address the underlying cause of any overspending you may have been doing regularly. By confronting the root of your overspending, you can make any adjustments your life may need.

Dedicates space for goal setting

Some budgets just ask that you put a certain percentage aside for your savings and debt, but zero-based budgeting allows you to set detailed instructions of what money goes where. You also have the option to put additional funds toward things like debt elimination when you spend less in other budgeting categories. You can also get more creative with your spending to hit your financial goals faster by cutting back or rerouting those dollars somewhere else.

The number one reason I personally love zero-based budgeting (besides having control issues) is that I can make sure I'm putting money aside for my financial goals and priorities. Because you create the basic categories and can be as detailed as you want, you can ensure you're putting money toward everything you need and want.

Zero-based budgeting forces you to be responsible with your money. You're in control, so mindlessly spending funds you don't have is more difficult. Thinking about how much money you've earned makes you wonder whether you need to spend the whole amount of money you put aside for new clothing or need to have ten different streaming services when you're hardly home to begin with. Because you're tracking everything and leaving less to chance, you're fully aware of where you stand at all times.

TIP

Make a vision board if you're having trouble putting money toward your financial goals. Grab a poster board from your local dollar store and print off images of items you want to purchase or trips you want to take. Glue the images onto the poster board and then hang it up where you're most likely to see it every day. Seeing your goals daily can help you stay committed to working toward them. My current vision board includes the cover of this book because I'm writing it, a few inspirational quotes, a list of publications I want to write for, and a picture of a Mercedes-Benz convertible. Hey, a girl's got dreams, too!

Considering the Cons of Using a Zero-Based Budget

It's not all rainbows and butterflies in Zero-Based Budgeting Land. In the following sections, I let you in on some of the downsides of using this system.

It's a lot of work

Lying to you is one thing you never have to worry about with me. I'm overly blunt and sometimes need just to stop while I'm ahead. So I'll go ahead and say it: Zero-based budgeting is a lot of work — like, a lot.

You have to continuously match up your expenses to your income, and you're also thinking about where every single dollar goes. Then you're wondering whether you assigned that expense to the correct category or forgot to account for that $1.37 you spent on that candy bar, all while being in bed at 1 a.m. Zero-based budgeting can take up a lot of mental energy you don't have, especially if you're a budgeting newbie.

It can be tough if your income is irregular

Having fixed categories that you assign regular amounts to may not work if you have an irregular income. In a perfect world, you could put whatever you earned in a business checking account and then pay yourself regularly into a separate account. So if you earned less one month than you usually do, no big deal. You'd still have a pot of money to dip into. But unless you have already established savings put aside, that's rarely how the process works. In reality, sometimes you're robbing Peter to pay Paul and vice versa. With your new budgeting skills, you can establish that dreamy business account I just described, but you may not be there yet.

It may make your variable spending stressful

Although zero-based budgeting can be flexible, it can also be rigid. Rather than giving yourself a pot of money and saying, "have at it," you're mentally stamping every dollar with a work assignment. This structure can leave you unable to take advantage of certain situations or opportunities because you didn't budget ahead for them. Say you're stressed out and feel like you need to grab dinner with a friend to sort out your thoughts in person. You may deny yourself that privilege if you're already over budget in that category, even though if you had just spent that $20 on drinks, you and your friend could have talked through a solution that allowed you to sleep better at night.

Sticking to a rigid way of tracking may also leave you feeling defeated if you go over your budget categories. Rather than using a general sum of money you can use to cover multiple categories, you're only giving yourself small increments here and there. Even outside of your sinking funds, stuff can come up that can wreck your budget. If you're having a challenging time being as proactive as this budget requires, you may feel like throwing in the towel early in the game.

Asking Yourself Whether Zero-Based Budgeting Will Work If . . .

You may be wondering whether zero-based budgeting is doable for you. In the following sections, I address two of the most common concerns I hear from people about this budgeting method.

You don't have the same expenses every month

You absolutely can work the zero-based budget system with varying expenses as long as you do the work while being focused. In addition to having one or more sinking funds (which I discuss earlier in the chapter) so that irregular expenses no longer surprise you, you can also sit with your planner/calendar and see whether you need to adjust your budget in real time based on upcoming events. Sometimes events and life situations do suddenly pop up. In these cases, you can transfer the funds from other categories to make your overall budget work for you, not against you.

Note: If you don't have the same monthly expenses every time and feel that your variable expenses come from one general fund instead, consider the 50/30/20 budget, which I discuss in full detail in Chapter 4.

You're not organized

Zero-based budgeting will be more challenging for you if you're not organized. It'll also be more difficult if you don't have the time to plan and commit properly. That doesn't mean any budgeting method isn't for you. It just means this one isn't.

REMEMBER

Although zero-based budgeting can motivate you to be more organized with your finances, it's okay if it doesn't. Shame isn't a motivating tool, and we already experience enough of that throughout life, so don't extend the same courtesy to your finances.

TIPS FOR ORGANIZING YOUR FINANCIAL LIFE

Being organized can be more challenging for some than others, especially if you're *neurodivergent* (your brain functions differently from what's traditionally considered "typical"). Here are some simple steps you can take to keep your financial ducks in a row:

- **Take time to file away the necessary paperwork and check on your financial accounts to ensure you don't need to take care of any issues right away.** If you're overwhelmed, ask for help. Believe it or not, some people love organizing so much that they'd be willing to do it for free if someone needed help. If you have a loved one or friend who has this strength, ask them whether they have time available to help you get organized. They may think of a more manageable filing system for you to implement, and having a second set of eyes is always helpful when dealing with clutter.

- **Establish a bill-paying system.** It doesn't have to be an elaborate ordeal, but taking time to pay your bills can help reduce late fees and interest if you're paying down debt. Write out a list of every bill and its due date and keep it on your desk. Every 1st and 15th of the month, look at your checking account to make sure each bill has been paid. If you have difficulty remembering, set whatever bills you can to autopay so you never miss one again.

Chapter **4**

The 50/30/20 Budget

I n their book *All Your Worth: The Ultimate Lifetime Money Plan* (Free Press), Senator Elizabeth Warren and Amelia Warren Tyagi first shared the concept of the 50/30/20 Budget Rule. Senator Warren created the 50/30/20 Budget Rule to help American families achieve greater financial stability.

The *50/30/20 budget* allocates money for all your financial needs, wants, and goals in a simple formula: 50 percent of your income goes toward your needs, 30 percent goes toward your wants, and the remaining 20 percent goes toward your savings and debt. This budgeting guideline should make people feel less stressed about money management because it's easier than other budgeting methods such as the zero-based budget in Chapter 3. It may also be a lot more flexible to follow and — dare I say it — fun. (And I have both Stephen King and my cat mentioned in my professional bio. I know about fun.)

TECHNICAL STUFF

Senator Warren is also credited as one of the creators of the Consumer Financial Protection Bureau (CFPB). The CFPB plays a significant role in enforcing responsibility for unfair lending practices and advocating for consumer rights. Every time someone commits fraud with your checking account, your financial institution can help you get your money back with regulations the CFPB has put in place.

REMEMBER

When I refer to "income" in this chapter, I mean your net income, not your gross income. Your *gross income* is the total amount of money you earn. Your *net income* is the amount of money you have left over after paying taxes and taking out any garnishments.

Setting up the 50/30/20 Budget

The 50/30/20 budget can be a great way for newbies and seasoned budgeters alike to get (back) on track without having to overhaul all their finances at once. This budget can help you get ahead financially without feeling the pinch.

TIP

Check out NerdWallet's free 50/30/20 budget calculator (www.nerdwallet.com/article/finance/nerdwallet-budget-calculator). You can enter your net income, and the budget total for your needs, wants, and savings categories will be calculated for you. Signing up for a NerdWallet account will allow you to track your monthly expenses.

Determine your income

The first step of setting up your 50/30/20 budget is just like the first step of any budget: You need to calculate your income. Calculating your income is the most crucial step because the rest of your budget is based on it. Figure out your monthly income first, as I explain in Chapter 2.

If you get paid irregularly, add your past six months of income together and divide it by six to get your average monthly income. This budget doesn't make you assign a job to every single dollar when it comes in, but you do put a certain percentage of your income into each category (or "bucket") of this money management plan, as shown in Figure 4-1.

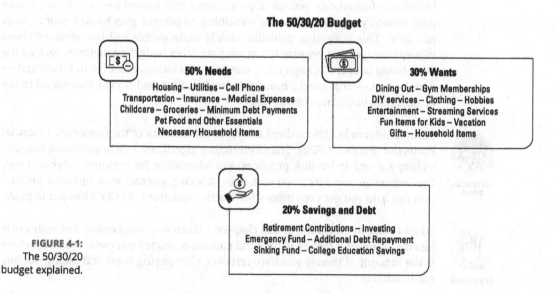

The 50/30/20 Budget

50% Needs
Housing – Utilities – Cell Phone
Transportation – Insurance – Medical Expenses
Childcare – Groceries – Minimum Debt Payments
Pet Food and Other Essentials
Necessary Household Items

30% Wants
Dining Out – Gym Memberships
DIY services – Clothing – Hobbies
Entertainment – Streaming Services
Fun Items for Kids – Vacation
Gifts – Household Items

20% Savings and Debt
Retirement Contributions – Investing
Emergency Fund – Additional Debt Repayment
Sinking Fund – College Education Savings

FIGURE 4-1:
The 50/30/20 budget explained.

Distinguish wants and needs

Confusing your needs with your wants (and vice versa) is easy. You need clothes, but you don't need expensive ones from a top designer. Food is a need, but shopping at the most expensive grocery store in town isn't. Your child may need supplies for school, but you can grab those items from the dollar store; they don't have to come from the fancy big box store. You get the picture.

One way to look at the difference is to consider whether not paying for the item will slightly inconvenience you or sincerely negatively impact you. If you have to clean your own house instead of having a housekeeper, that's likely an inconvenience. If you can't afford to refill your monthly prescriptions, that's your life being negatively impacted.

TIP

That's not to say that you need to focus only on your needs; you're human and can't live off ramen noodles forever. I just want to point out how essential differentiating your wants and needs is and how you can practice responsible *discretionary spending* (voluntarily spending money you don't need to). I mean, you *are* dedicating at least 30 percent of your budget to the fun stuff in this system. You can at least make your wants percentage stretch to give you the most bang for your buck.

Determine your 50 percent needs

Needs are things that you can't skimp out on without experiencing dire consequences. Humans need both food and shelter to survive. I need gas in my car to get around, while you may need a subway pass to get to work. You can include both fixed expenses and variable expenses in the needs category. You can read more about fixed and variable expenses in Chapter 2.

Here are some things that may qualify as a need:

>> **Rent or mortgage**

>> **Property taxes and HOA dues**

>> **Utilities like electricity, water, Internet, and cellphone service**

>> *Note:* Internet is also considered a need if you're a remote worker or have children who have homework. Heck, I think access to the Internet is a need for anyone because of how much of daily life now depends on it.

TIP

>> **Minimum payments on loans and other lines of credit, such as a car loan or student loans, so that you stay in good standing**

If you have federal student loans, you can qualify for what's known as an Income-Based Repayment Plan (IBR). The IBR states that you can't pay more than 10 percent of your total income toward your student loans.

>> **Groceries**

- **Food:** I'm talking traditional vegetables, grains, and protein, not meal-prep kits or fancy premade dishes from the hot food section or salad bar.

- **Personal hygiene products as well as grooming services that are essential such as haircuts.**

- **Any needed household cleaning supplies such as laundry detergent and dish soap.**

>> **Transportation expenses such as gas and passes to ride public transportation**

>> **Insurance such as auto, rental, or homeowners and medical and/or dental premiums not covered by an employer**

>> **Prescriptions, therapy, and any doctor co-pays or medical/dental deductibles**

Note: I firmly believe that if you need therapy, you put it in the need category. Therapy is necessary for a productive and happy you, and it can also prevent you from spending money on poor choices because of a lack of better judgment. I discuss ways to save on treatment in Chapter 14.

>> **Childcare and other expenses related to caring for dependent children**

>> **Current educational expenses for you or your child, such as tuition, books, and parking passes**

>> **Office supplies and equipment that are vital to your earning an income**

>> **Professional licenses and dues**

>> **Clothing (within reason)**

>> **Pet supplies, including food, medicine, cat litter, animal bedding, and required veterinarian visits**

>> **Urgent household repairs that directly impact safety and well-being**

REMEMBER

This isn't a complete list of needs because your situation is unique, but it's a good general list of what people can and can't live without. If not paying for it would significantly impact your life, it's on this list.

If you need help figuring out what to include in your living expenses, consider asking a close friend or someone you trust. They may provide some insight into situations you didn't think to consider.

Review your spending analysis to make sure you don't forget anything. (Refer to Chapter 1 if you haven't completed one.) Note that all your needs may not fit within 50 percent of your income; if that's the case, check out the later section "Example two" for some suggestions on reducing your needs expenses.

TIP

When possible, prioritize wellness in your budget. If you're struggling to find the money, take advantage of free or low-cost resources such as contacting local community health services, watching exercise or yoga videos on YouTube, checking out books from your local library, and downloading meditation apps.

Evaluate your 30 percent wants

This category is just as it sounds: It's all about the fun stuff. If you want something that's not vital to your survival, it goes in here. Another way to look at it is as all the spending you do that doesn't necessarily fit in the needs category in the preceding section. Some examples include the following:

>> **Household decor items, like candles**

>> **Furniture**

>> **Services you can do yourself, such as house cleaning, meal prepping, and landscaping**

>> **Cosmetic procedures like Botox, chemical peels, facials, and adult braces**

   Adult braces aren't always for cosmetic reasons but are usually not covered by dental insurance. You can also include grooming services you can do yourself, such as pedicures and hair removal.

>> **Makeup**

   Note: As I explain in Chapter 2, depending on circumstances, makeup can sometimes qualify as a need. But in most cases, it's probably a want.

>> **Expensive clothing and shoes**

>> **Gym memberships**

>> **Subscription boxes, such as those containing food, beauty products, hobby items, and so on**

>> **Items needed for hobbies, such as certain supplies or magazines**

>> **Things you randomly collect, like stuffed animals**

- » Continuing education, like online classes
- » Streaming services
- » Dining out
- » Takeout coffee
- » Child-related expenses such as toys, extracurricular activities, and entertainment
- » Pet toys (and anything else your furry friends don't need to survive)
- » Vacations
- » Gifts
- » Concerts and other outings with friends
- » Annual passes to places like the zoo and local museums
- » Decorations for holidays
- » Parties

Yes, streaming services are considered a want because you don't need them to survive, especially when so many free channels are available over an antenna. Entertainment isn't a need, no matter how much people try to convince themselves that it is. And buying that coffee for your commute isn't a necessity, even when you feel like a quick caffeine boost is what you *need*.

REMEMBER

It's okay to want stuff. Yeah, I said it. I may get my finance street cred checked next time I go to a conference, but I like spending money on stuff for my paper planner. Getting to decorate a page according to my goals and plans for that particular day brings me joy. They're just adult stickers that make me giddy. Your wants should bring you joy, too. Life is too short for them not to.

Save 20 percent for retirement and future expenses

The last category of the 50/30/20 budget is dedicated to your future financial responsibilities. In this category, you include saving for your retirement as well as any expenses you may have in the future. Here are some examples of things you can put your 20 percent toward:

- » Retirement accounts like your 401(k), 403(b), and IRAs
- » Investing, such as index funds and bonds, that you do outside of retirement accounts

>> **Establishing an _emergency fund_**

An emergency fund is a separate amount of money that is intended to cover your bills in case of job loss or another major expense, such as a needed home repair or medical bill. (See Chapter 8 for more information.)

>> **Sinking funds for annual expenses like car registration, gifting, and healthcare-related costs such as insurance deductibles**

For more information about a sinking fund, see Chapter 3.

>> **Fun extras for your child, such as paying for summer camp when it isn't needed for childcare**

>> **Your child's future college or technical education**

>> **Additional payments on your debt, including loans financed through a financial institution or from an individual, credit card debt, and old medical bills**

>> **Future taxes**

>> **Tithing (see the tip below)**

>> **Unexpected expenses that aren't part of your regular budget, such as car and home repairs and emergency pet care**

TIP

Some people may consider tithing a need instead of budgeting for it within their savings. How you decide to account for it in your budget is totally up to you. Just be aware that you'll need to decide how the expense will be categorized — monthly or periodically.

The opportunities are endless here, and you can decide how you want to save. Maybe one month you're feeling spicy and throw an extra $100 on that annoying credit card debt that you've had for several months. Then the next month, you stash some additional money aside in your kid's college fund because they just announced they want to be a doctor. You don't need to be a doctor to know that medical school is expensive, so you're adding the extra $100 there instead.

As a self-employed person, I'm currently focusing this category on a cash buffer in my business checking account so that I can start to pay myself a regular income out of savings instead of living off an irregular one. I also have a special-needs pet who often needs unplanned-for medical care. It ain't for the weak, but just like anything else in my budget, I make room for the things that matter the most.

REMEMBER

I can't stress enough how much an emergency fund can save you from all types of stressful financial situations. It can mean the ability to get your car fixed so you and your family have reliable transportation. It can determine whether your pet can come home from the vet with medicine after a successful procedure. It can even mean that you can walk away from an abusive situation. (*Note:* If you or someone you know is in a domestic violence situation, please call the National Domestic Violence Hotline at 1-800-799-7233. You can also go online at www.thehotline.org.)

I also love considering the savings category the "preparing my future self" category. Although I may not like that I'm unable to travel to the beach or buy a coffee, future me is going to appreciate having an easier retirement thanks to the sacrifices current me is making. Is it easy? Heck no. Sometimes I feel deprived when I see my peers taking expensive vacations. But I can use it as motivation to make more money so I can travel, too!

Explore real-life examples

The following sections crunch some numbers for hypothetical 50/30/20 budgeting scenarios.

Example one

Say you take home $4,000 a month after taxes (see Figure 4-2). If you use the 50/30/20 budget rule, you're spending roughly the following for each category:

Needs (50 percent) = $2,000

Wants (30 percent) = $1,200

Savings (20 percent) = $800

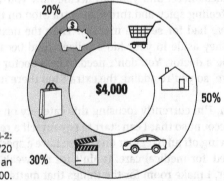

FIGURE 4-2:
A 50/30/20 budget for an income of $4,000.

Now assume your needs breakdown looks like this:

Rent/mortgage = $1,200

Utilities = $200

Transportation = $200

Groceries = $300

Other = $100

Total = $2,000

To cover your needs with 50 percent of this income, your expenses need to be $2,000 or less, so you're on track so far.

Maybe your wants look like this:

Streaming services = $50

Dining out = $200

Cleaning service = $100

Entertainment = $200

Travel = $400

Lunches out with co-workers = $100

Child's extracurricular activities = $150

Total = $1,200

That matches the maximum 30 percent you've budgeted for this category. All that's left is to track your savings:

Investing = $250

Emergency fund = $100

Sinking funds = $200

College savings account (529 plan) = $250

Total = $800

That's exactly what you've budgeted. All your actual spending matches the target numbers, making your $4,000 income sufficient. Way to go, hypothetical you.

TIP

You can always play around with the percentages. You may not need 30 percent of your income for your wants, and you can reallocate that extra percentage to one of the other buckets. Consider whether you need to put 30 percent of your income toward your wants. In this scenario, you've allocated $1,200 for fun money, but you can always play with the percentages. For example, you may want to put more money aside for any goals you may be pursuing, increasing the 20 percent bucket by funneling some of your wants money into the savings category. Start small and move the needle little by little. You'll be surprised how much you can save when you put your mind to it.

TIP

Financial goals are plans you want to accomplish with your money. It can be something such as buying a new wardrobe to saving for a down payment on a home. Just like regular goals, they require actionable steps you can take to achieve them. See Chapter 16 for more information.

Example two

Your needs may not always fit the 50 percent allocation this budget provides. Using $3,600 as your monthly income (see Figure 4-3), your categories break down this way:

Needs (50 percent) = $1,800

Wants (30 percent) = $1,080

Savings (20 percent) = $720

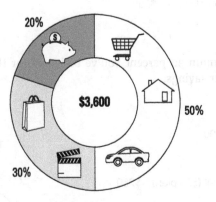

FIGURE 4-3:
A 50/30/20
budget for an
income of $3,600.

Now say your needs look like this:

Rent = $1,600

Utilities $250

Groceries = $225

Transportation = $125

Other $100

Total = $2,300

Your needs are $2,300 a month, or approximately 64 percent of your income. Fifty percent of your income isn't going to cover your needs sufficiently, so you're going to be over budget. One solution is to allocate a different percentage to your wants and savings to accommodate your living expenses adequately.

WARNING

Another solution is to see whether you can reduce your needs spending, because paying a large percentage of your income toward only needs can be risky. The more money you need to survive, the more you need to adequately plan and save in your emergency fund to help prevent financial catastrophe in case of job loss. Look to see whether you can reduce any expenses in your needs category. Try to downsize your lifestyle by finding cheaper living accommodations and utilizing any discounts you may qualify for.

You can also consider increasing your income by earning extra money from a part-time job or side gig in your free time. (Chapter 2 has more on income streams.) Even earning an extra $100 a week (after taxes) equals at least $400 a month to add to your main income.

TIP

No matter what you try, you may not be able to keep your needs under the assigned 50 percent total. Squeezing a square peg in a round hole can be frustrating, no matter how much you try. Don't beat yourself up, especially when plenty of other budgeting methods are out there for you to try on. Check out the other chapters in Part 2 for more options.

THE BOTTOM LINE

Having three main categories to balance rather than several can be much more manageable when you're starting your budget journey. It still provides structure but not so much that you feel it's rigid and constrictive. If you're too strict, you may get turned off and stop using your budget altogether. However, identifying whether you have any spending habits you need to improve can be more problematic with a 50/30/20 budget.

Because the 50/30/20 budget is more flexible than other budgeting methods, you have to worry only about setting expenses to percentages and not specific amounts. Instead of overcategorizing, this approach has general spending buckets that you don't need to overanalyze. Less stress overall means it's a budget you're more likely to stick to. That's a good thing.

Looking at the Pros of Using a 50/30/20 Budget

In this section, I lay out some of the advantages that come with the 50/30/20 budgeting method.

It's simple

Other budgets can seem overwhelming with all their steps and categories. But the 50/30/20 budget is pretty easy. You have only three categories to fill and monitor throughout the month. You don't need to monitor every purchase or handcuff yourself to spreadsheets. You don't feel deprived of lunches out with co-workers or grabbing tickets to the last-minute event your friends invite you to.

REMEMBER

Different stages of your life may require you to use different budgeting methods. The best way to succeed is to use what works best for your current situation. You may be in a stage now without a mortgage or dependents and the 50/30/20 is a good choice. But as you take on more responsibility or your goals change, you may need to adjust your method.

It creates financial responsibility from the get-go

The 50/30/20 budget forces you to be financially responsible without thinking about it. Designating 50 percent of your income to necessities or living expenses is a significant financial move. It gives you more control over the other parts of your life, including your future plans, by allowing you to save a good percentage of your income. And it gently forces you to live on less of your income. The less dependent you are on your income to cover your living expenses, the less an unexpected job loss may affect you.

It works regardless of your income level

Another cool thing about the 50/30/20 budget is that you don't need to make a certain amount of income to enjoy the benefits. Because you're not overcategorizing items, you're able to avoid the stress that comes with having to assign every category a dollar amount. There is no additional pressure from overspending in a category as long as it's within the allocated percentage. No matter your income, living on 50 percent is always a good thing. The lower your living expenses are, the less you'll need to worry about coverage in case of a loss of income.

You can include fun in your budget

Thirty percent of your income is now bookmarked for fun! How cool is that?!?! I know the exclamations may seem a bit extreme, but I want to emphasize how much money you have to enjoy your life as you see fit with this method. As long as you can fit your expenses within a certain budget amount, you can watch your fancy streaming platform while eating some delivery and then grab a coffee on your way to work the next morning, all without any guilt.

You can enjoy a higher tier for your streaming service without having to nickel and dime your rate or see whether you can do without. You can get a gym membership and new gym shoes while you're at it. This budget is flexible so that you can be, too.

TIP

You can include even more fun in your 30 percent if you work to make your money stretch. You can almost always find a cheaper way to do something. Try using services like Groupon or look for free community passes to the zoo, state parks, museums, and so on at your local library. Chapter 16 provides a few suggestions for finding inexpensive ways to include "fun" in your budget. If you're trying to make your 30 percent go farther with the littles, just do an Internet search for "Free things to do with kids + [city you live in]," and a list will pop up — trust me!

Your financial goals are a priority

The 50/30/20 budget forces you to focus on your financial goals. Paying off debt so you can pay less money in interest fees over time is an excellent use of this category, as is paying any extra on loans that may have lingered.

REMEMBER

Having debt doesn't make you an awful person, but it can reduce opportunities to use that money in another category of your budget. For example, say a significant part of your needs allocation goes toward your student loan. If you put your 20 percent savings allocation into paying off that debt sooner, you free up room in your needs category so that if, say, your dream job opens up but at a pay cut, you're in a position to seize that opportunity, trim your needs budget, and live within those reduced means.

Setting aside 20 percent of your income can help you with saving for your retirement. If you automatically know you should be putting a monetary amount toward the future, you can set up deductions with your employer to automatically deposit money into your 401(k).

You can also set up automatic deductions for paying off your debt and a high-yield savings account (HYSA) to save for a rainy day. Bonus? If your HYSA is used to save money you were going to save anyway, you can be making interest for free! I recommend checking out Capital One's HYSA at www.capitalone.com/.

Another avenue is to use part of that 20 percent to put money aside for a down payment on a home or other major life events like a wedding. You can ensure your emergency fund is adequately stocked up for a rainy day or to cover all your bills if you're taking unpaid parental leave. (See Chapter 13 for more information about parental leave.)

Checking out the Cons of Using a 50/30/20 Budget

Just like any budgeting method, the 50/30/20 system has a few cons you need to be aware of, too.

Your categories may not match the percentage assigned

Just as your needs may not match up to 50 percent of your allocated income (as I illustrate in the "Example two" section earlier in the chapter), your wants and savings may not track to their respective percentages. Here are some possible reasons you exceed any of these three categories:

>> **You live in an area with a higher cost of living.** If you're paying more for housing, you may also be paying more for utilities, pushing your needs above 50 percent. In some places like New York City and San Francisco, finding an inexpensive place to live isn't easy or even doable. I know people who commute one hour by train each way from Pennsylvania to New York City because they can't afford to live in NYC.

>> **Your income is lower than average (for your state), making saving according to percentages difficult.** You can quickly max out the first and possibly second budgeting categories when you're earning less than the average income according to your state. In this case, this budgeting method may be an unrealistic option for you.

>> **It doesn't count for times of inflation, when basic expenses can sky-rocket.** Goods like groceries, gas, and household items fluctuate depending on the current state of the economy. Living on less than 50 percent is easy when inflation rates are low and more challenging when they're higher. For example, if you have a large family to feed, doubling your grocery expenses because of inflation may be a significant hit to your budget.

- **You have a higher percentage of needs going toward expenses like childcare.** Because of childcare's costs, the United States is one of the most expensive countries to raise a child in. Childcare subsidies can help but are hard to qualify for even if childcare takes up almost half your income. Childcare costs are usually determined by state and the general costs of living. According to a 2022 Cost of Care survey by Care.com, 51 percent of parents surveyed said they're spending more than 20 percent of their household income on childcare.

- **You're paying off a lot of debt.** Student loans in particular can take up a substantial amount of anyone's income.

- **You're trying to save for an early retirement.** The earlier you're trying to leave the workforce, the more of your income you need to designate toward savings and investing. You may be looking at putting between 40 and 50 percent of your income toward savings to hit these financial goals. I've known people who managed to save 75 percent of their income. I don't know how I feel about the lifestyle choices they had to make to get there, but I know they were able to do it.

- **You're behind in retirement savings.** If you're behind in retirement, you need to save more money, too. Depending on how long you have until you retire, you may need to take advantage of catch-up contributions to your 401(k). You may also need to be investing additional funds as much as possible or even trying to pay off your mortgage.

REMEMBER

Determining how to categorize your wants and needs can be difficult, which can skew the percentages in this budget. Check out the earlier section "Distinguish wants and needs" for more on how to differentiate between the two.

You may use your fun budget for junk you don't need

If you're like me and have a complicated history with shopping, giving yourself 30 percent of your income to spend on whatever tickles your fancy may be downright dangerous. I can't give myself an online shopping budget category because I know in the deepest part of my heart that I'll spend every cent of it. I won't even need anything, and I'll still make sure I spend every penny out of that sucker. If you don't believe me, ask my dog, Annie. She's the recipient of a floral scarf she can't keep on for more than five minutes.

Buying things indiscriminately means you eventually accumulate a lot of junk you don't need or even want. Looking around your house and seeing everything that was once money sitting in your checking account can be disheartening. As much as you tell yourself you can sell it online, no one will buy your $1,000 couch for $900 — no one.

Spending money on stuff that doesn't matter just because you can may mean you ultimately take longer to hit your financial goals such as saving for your future, making a big purchase you're eyeing, or even taking a fancy trip you've been dreaming about for years. Look around your house and add up how much the junk you don't want costs you. If it's ten bucks, no big deal, but hundreds of dollars could've been a plane ticket to somewhere cool if you'd funneled it into your savings category instead of spending it on frivolous wants.

TIP

To resist impulse buys, try instituting a waiting period. Every time you want to purchase something, put it on a list along with its cost. Then come back 48 hours later to see whether you still want it. You can also create wish lists at your favorite online retailers to reference later for a more conscious spending experience. Ask me how many scarves Annie has now.

Finding guidance for savings is difficult

You know that you have 20 percent of your income to work with automatically, but this fact doesn't mean you know where that money should go. The budget doesn't come with guidance on what you should save for first or pay off next or recommendations on different investment vehicles that you could be taking advantage of given your current life situation.

TIP

If you're new to investing, check out Investopedia (www.investopedia.com). Investopedia covers essential money topics such as how to manage your money and pick a checking account, but it also dives deep into explaining different ways to invest your money, including options like exchange-traded funds. You can also find out more about the different retirement accounts available.

Evaluating Whether a 50/30/20 Budget Will Work If . . .

The 50/30/20 budget isn't for everyone, but it may be right for you. Or not. The following sections explore some common scenarios.

TIP

Different stages of your life may require you to use different budgeting methods. The best way to succeed is to use what works best for your current situation. You may be in a stage now without a mortgage or dependents and the 50/30/20 is a good choice. But as you take on more responsibility or your goals change, you may need to adjust your method.

You have a variable income

Okay, here I go, having to be the realistic personal finance columnist again. If you have a variable income, I honestly don't think the 50/30/20 budget will work for you. This budgeting method works best if you have a stable income. A *variable income* means you get paid irregularly and have different amounts of money coming in at different times. Having a variable income is perfectly fine. I'm paid this way.

The issue with the 50/30/20 budget in this situation is that because your income varies every month, so does the amount of money you can assign to your needs, wants, and savings. But what you actually spend on those categories, especially needs, doesn't automatically change accordingly. If you have a slow month, you may be looking at trying to cover your needs with far less than is realistic or doable. In this case, you should consider other budgeting methods in Part 2.

You're new to adulting

Yes, the 50/30/20 budget can work for you. For starters, it's better than having no budgeting method. Any type of budgeting when you're first starting in the real world benefits you. You need to know your overall expenses, the difference between wants and needs, and the types of savings you can pursue. It also helps you designate money for your debt.

I love the 50/30/20 method for those just starting because it's a good rule of thumb to start your money journey. You figure out how to live on half your income and how important considering needs versus wants is. If you need to live on more of your income, this technique can motivate you to lower your expenses to fit within the 50 percent threshold. Getting into the habit of routinely trying to lower your expenses can set you up to save money throughout your life.

You also have designated fun money, so you don't feel as restricted as you may with other budgeting methods. Life is about balance, so why wouldn't you want that for your budget? The 50/30/20 budget creates this freedom and allows you to put money toward saving for your future.

Chapter 5

The Envelope Budget

One of the scariest things I've done in my life is decide to pursue self-employment. I'd worked in the nonprofit sector for more than 20 years and loved it most of the time. Being on my own since age 15 meant that a steady paycheck was what security looked like to me, and I had a hard time letting that go. Without steady pay, my income took a significant hit. Suddenly, I was more anxious about money than I had been in a long time.

Determined to make my money last while I worked on securing clients, I decided to try out the envelope budget system. *The envelope budget method* (also referred to as *cash envelopes* or *cash stuffing*) is an effective way to monitor your cash flow visually and interactively. Like the zero-based budgeting method I discuss in Chapter 3, you assign a dollar amount to a list of categories that your expenses fall under. However, the envelope budget doesn't require you to sort through your checking account to track expenses or sit in front of a spreadsheet to determine how much you have left to stretch until the end of the month.

After you've determined the amount of money for each category, you withdraw the amount of cash you've budgeted for from your checking account and put it into envelopes assigned to those categories. Then you're allowed to spend the cash in your envelopes however you see fit. But that's it — no debit or credit card for everyday expenses. When your cash is gone, it's gone. You're out of money until the next payday, when you can refill your envelopes again.

This method of budgeting can help you become more disciplined with your spending. You're physically handling the money from your checking account, so your cash becomes tangible — physically handing it over for purchases rather than using your debit or credit card. Otherwise, you'd have to deal with a credit card statement that arrives later.

My goal when choosing this system was to focus on my needs until I had a regular income again and then go from there (for details on needs versus wants, see Chapter 4). This budgeting system seemed to provide firm boundaries, which I needed if I was going to make my cash flow stretch. Surprisingly, it not only worked but also has become one of my favorite budgeting methods.

Research has shown that, as a society, we hate the feeling of parting with physical cash. This theory is known as the *pain of paying concept*, which means you experience a feeling of loss when you spend your physical money for a product or service. Conversely, other studies have shown that spending with credit cards doesn't provide that immediate sense of consequence. Swiping a piece of plastic doesn't hit your brain the same way, because that's a problem for future you.

REMEMBER

Money is emotional, and people don't like feeling the consequences of their spending, but immediate consequences can be a reliable learning tool, especially regarding your hard-earned cash. The envelope budget forces you to deal with these effects in a way that debit and credit cards don't.

This effect is especially true for me. I've learned as I've gotten older that I'm a visual learner. The envelope system lets me see the money leaving my account and allows me to feel the pain of paying, which prohibits any unnecessary spending. Because I'm less likely to spend money with this method, coming in under budget is even easier for me.

Setting Up Your Envelope Budget

The envelope budget method is an easy way to put money aside while taking care of both your fixed and variable expenses. It also helps you not spend more than your income, so you don't have to deal with a deficit later on.

REMEMBER

Fixed expenses stay the same every month, while *variable expenses* can fluctuate. I cover the differences between fixed and variable expenses in Chapter 2.

Envelope budgeting requires you to be disciplined with your spending without even realizing it. Its simplicity means you're more likely to stick with it, which is a huge plus for any budget.

REMEMBER

The envelope budget method doesn't work unless you hold yourself accountable. That means being honest with the cash you have at hand and how you're spending it.

TIP

If you love the envelope budgeting method but for whatever reason don't have easy access to cash, try the Goodbudget app for your phone or online browser. You can assign cash to virtual envelopes and track your spending through the app. Goodbudget immediately updates to let you know how much you have left in your categories, and you can set alerts for when a category gets too low. You can plan for future spending, check on your debt progress, and sync categories with your partner or other family members.

Determine your expense categories

First things first: Make a list of all of your expenses, both fixed and variable, as I lay out in Chapter 2. Group your expenses by category.

Some ideas for categories include (but aren't limited to) these:

- » Groceries
- » Dining out (takeout meals and coffee; see the tip below)
- » Entertainment (magazine subscriptions, concerts or movies, hobby supplies, streaming services, books)
- » Date night
- » Pets
- » Children (allowance, money for toys and entertainment)
- » Transportation
- » Medical
- » Household items
- » Adult allowance
- » Miscellaneous (anything you forgot or pops up that is not covered in another envelope for that budgeting period)
- » Hygiene and beauty
- » Services (housekeeper, landscaper, massage therapist)
- » Travel
- » Gifts

>> **Home decor and related projects that are not repairs**

>> **Tithing**

>> **Rent or mortgage**

>> **Insurance (rent/homeowners, car, medical, dental)**

>> **Utilities**

>> **Debt (credit cards, student and automobile loans, other types of debt)**

>> **Sinking funds (car maintenance, future holiday celebrations, medical procedures, emergency funds; check out Chapter 3 for more info)**

TIP

Some expenses may qualify under more than one category, but be careful to only use one category. For example, getting drinks or buying coffee makes sense under dining out or entertainment. Either choice is fine as long as you apply it consistently in one category.

For example, I place all my streaming service subscriptions under my entertainment category. I also group anything else I do for fun in this category, like supplies for hobbies or concert tickets.

After you've created categories, assign a dollar amount to each one according to your income and financial goals. You want to see which category has the most variable expenses along with how much you are spending. High variability indicates that a category should have a cash envelope for better money management. If it's a fixed expense, such as rent or utilities, dedicating an envelope to it doesn't make sense because you have no control over the amount being spent.

At this point, assign a dollar amount to each category. A sample list may look like this:

Groceries: $200

Dining out: $150

Medical insurance: $100

Gas: $50

Entertainment: $125

Gifts: $50

Total: $675

Note: You'll need to subtract the expenses that are withdrawn automatically from your account. Using the sample expense categories above, subtract your $10 monthly Internet radio subscription from your entertainment category.

Because that $10 is coming out of your account automatically, you don't also put it in the associated envelope so you aren't spending money you don't have. In this case, $125 − $10 = $115 leftover for the entertainment envelope after you subtract the expense.

REMEMBER

Don't budget more for your expenses than you make in income. If you need to, list all the income you'll earn during a month to remember how much you can responsibly assign to each category. Subtract your expenses from your income. If you have extra leftover, you're in great shape. If you come up negative, go back and crunch your numbers again. You need to cut back your spending or determine ways to increase your income.

Create the cash envelopes

You need a stack of envelopes. If you're just starting, I find the dollar store envelopes the most cost-effective. If this system works for you, you can invest in higher quality envelopes later.

Grab a marker or pen and label your envelopes the categories you've listed (see the preceding section). Each category should have its own envelope. Don't put multiple categories into one envelope, or this budgeting method won't work. Be sure to also create an envelope labeled "to deposit." You don't put any money in this packet upfront, but you need it ready for cases where noncash purchases are unavoidable, as I explain later in the chapter. Figure 5-1 shows you what your envelopes may look like.

Every paycheck, you'll refill your envelopes. I refill my envelopes biweekly because that's what works for me with my irregular income. If you get paid monthly, you could do this as well to help keep your cashflow consistent throughout the month.

Next, look at how much cash you need for each envelope. Because you need to withdraw cash from the bank or ATM, you have to determine how many bills you need in specific denominations. For example, if you have $50 budgeted for gas, you need to withdraw a $50 bill or two $20 bills and one $10 bill. If this math seems like too much work, just deal in numbers that you can take care of with $20 bills. So instead of assigning $50 for gas, you'd round down to $40 or up to $60.

TIP

One of the things I love about the cash envelope system is that you can be as creative as you want. You can find cash envelope templates and assembly instructions for free on many websites by just searching for "free cash envelope template." I design my cash envelopes by using Canva (www.canva.com). It's fun and free and lets me be creative! You can also check out sites like Etsy (www.etsy.com) for templates you can purchase and then print out. (Just be sure you're taking that money from the correct category.)

Your Cash Envelopes

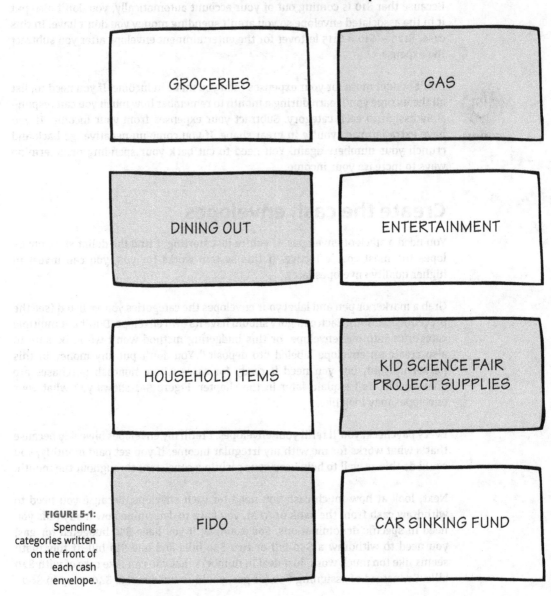

GROCERIES

GAS

DINING OUT

ENTERTAINMENT

HOUSEHOLD ITEMS

KID SCIENCE FAIR
PROJECT SUPPLIES

FIDO

CAR SINKING FUND

FIGURE 5-1:
Spending
categories written
on the front of
each cash
envelope.

After you've taken out your money from the bank, fill each envelope with the amount of cash assigned to its category. Now you're ready to start using your envelope budget.

Spend from your cash envelopes

Going forward, all spending comes from your envelopes if you can possibly help it. You're now basically ignoring the debit and credit cards in your wallet like a bad date that just won't go away.

TIP

Don't leave all your cards at home, however. Even though you're not using them, bring them with you in case of emergency. If a tire blows out while you're driving home, you most likely won't have enough cash handy to have it repaired. Having your credit or debit card with you can prevent you from scrambling to take care of a problem.

Whenever you make a purchase, go into your corresponding envelope and pull the appropriate amount of cash out. Every time you make a purchase, write the expense on the back of the envelope. Doing so helps you know how much cash you have on hand. So if you've budgeted $60 for gas and then spend $30, mark that down so you know at a glance that you now have $30 left in your gas envelope, as shown in Figure 5-2.

Cash Envelope Spending

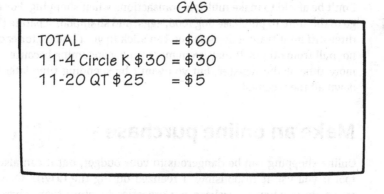

GAS

```
TOTAL                = $60
11-4 Circle K $30 = $30
11-20 QT $25      = $5
```

DINING OUT

```
TOTAL                           = $150
11-1 Starbucks $6.40            = $143.60
11-8 Dinner w/ friends $40      = $103.60
11-11 Starbucks $6.40           = $97.20
11-18 Company lunch out $20     = $77.20
11-20 Drinks at new bar $30     = $47.20
```

FIGURE 5-2:
Spending written out on the back of your envelopes.

You don't need to take all your cash envelopes with you all the time. If you're running to the store for household items only, taking just the envelope for that category makes sense. That way, your money is less likely to get lost, spent improperly, or, worst-case scenario, stolen. If an emergency pops up, you can use your debit card and move cash around later.

When you spend all the money in a given envelope, you're done. You have no more cash left to spend in that category until your budget resets. When your budget starts over, you can then add additional cash to the envelope.

If you run out of cash in one envelope, you may be tempted to start borrowing funds from others. Stop right there! When you start borrowing funds, you're screwing up your entire budget. The point of a budget is to keep you accountable for your spending. Borrowing here and there can lead you back to old habits that you're trying to change.

If overspending seems to be an ongoing problem, reevaluate how much money you've designated in each category and see whether you need to increase the amounts. Staying flexible when following this (or any) budget is the key to being successful.

Don't be afraid to make multiple transactions when shopping. For example, if you go to the store to purchase dog food, eggs, and shampoo, separate those items into three different transactions so you can stick to your budget for each category and not pull from others. It may seem more time-consuming because you're spending more time at the register, but you won't be spending time later trying to track down all the receipts!

Make an online purchase

Online shopping can be dangerous to your budget, but it can also be a fantastic tool if you use it responsibly. I realized during the COVID-19 pandemic that I spend more when I purchase my groceries in-store than when I shop online. Turns out I'm not tempted to pick up as much junk online as I am when I'm browsing the aisles. And sometimes items are cheaper and easier to find online, especially if you live in a more rural area. Some things just aren't available at brick-and-mortar locations, and online purchases are unavoidable.

When you're shopping online, determine what category the spending falls under and subtract the money you've spent from the appropriate cash envelope(s). Place the cash into your to deposit envelope. When you remove the cash from the original envelope, you signal to your brain that this money has been spent. You can either redeposit the funds from your to deposit envelope or keep the cash and apply it to next month's cash envelope.

For example, after I purchase my groceries for delivery, I go into my grocery envelope, take out the cash I spent, and transfer it into my to deposit envelope so I don't accidentally spend the money again. I usually collect the cash I spend online monthly and then deposit it later. I tried to use it for other envelopes for the next cycle, but then it got too confusing.

If you have cash left over at the end of your budgeting period, use it how you see fit. Here are a few options:

» Roll over the cash into the same category, giving you more wiggle room for an upcoming purchase in that category.

» Add it to a sinking-fund envelope to help save up faster.

» Transfer it into your to deposit envelope and then put that cash aside for financial goals, like investing or saving up for that trip you've been meaning to take.

Analyze real-life examples

If want to implement an envelope budget, try your best to predict accurate and realistic spending categories. The following sections review a few real-life example cash envelope categories with amounts for each envelope.

Example one

Here's an example of what a category breakdown may look for a twentysomething who's budgeting for the first time:

Groceries = $150

Dining out = $200

Coffee = $30

Rideshares = $40

Entertainment = $150

Beauty = $100

Sinking funds for emergencies = $100

Household Items = $75

Pet = $50

Clothing = $75

Total = $970

This person needs to withdraw $970 from their checking account to fill their cash envelopes. For easier reference, they may withdraw $1,000 and set the extra $30 aside in a miscellaneous envelope.

Example two

Following is an example for a married couple:

Groceries = $300

Gas = $100

Dining out = $200

Date night = $100

Individual allowance = $200

Household items = $200

Miscellaneous = $200

Total = $1,300

Because this amount comes out to an even number, the couple should have no issue withdrawing the funds needed from an ATM.

Example three

Here's what cash envelopes may look like for a family of four:

Groceries = $600

Transportation = $200

Childcare = $300

Allowances = $400

School fees = $50

Clothing = $200

Dining out = $400

Household items = $200

Entertainment = $200

Total = $2,550

This family needs to withdraw $2,550 for their cash envelope needs. They may need denominations other than $20 bills to help accommodate expenses that their children may have, such as school fees for clubs and field trips.

TIP

Speaking of kids, the envelope budgeting system can be a great way to teach children about money. Explain the difference between saving and spending and then let them allocate their allowances and any cash gifts they receive between the two. Then let them spend their money as they see fit. They'll realize the more they impulsively spend, the less they have for a bigger-ticket item. By making money tangible, you make it easier for them to reach their goals.

Perusing the Pros of Using an Envelope Budget

As I note earlier in the chapter, the envelope budgeting method is a great way to stay disciplined without having to focus on every single detail. Discipline is hard enough in all areas of your life, so why add that stress to your finances?

But that's not all! The following sections outline even more advantages to using this budgeting method.

REMEMBER

Every single financial action you take in the here and now affects your future self. If you consistently take care of your teeth today, you help your future self to avoid costly dental visits. When you put the extra $25 left over in one of your envelopes into your 401(k) instead of blowing it online, your future self can relax a little more in retirement. When you go into debt for purchases you can't afford, your future self eventually pays the consequences instead of enjoying a financially comfortable life.

It's easy to maintain

An envelope budget is one of the easiest budgeting methods to stick to in the long term because you see right in front of you how much money you have to spend. By making your cash tangible, you have a personal interaction with your money that no other budgeting method can provide. After you empty your envelopes, you know you're out of funds to spend in those categories until your next payday. This approach is a great way to refocus on yourself and your goals at no additional cost to you.

The added benefit of sticking to your envelope budget is that it allows you to stay in your lane regarding your spending. Using credit cards can compromise your financial future if you don't use them responsibly. When you aren't tied to tangible cash, making a purchase and then just paying it off "later" is easy. But if you can't afford to cover the entire purchase within the next payment period, you're then spending money on interest. Even if you manage to pay it off, you risk not being able to afford your expenses because you cleaned out your cash flow.

It helps with overspending

As I explain earlier in the chapter, the pain of paying triggers your brain to feel a certain kind of pain every time you physically hand over cash. When you're in pain, your *fight-or-flight response* (a genetic holdover from your caveman ancestors that's meant to protect you from threats) is fully activated. Your mind starts subconsciously assessing the situation, allowing you to spend less cash.

Envelope budgeting helps you quickly decide what is (and isn't) working in your budget. You automatically know if you're spending too much and can assess that information in real time rather than later when reviewing your bank statements. If you realize you've depleted an envelope too quickly, you can go over your current spending to see what you did and then adjust the next budget accordingly.

Having a limited cash supply can prevent you from making impulse purchases. Seeing the cash dwindle over a short period can make you second-guess your purchases. You become hyper-aware of how much cash you have on hand and how much buying unnecessary items can take away your ability to cover important expenses.

Because you can't casually whip out your credit card for non-emergencies, you aren't able to charge things you can't afford with the promise that you'll pay for them later. You're forced to hold yourself accountable. Immediately, you're facing the consequences of your actions if you overspend rather than pawning it off on future you.

REMEMBER

The envelope budget requires that you spend time in reality. With access to your current cash, you know what you can and can't afford at any time. No longer is your cash something that's represented when you look at a computer screen. It's right in front of you at any given moment.

It helps build frugality and resourcefulness

When money becomes a tangible item, you're less likely to hand it over as willingly as you were before. Having a harder time parting with your cash can include new and healthy habits, such as practicing frugality and being resourceful.

One way to start becoming more frugal is to look for free hobbies or entertainment to stretch your cash further. Go to your local library and/or check out its website or app to see what's available. Try hiking on local trails or check out the park close to your home. Investigate whether your city offers free admission days to local museums. Have friends over for a potluck.

Being on a limited cash diet can also make you more resourceful. Instead of buying new clothes, you have to look at what outfits you can make work with what's in your closet. You think about new meals you can make with ingredients you already have on hand or base your shopping around sales. You may find that you need much less to live on than you originally thought.

TIP

Resourcefulness is a skill that can benefit you in all areas of your life. Being resourceful can force you to start thinking outside the box and finding new solutions to solve problems. You start to see new opportunities everywhere. The more opportunities you see, the more likely you are to achieve your goals.

Considering the Cons of Using an Envelope Budget

Cash can be your best friend, but it can also inhibit you financially. For one thing, cash can only go so far. Plus, credit cards have certain advantages you won't be able to take advantage of on an envelope budget.

You miss out on credit card perks

Many people look forward to using credit cards because those cards have perks tied to them. For example, many credit card providers reward you with points every time you spend money on that card. You can then redeem those points for merchandise, gift cards, and sometimes even free airline tickets and hotel rooms. Many people can cut their travel costs or even travel for free on credit card rewards (a process known as *travel hacking*).

Cash back is another bonus that comes with some credit cards. Credit card companies who offer cash back refund you a percentage of the money you've spent in certain categories. For example, if you get 1 percent cash back on gas and spend $100 dollars in that category, you get back $1. Different companies offer different incentives, and the percentages can change from time to time.

TIP

For situations where you can't avoid using credit cards, ensure you use any rewards you earn to your advantage. Don't treat cash back as a freebie; pay off that purchase within the billing cycle. Then, treat the cash back reward as new income. You can use it toward a savings goal, to pay off another debt, or to fill one of your budgeting envelopes.

REWARDS WITHOUT CREDIT CARD DEBT

You can receive travel rewards without using credit cards. Major hotel chains such as Marriott or Hilton often have loyalty programs that let you earn points by staying at the hotels or booking travel packages that include a hotel stay, car rental, and flight. And some airlines, like Southwest, allow you to accumulate points to use for free flights.

You can also get cash back rewards from designated retailers. Major banks like Capital One and Wells Fargo allow you to go through their dashboards while you're online shopping. Click the link for your favorite stores and get cash back after completing a purchase. You can also utilize shopping programs like Target's Debit Red Card. When you link your Target Red Card to your checking account, you instantly get 5 percent off the entire store with very few exceptions. **Remember:** You'll need to keep track of your spending when using this type of store debit card by recording the dollar amounts on your cash envelopes. You can withdraw the cash from your envelopes to deposit into your checking account later.

You may find it too restrictive

One of the main reasons the envelope budget works is because it restricts your cash flow. But because borrowing from other envelopes is discouraged, you can be left struggling until your next payday if you spend more than you expected in a category.

Another restriction is a new business trend toward not accepting cash. Theme parks, hotel chains, and stadiums are just a few examples of venues that increasingly require cashless payments. If you have to use a card at a cashless business, remember to take the money out of the appropriate envelope(s) later, as I explain in the earlier section "Make an online purchase."

Cash can be stolen or misplaced

When you're not using a credit or debit card, you don't have to worry about fraud. What you do have to worry about is making sure the cash you're using for your envelope budget is in a safe and secure place.

If someone steals your credit card, you can cancel it and request a new one immediately. But if someone takes your cash, it's nearly impossible to replace unless you have concrete evidence of who stole it.

You can also misplace cash if you're absent-minded or leave your envelopes lying around. How often have you tried on your winter coat for the first time in months and found a few bucks (or, if you're like me, a twenty or two) in one of the pockets?

Asking Yourself Whether the Envelope Budget Will Work If . . .

If you're wondering if the envelope budget is for you, I understand. It can be a lot to get used to at first. In the following sections I've referenced concerns that I've heard from people when it comes to this budgeting method.

You struggle with planning ahead

The best budgets can go sideways. Life happens. Sometimes your original plans fall through and come with more expensive replacements. Or maybe you're transitioning through different stages of your life, such as graduating college or returning to the workforce.

If you spend less than your budgeted amount in a given month, add the leftover money to next month's envelope. So if you spend only $37 on the pet category one month, you'll have $63 in that envelope the next month ($50 monthly allocation plus $13 extra from the previous month). If you always roll the cash over this way, you'll be able to take care of a higher expense month without pulling cash from somewhere else.

TIP

Here are a few other ways to help plan for your variable expenses as much as possible:

>> Because you have to plan ahead to use the envelope system, use that mindset to your advantage. Check your calendar to ensure you've accounted for every event, outing, and so on, you have planned. Include plans that are still maybes. This way, you have the flexibility to say yes if they become concrete.

>> Take time to inventory things around your home. At least once a month, check your stock of personal products and everyday household supplies. By keeping an eye on items you need to replenish, you can allocate an accurate amount of cash to that category. This strategy can also help you purchase items ahead of time so you aren't running out of several products at once.

>> Stay on top of your finances by creating a miscellaneous envelope. This envelope can be a catchall for expenses you aren't expecting or categories that go over their allotted amounts through no fault of your own. This way, you're not reaching for a credit card to make up the deficit.

You need to share cash with your partner

The envelope budget can have the same benefits I lay out earlier in the chapter for partners as well as individuals. It can help you as a couple keep from overspending, stay accountable to each other, and hit your shared financial goals. When you use it effectively, you can manage your cash flow and become more resourceful, which can increase financial stability.

To use the envelope budgeting method with your partner, you need to work together as a team. You *both* need to be involved with your budget, spending, and all the expenses because you both need to know how much money you're allocating to work toward your common goal.

First, create your household budget. Decide together what amount to allocate to all your envelopes so that you're both aware of how much money you have to spend. Depending on how merged your finances are, deciding where the cash should come from may be a good idea. If you don't have a joint checking account, you can predetermine how much cash should come from each person and then fill the envelopes that way. You can find the basics on putting together an envelope budget in the earlier section "Setting Up Your Envelope Budget."

After you've assigned your cash, discuss who'll be spending it. For example, if you both need gas, you want to make sure you both have access to the envelope you've designated for that category. You can take turns holding the envelope or keep it in one spot to pull from as needed. If all else fails, you can split the cash into two individual envelopes.

TIP

If you or your partner does the majority of shopping in one area, like groceries, that person may just hang on to the envelope instead of the two of you passing it back and forth. My fiancé would rather go to the dentist than the grocery store, so I handle the groceries envelope. This arrangement works for us because I can stay under the budgeted amount I set aside and be mindful of how much we're spending so I can reassess to make sure our budget is working.

You can also make sure you and your partner each have an allowance category. This money you can spend guilt-free without having to check in with each other ahead of time. An allowance can also be a great way to avoid conflict with your partner about spending habits that you don't necessarily agree on but that aren't affecting your overall finances. The amount you choose for an allowance is up to you, but you can always start off with the same amount and then go from there.

TIP

Go on a money date with your partner. Pour a beverage of your choice and go over your joint spending for the month. This will help you ensure that you're both involved and know where your money is going.

IN THIS CHAPTER

» Putting together a pay-yourself-first budget

» Checking out the advantages and disadvantages of using a pay-yourself-first budget

» Tackling situations where this budget may or may not be right for you

Chapter **6**

The Pay-Yourself-First Budget

Budgets usually focus on your expenses. You always want to make sure you have your bases covered while still providing room for fun and for your financial goals. But because you concentrate on your expenses rather than your goals, you don't always accomplish those objectives. It happens to everyone, me included. I often tell myself that anything I have left over after I pay my expenses can fund my goals, but then I spend everything because I forget about my plan. Sound familiar?

If you struggle with meeting your financial goals, both short-and long-term, the pay-yourself-first budget may be the answer. The *pay-yourself-first budget*, sometimes known as *reverse budgeting*, makes your financial goals a priority by focusing on them first rather than your expenses. Whatever you have left is what you then use to cover your fixed and variable expenses.

By zeroing in on your goals first, you make sure they get covered no matter what. You aren't wondering about your retirement or whether you have enough money to cover the deposit on that new apartment you want. Instead, you feel confident that you're getting stuff done. You can sleep better at night and, most importantly, enjoy the money you have right now. You're taking care of yourself, which is why a lot of certified financial planners are huge advocates of pay-yourself-first budgeting.

REMEMBER

Because the future hasn't happened yet, you may tend to think of your future self as a stranger. How many times have you told yourself that an issue is a future *you* problem? But future you matters, and budgeting today in a way that accounts for your future needs sets you up for success.

Setting Up the Pay-Yourself-First Budget

The pay-yourself-first budget setup may seem counterintuitive initially. You're used to covering your expenses and then saving and spending the rest. But with this budget, you make sure your savings are the first item you take care of — your fixed expenses and your variable spending are secondary.

As I explain in the following sections, you first decide what percentage of your income you want to pay yourself. You then find an automatic way to put money toward your goal; only after you've paid yourself do you take care of your fixed and variable expenses and freely spend the rest of your income.

Figure out your financial goals

The first step in using the pay-yourself-first budgeting method is to decide what goals you should be working on. Doing so helps you decide how much you pay yourself monthly. You can't save for anything without having an actionable goal in mind to achieve it. When you set a goal to manage your finances, you're more likely to get there.

A great way to set financial goals for yourself is to set some uninterrupted time aside and brainstorm (See Figure 6-1). Here are some questions to ask yourself:

>> **Where do I want to be in one year, five years, and ten years?** By imagining where you want to be in these time frames, you can start to think about what financial goals you need to set to get you there.

>> **Have I been meaning to have anything repaired?** Sometimes you put maintenance off because it costs money you don't think you have. Does your car need new tires? Does your house need some electrical work? Getting such items repaired may be a financial goal you want to work on.

>> **How much money is in my emergency fund?** Making sure you're properly covered for all emergencies should be a priority if it's not already. Check out Chapter 8 for more on emergency funds.

>> **Do I have any debt?** If you have any credit card debt (or student loan debt, or any debt) to pay off, taking care of that is a great financial goal.

TIP

Many budget experts recommend that you focus solely on debt repayment first so you can eventually move on to your other financial goals. But I say that your future self can't rely on your intention to save "one day." You can save money *and* pay off your debt at the same time.

>> **Can I retire on time?** Retirement will be here before you know it, so checking the status of your retirement accounts is necessary before you start a new budget.

>> **Do I have any bucket list items I want to accomplish?** As I mention earlier in the chapter, having the money you can spend on fun is extremely important. Spending on your dreams is important, too.

TIP

Another great way to work on financial goals, or goals in general, is to break them up into short-term, mid-term, and long-term time frames.

>> **Short-term:** A *short-term goal* is one you can accomplish in six months or fewer, like saving for your child's birthday party.

>> **Mid-term:** You can accomplish a *mid-term goal* within a year or two, such as paying for a wedding or a down payment on a house.

>> **Long-term:** *Long-term goals* are those you can complete within five to ten years or longer, like saving $100,000 for retirement.

You're more likely to accomplish a short-term goal and then transfer that motivation to your next goal. This momentum can have a trickle effect on your other goals over time. In Chapter 16, I provide more information to help you set up your financial goals for the future.

Calculate how much you need to save

After you've decided what goals to work on, as I explain in the preceding section, figure out the monthly amount you need to save to progress toward accomplishing them. One of the ways I determine how much I need to save each month toward my goals is by looking at what the time frame each one has. Then I divide the time frame by how many months I have to accomplish it. For example, I want to save $1,000 to redecorate my outdoor patio (true story). If I want to be able to enjoy my patio in five months, I need to save $200 a month to hit my goal on time.

You can also use this method to break up larger amounts you want to prioritize, like retirement. If your goal is to invest $6,000 into your 401(k) this year, divide $6,000 by twelve months. By using this method, you know that $500 a month would have you hit your yearly retirement goal.

Financially Savvy Goals

Retirement

☐ Decide what lifestyle you'll be pursing in retirement

☐ Max out your employer's retirement account contribution

☐ Open a Roth IRA

☐ Create a will and trust

☐ Live off a mock retirement budget

☐ Keep an eye on your Social Security account

☐ Secure life insurance

☐ Look into long-term care

☐ Downsize your home

Investing

☐ Buy your own home

☐ Become a landlord

☐ Buy a vacation property

☐ Learn about the stock market

☐ Create an investment strategy

☐ Open a brokerage account

☐ Hire a financial planner

☐ Learn the difference between index, mutual, and electronically traded funds

☐ Start your own business

☐ Open a 529 savings plan for your loved one

☐ Create a custodial Roth IRA for a dependent

General

☐ Conquer your budget

☐ Save a $10,000 emergency fund

☐ Buy a car in cash

☐ Pay for a wedding in cash

☐ Plan an anniversary party

☐ Take a trip to another country you've always wanted to visit

☐ Remodel your home

☐ Buy a nice piece of art

☐ Donate to a nonprofit to honor a loved one who has passed

☐ Start a scholarship fund

☐ Offer to help a loved one you know who will not take it for granted

☐ Take up an expensive hobby

☐ Learn new financial concepts

☐ Work on your money mindset

☐ Learn how to make credit card rewards work for you

☐ Max out your earning potential

☐ Go back to school

☐ Read a personal finance book

☐ Start llama farm

Debt

☐ Pay off your student loans

☐ Squash that car loan

☐ Work on your credit score to qualify for prime financial products

☐ Take care of any government debt like taxes

☐ Clear up any lingering credit card debt

FIGURE 6-1: Brainstorming examples of financial goals.

REMEMBER

Compound interest is your friend when it comes to retirement, and the younger you start saving, the smaller the amount you need to contribute over time, as Figure 6-2 illustrates. Although you can make catch-up contributions when you're closer to retirement age, you have to save more overall.

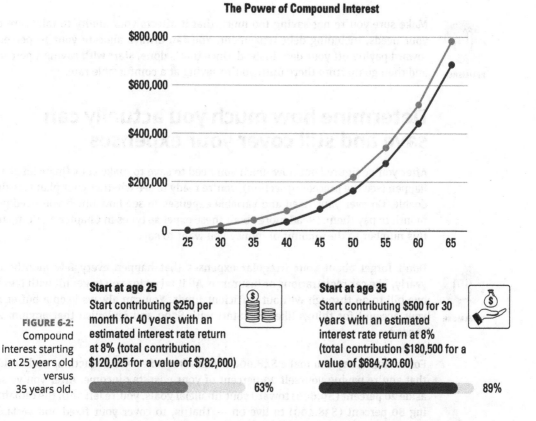

The Power of Compound Interest

FIGURE 6-2:
Compound
interest starting
at 25 years old
versus
35 years old.

Start at age 25

Start contributing $250 per month for 40 years with an estimated interest rate return at 8% (total contribution $120,025 for a value of $782,600)

63%

Start at age 35

Start contributing $500 for 30 years with an estimated interest rate return at 8% (total contribution $180,500 for a value of $684,730.60)

89%

Another way to figure out how much you should pay yourself is to choose to save a certain percentage of your income. Saving at least 10 percent is recommended, but you can always save more. If you can't save 10 percent, save some percentage, even as small as 1 to 2 percent, and work your way up.

For example, if you want to start saving 10 percent of your $4,400 income, you'd put $440 toward one of your financial goals. You can also divide the percentage among goals to work on them simultaneously. Take 5 percent of your income (or $220) toward retirement and then the remaining 5 percent toward another goal, such as saving for a house.

After you've allocated for your goals, you can spend the rest of your money on your other expenses. If you saved 10 percent of your income, you'd have 90 percent to cover the rest of your spending.

TECHNICAL STUFF

This amount isn't a reality or a possibility for many, but I personally know people who can save between 25 and 50 percent of their incomes. It's not easy, but by using the pay-yourself-first method, they've figured out a way to get it done so they can accomplish their goals.

REMEMBER

Make sure you're not saving too much that it affects your ability to take care of your needs, including debt repayment. You can always allocate your 10 percent toward paying off your debt instead. Once that's done, start with saving 1 percent and then go up from there until you're saving at a comfortable rate.

Determine how much you actually can save and still cover your expenses

After you've figured out how much you need to save to make your financial goals happen (see the preceding section), you're ready to see whether your plan is really doable. Go over your fixed and variable expenses to see how much you need per month to pay them. (Read more about these expense types in Chapter 2.) Compare this number to the amount of money you want to save.

REMEMBER

Don't forget about your irregular expenses that happen every few months or yearly, like car registrations or insurance. All it takes for you to get hit with fees is one bill to go through without sufficient funds. You can always keep a buffer in your account for things like this. Start with $500 and replenish that amount as needed.

For example, say you make $48,000 a year after taxes and deductions and decide that you're paying yourself 20 percent of your post-tax income. After you've set aside 20 percent ($9,600) toward your financial goals, you're left with the remaining 80 percent ($38,400) to live on — that is, to cover your fixed and variable expenses.

TIP

Take advantage of any employer-sponsored savings options available to you. Pre-tax deductions to a 401(k), Flexible Savings Account, or Health Savings Account. These options can not only help you save for retirement and future medical-related expenses but also the amount of taxes you'll pay will be lower; your income has been reduced because of the pre-tax contributions.

If you can't pay your expenses with the amount left over after you fund your goals, you have three options:

>> Earn more income.

>> Cut your expenses or the amount you want to save.

>> Do both of those things.

Choosing which option to use depends on what season of your life you're currently in. You can read more about cutting expenses and finding other income streams in Chapter 2.

You can play around with the percentages or amounts you want to save until you find something that works for you. Even though you may want to start saving a huge amount right out of the gate, that goal may not be realistic. If prioritizing your financial goals leaves you with nothing left, cut back. You want to be slightly uncomfortable so you grow but not to the point where you might be sacrificing your credit rating by not paying your bills on time or your health because you're eating ramen for every meal.

TIP

Paying yourself first is easy with automation. You can use payroll deductions or set up automatic payments with your loan provider. Sometimes, you can snag discounts by setting up automatic payments and transfers. For example, some student loan providers take off a partial percentage of your interest rate if you set up an automatic payment from your checking account through their platforms. The more you automate, the more time, and money, you end up saving.

When you've worked out a doable arrangement, sit back and enjoy your progress. Because you've already taken care of your priorities, you shouldn't have much left to do. Don't forget that you can adjust your percentages as needed. Budgeting is never set in stone. Instead, consider it a working document for your finances.

Explore real-life examples

Paying yourself first doesn't have to be complicated or difficult. Say you have a monthly net income of $4,000. (*Net income* is how much you earn after taxes and any other deductions/garnishments.) You want to prioritize an emergency fund and a vacation with your friends. You decide to put aside $250 for an emergency fund and then another $250 for your vacation. After you save this amount, you have $3,500 to cover your fixed expenses, variable expenses such as groceries, and debt repayment.

Or say you have an income of $3,000 and feel that using percentages seems more doable. You can start saving 10 percent toward your retirement, 5 percent toward your student loans as an extra payment, and another 5 percent toward a down payment for a house. You're putting aside a total of 20 percent of your income, or $600. You'd have the remaining 80 percent, or $2,400, to cover the rest of your living expenses.

For monthly income examples using a pay-yourself-first rate of 10 percent, see Table 6-1.

TABLE 6-1

Pay-Yourself-First Examples

Monthly Income	Pay Yourself 10%	Income Remaining
$2,500	$250	$2,000
$3,000	$300	$2,700
$4,000	$400	$3,600
$4,500	$450	$4,050
$5,000	$500	$4,500
$6,000	$600	$5,400

You can make automatic or manual transfers per paycheck, but the most important part of this budget is consistency. Consistency can look like sitting down every paycheck and going over your goals. It can be initiating transfers on a certain day. If you can do something that moves you closer to the finish line, make it part of your routine.

Understanding the Pros of Using a Pay-Yourself-First Budget

Every budgeting method has its benefits, including this method. If the advantages in the following sections sound good to you, this budget may be a good choice.

REMEMBER

One great thing about this budgeting method is that your variable spending doesn't come with shame attached to it. I'm 100 percent certain, even without being a therapist, that shame is one of the worst things you can feel on the planet. And you see a lot of shame in personal finance that shouldn't be there, especially around spending.

Financial goals are easier to stick to

One of the best things about the pay-yourself-first budgeting method is that your goals come first. When you put your goals first, they're easier to accomplish.

Paying yourself first means you hit that goal every single month. No more waiting anxiously to see whether you're going to be able to save money for your goals. You've already made a point to fund those goals.

Focusing on saving now sets you up for success in the future. This budgeting method helps make sure you're taking care of your future self.

REMEMBER

Whether you like them or not, your habits become your routine. The sooner saving becomes a habit, the more you'll be able to do it. If you get into the habit of spending money, you'll continue to spend money. If you regularly save money, you'll continue to save money.

By focusing on your financial priorities, you can feel more at ease. That emergency fund you've been meaning to start? Funded! Saving for retirement? That's been handled. Worrying about your finances less means you have more time to enjoy other areas of your life.

It helps you prioritize saving

Saving a set dollar amount or percentage of your income can motivate you to save more money as time goes on. If you're competitive like me, you can turn it into a game with yourself. Did you save 10 percent last month? Shoot for 11 percent this month. You started by saving 1 percent? Aim for 2 percent the next month.

When you make saving money into a game, you subconsciously start to find ways to slash your expenses. Every dollar you don't spend is a dollar you can now save. If you make $4,000 a month and start to save 10 percent in January, you'll have $4,800 by the end of the year. If you somehow raise it to 11 percent starting in February, you end up with $5,240 instead. That's almost $500 extra dollars you found just by decreasing your expenses by 1 percent!

It's low stress

The pay-as-you-go budget is an easy way to put your finances on autopilot without too much thought. With other budgets, you check your spending more often to make sure you're keeping your spending in check. With this budget, your spending is under control without your having to obsess over it.

As long as you're taking care of your financial priorities, you have no need to stress over the rest of your expenses. Your money is meant to provide you with options. One of those options is being able to enjoy your life. You can do that and take care of business all at the same time with the pay-yourself-first method.

Considering the Cons of Using a Pay-Yourself-First Budget

Like the other budgeting methods discussed in the previous chapters, the pay-yourself-first budget can have disadvantages, especially if you need more control over your spending. The following are a couple things to consider.

Saving even a small percentage can strain your quality of life

Figuring out what percentage you can afford to save without squeezing yourself too thin can be tough. You may not have as much wiggle room as you assumed. Being uncomfortable is one thing, but actually suffering is another.

Of course, deducting your saving automatically off the top doesn't mean you'll suffer the rest of the month, but not giving yourself enough money to cover all your expenses may cause some discomfort. Sometimes cutting your expenses takes time, and, as I mention earlier in the chapter, not everyone can reduce their expenses. If you're immediately facing a deficit, you need to reduce the amount of money going toward your financial goals.

You may need more structure

If you love a routine and structure, the pay-yourself-first budgeting method may not be for you. Because it doesn't offer any rules besides focusing on your financial goals, you may find yourself lost in other areas of your budget, like your fixed and variable expenses.

Without a guideline of what to spend on your expenses, you may be overspending in one or more budget categories. If your rent is a few hundred dollars more than it needs to be, who cares? You can afford it because you've already taken care of your goals.

Losing track of your spending can cause you not only to overspend but also to underspend. Having a general pot of money to draw from can be liberating, but it can also be inhibiting. Not knowing how much money you can spend in a given category can make you feel like you need to buy cheap items when quality items are better in the long run and actually within your budget.

Evaluating Whether the Pay-Yourself-First Budget Will Work If . . .

The following sections answer some of the most common questions I hear when people consider this budgeting method.

You get overwhelmed easily

The pay-yourself-first budgeting method may not be for you if you get overwhelmed easily. It requires you to think about big-picture questions (head to the earlier section "Figuring out your financial goals"), price out your goals, and really critically analyze which objectives are your biggest priorities. Tackling these future-facing tasks can be difficult if you aren't in the right mindset or you already feel like you're currently at capacity in your day-to-day life.

You're organized

Yes! This budgeting method can totally work for you. Prioritizing your goals is just the kind of financial strategy that many organized people love. Organized people hate wasting time and resources, which includes money.

To reach your goals, you need to be organized. I find that organized people tend to be motivated people. (Why else would I — uh, I mean "someone" — lug a planner around and make sure everything was color coded?) You need to think about what you want your outcome to be and then be able to break your goal down into actionable steps. You can easily add actionable steps to your to-do list (maybe even in your planner!).

REMEMBER

Just because this budget *can* work for organized people doesn't mean it *will* work for every organized person. If your brand of organization is that regularly reviewing your spending keeps you accountable to how you use your money, another budgeting method may work better for you. Note that you can also use the pay-yourself-first method within other budgeting methods. For example, you can pay yourself first and then categorize the rest of your spending using a zero-based budget (see Chapter 3), 50/30/20 budgeting (Chapter 4), or cash envelopes (Chapter 5). This way you can ensure you're making every penny count in your budget.

TIP

Don't be afraid to write your expenses down if you prefer pen-and-paper documentation. I've tried to use apps and spreadsheets with the best of intentions, but then I get frustrated. Instead, I write my spending down in my planner. Tracking my daily expenses this way makes me feel more connected to my finances.

You have a lot of debt

Yes! Many people feel that if you're in debt, nothing else should be your priority. This mindset frustrates me! I couldn't disagree with something more.

Debt does *not* make you a bad person. Sure, sometimes you can get caught up in spending above your means. Sometimes you have to make mistakes to learn.

REMEMBER

However, not all debt is created equal. Emergencies are never preplanned, and the result may cause you to acquire some debt. You can't plan or prepare for every situation you'll encounter, so sometimes a payment plan is necessary to get you back on track with your financial goals.

You can jeopardize your future when you focus on debt repayment only. Retirement may seem far away, but it will show up one day — sooner than you think. Government programs like Social Security can help as a safety net, but even then you may end up short. What if you can't go back to work?

Wanting to plan life events while you're in debt isn't wrong, either. You should be able to buy a house, plan a wedding, or work toward another financial goal as long as you're caught up on your debt repayment. You can't live on pause because some financial guru told you to — even me!

If you want to start using the pay-yourself-first method, ensure you can cover all your current payments toward your debt. After you're covered, pick one financial goal you can work toward that's unrelated to your debt. Work on your emergency fund, save for a trip, or start putting money aside for a home improvement project. Start with a small amount or percentage of your income and then go from there.

As I mention earlier in this chapter, you can save *and* pay off your debt at the same time. It's not one or the other. Yes, you pay more in interest and fees the longer you take to pay your debt off.

However, don't sacrifice your entire happiness for it. Your future self is important and deserves to be taken care of. Having a health scare or needing a new car doesn't mean you can't work toward your retirement. It doesn't mean you can't save toward your parental leave. Don't put your life on hold because you want to save a few dollars by not paying the debt's interest rate.

Chapter 7

Tips for Creating a New Budget

The word has gotten a bad rap over the years, which makes me sad because I love budgets! Budgeting is one of the key financial tools you need to understand to succeed financially. If you have no idea how much money you have coming in or where you're spending it, you can't make a budget work. I believe proper budgeting gives you more options for how you spend your money. Knowing what you can and can't spend your money on? Option. Being aware of how you're doing with retirement contributions? Option.

When you use a budget, you plan for your future. You're taking charge of your life and leaving fewer things to chance. I know, however, that being in control and taking charge of your money can be overwhelming if you've never done it before. Fear of the unknown can paralyze people, especially regarding their finances. Particularly when you grow up without great financial role models, knowing what you're supposed to do or even avoiding picking up those habits is tough.

In this chapter, I share some budgeting guidelines that have helped me and millions of other people live the lives of our dreams. They may not all apply to you or your situation, and that's okay, too. One of my favorite sayings is "Take what you want and leave the rest." That works for all areas of your life, including personal finance. It's personal and yours to call the shots.

REMEMBER

You may already be budgeting without even realizing it. If you send money to your retirement account and live off the remainder of your income, that's the pay-yourself-first budget (see Chapter 6) or the 50/30/20 budget (Chapter 4). If you give yourself a cash allowance for lunch, that's the envelope budgeting method (Chapter 5). And if you make a list of categories to track your spending, that's zero-based budgeting (Chapter 3).

Determining Your Budget Categories

The categories you choose can make or break your budget. That sounds pretty dramatic, but I feel comfortable being direct with you knowing you bought this book for a specific reason.

When you create categories for your spending, you're creating a spending plan. Creating a spending plan is what's going to get you where you want to be: making your money work for you rather than against you.

Planning ahead for the month

The first step to figuring out what spending categories to use in your budget is to plan ahead for your month. Planning keeps you from wasting time and money, two of your most precious resources. Forgetting events, appointments, or renewal fees can all derail a budget. When you plan, you're fully aware of what you have coming up and can allocate money accordingly. For example, if you have a lot of upcoming get-togethers with friends, you can plan ahead by putting additional money into your entertainment category and cut back elsewhere.

Meal planning is a great example of planning ahead. Every week you make a list of meals to cook and then write out the ingredients you need. You shop for everything at once, meaning you make fewer trips to the grocery store. Knowing what you're eating every night ahead of time also means less money spent dining out.

Similarly, when you know you have something on the horizon, such as a birthday gift, you can shop around for the best deals. Because you aren't making a last-minute purchase, you aren't paying for convenience and forfeiting quality. Bonus: Planning ahead for an event also allows you to save for it a little bit at a time rather than all at once.

Here's how to make sure you have an eye on everything you may need a category for:

1. **Make a list of your fixed expenses.**

   I recommend investing in a planner you can write in or using a calendar app.

2. **Add each expense on the due date within the calendar.**

   Look over your expenses to account for any irregular ones you may have forgotten about.

3. **Write down any upcoming appointments, birthdays, and social events that will cost you money and note how much money you'll likely need.**

   The calendar entries give you an idea of how much money you'll need to spend during the month to compare with your monthly income.

REMEMBER

You need to be aware of how much income you'll have so that you can accurately budget your categories. If your categories add up to more than your income, you may need to cut back on your upcoming spending.

TIP

Keep a running list in your Notes app of gifts you need to buy. When you know you need to buy a particular gift ahead of time, you're more likely to spend less money. List each recipient (by name), things they like, and the occasion so you're not racking your brain for the details later. For example, I know one of my best friends is obsessed with Star Trek. While shopping, I randomly found some Star Trek socks at the dollar store. Now she'll have multiple pairs of Star Trek socks for Christmas, and I've avoided the stress of finding a last-minute gift.

Reflecting on fixed and variable spending

Figuring out where your money goes and seeing where you want it to go can be empowering when determining your budget categories. My money has told me a lot about myself over the years. Some things have been good, like the fact that I established a scholarship fund with a previous employer. Other revelations have been bad, like the time I flew across the country last minute, paying an exorbitant amount of money on an airline ticket only to receive bad news after I arrived at my destination. That one particularly stung.

Your fixed and variable spending can tell you a lot about yourself: your habits, preferences, what you value the most. For example, I value self-development, and the proof is in my therapy expenses, medications for my mental health, and a few subscription boxes I use to take time out for myself. If you value health, you probably spend money on healthy meals and maybe a gym membership. If your rent is a large percentage of your budget, that may be because where you live is important to you.

TECHNICAL STUFF

Speaking of rent, a good rule of thumb is to not spend more than 25 to 30 percent of your take-home pay. If you live in a big city with high rent, don't feel bad that you're spending more than "recommended." You need shelter and can always balance your budget differently. If you want to aim for 25 to 30 percent, consider living with a roommate.

REMEMBER

Spending your money on things you value can help make you happier and more fulfilled. To get a sense of how your money reflects your values and, by extension, what are likely good budget categories for you, consider asking yourself the following questions:

>> What am I spending my money on?

>> Is my spending productive or helpful?

>> Am I happy to see that I've spent money on _____?

>> What values does my spending reflect?

>> What is my money saying to me?

>> How do I feel about how much I've spent on certain items?

>> Do I get emotional when I think about my spending habits?

>> Do I shop to make myself feel better?

>> Do I hide my purchases from others?

>> Am I an impulsive shopper?

>> Do I spend more on wants than on needs?

>> Do I often pay for convenience?

>> Am I planning for my future?

>> Is anyone in my life receiving financial assistance from me?

>> Am I receiving a financial assistance from anyone?

These are all great questions to get you started on your money reflection journey. Remember to take breaks if you get overwhelmed thinking about where your money goes. Just trust the process. Work your way through so you can develop your financial categories appropriately to make your money work for you.

TIP

If you really want to get in touch with how you spend your money, start a spending journal. Every day, write down your expenses and any emotions or thoughts tied to them. You may be surprised at what feelings come up. For example, when I see a lot of Starbucks purchases in my budget, I know that I'm physically exhausted. I use that information to cut back on my coffee purchases and take time to rest properly.

Compiling a list of budget categories

You can split your budget among many different categories. Here's a list of some general categories and the kinds of expenses that may fall into them to get you started.

REMEMBER

You don't have to make your budget complicated. The categories I list here are just the tip of the iceberg. You may find that this number of categories is too many and want to make it simpler. Do what feels right for you and your money. The important part is that you stick to it.

» **Home**

- Mortgage or rent

- Property taxes and HOA fees

- Homeowners or rental insurance

- Warranties

- House maintenance such as landscaping, pool, and cleaning services.

- House repairs

- Appliances

- Furniture

- Household decor

- Cleaning supplies

- Security camera services

» **Utilities**

- Electricity

- Water

- Your home's gas bill

- Trash pickup

- Internet (I consider this item a utility because many people need it for work and school)

- Cellphone

» **Transportation**

- Gas

- Vehicle payment (if not listed under debt)

- Vehicle insurance
- Vehicle maintenance, such as oil changes and repairs
- Vehicle registration
- Public transportation
- Highway tolls
- Parking fees
- Rideshares such as Uber and Lyft

>> **Food**

- Groceries
- Meal-prep services such as Blue Apron
- Personal shopping services like Instacart
- Meal delivery like DoorDash and Postmates
- Dining out

>> **Children**

- Baby formula and food if outside of regular groceries
- Daycare
- Child support
- Diapers
- Clothing
- Personal hygiene items
- After-school care
- School fees
- School supplies
- Gifts
- Toys
- Club or sports fees

>> **Medical**

- Medical, dental, and vision insurance
- Co-pays
- Flexible spending account or health savings account

- Doctor visits
- Dental exams
- Hospital stays
- Medical testing
- Medications
- Therapy sessions
- Medical supplies and equipment
- Supplements and other alternative medical visits

» Pets

- Pet food
- Veterinarian visits
- Medication and supplements
- Pet insurance
- Grooming such as nails and haircuts
- Boarding or pet sitting
- Cat litter
- Clothing and toys

» Personal

- Hygiene products
- Grooming services such as haircuts and aesthetician visits
- Massages and other spa visits
- Makeup and perfume/cologne
- Clothing
- Shoes
- Accessories

» Entertainment

- Streaming services like Netflix and Hulu
- Media subscriptions such as Kindle Unlimited and Spotify
- Alcohol
- Admission fees

- Concerts and other performance shows
- Subscription boxes
- Supplies for hobbies
- Social outings with friends
- Video games and gaming devices
- Movie theater tickets

>> **Party planning, gifts, and donations**

- Birthday gifts
- Gifts for special occasions such as weddings, baby showers, and graduations
- Holiday gifts
- Food and decorations
- Cards
- Wrapping paper
- Shipping materials
- Charitable giving
- Tithing
- Fundraising

>> **Travel**

- Plane tickets
- Baggage fees
- Hotel accommodations
- House rentals
- Rental cars
- Local transportation
- Food
- Special outings
- Souvenirs

>> **Insurance/future-planning**

- Life insurance

- Short-term and long-term disability insurance
- Long-term care insurance
- Caregiving
- Nursing or retirement home
- Estate and trust legal fees
- Burial expenses

» Savings

- Retirement contributions
- Brokerage accounts
- Treasury bonds
- College fund
- Emergency fund
- Moving expenses
- Automobiles
- House down payments
- Weddings
- Graduation (expenses not covered in other categories)

» Debt

- Vehicle payments (if not listed under transportation)
- Student loans
- Credit cards
- Personal loans
- Medical debt
- 401(k) loans
- Payday loans
- Title loans
- Debt settlements
- Court judgments such as restitution or alimony
- Legal fees
- Back taxes

Using the Right Tools

One of the key components of budgeting is to make sure you're using the right tools to track where your money goes. Whatever budgeting method you decide to use, you need to know in general where you're spending your money so you can allocate the proper funds for your categories. (For more on figuring out what categories to use, head to the "Determining Your Budget Categories" section earlier in the chapter.)

Tracking your money with budgeting software

An easy way to keep track of your budget is by using budgeting software that you download to your computer desktop or access online. When you use budgeting software, you can relax and have it do the calculations for you. Letting go of manually tracking every monetary transaction can help you free up mental space to focus on something else.

TIP

When picking out budgeting software, make sure it supports a budgeting method you want to try and will stick with in the long run. For example, if you want to use the zero-based budgeting method (see Chapter 3), don't pick a budgeting program that focuses on the envelope method (Chapter 5). You also want to ensure the software doesn't share your private information with third parties.

REMEMBER

Don't forget to factor in any associated costs for using budgeting software. A lot of free budgeting software and apps are available, so you don't have to spend money to manage your money. But paid subscriptions to budgeting software and apps can unlock more features to help manage your finances and save money over time.

The budgeting software options in the following list all have downloadable apps from Google Play and the Apple App Store; however, the focus here is on budgeting programs that you can access online or download to your desktop.

>> **YNAB (You Need a Budget; www.youneedabudget.com):** YNAB is a great software for zero-based budgeting because it stresses that you give every dollar a job. You can see your money all at once by linking the program to all your financial accounts. This overall budget snapshot can help you see whether your money is going where it should be.

>> **Mint (mint.intuit.com):** Mint is an app but its software is great and has additional features you can use. Like YNAB, Mint has the ability to help you sync all your financial accounts. Mint automatically categorizes your expenses,

so that's one less thing you need to do. It also tracks the bills you've paid and alerts you when you're going to be late with a custom setting you can put in place. I love the ease of Mint, including its automatic updates.

>> **Quicken (`www.quicken.com`):** Quicken is one of the oldest players in the budgeting software game. It scans your transactions and assigns them to the categories you set up. You can assess your spending to see whether you're hitting your financial goals. Quicken offers a few different tiers of software so you can figure out which one works best for you. The thing I love about the Quicken tiers is that one helps you grow your investment portfolio. This feature is great for the pay-yourself-first budgeting method (see Chapter 6).

>> **Tiller (`www.tillerhq.com`):** If you love spreadsheets, Tiller is for you. The Tiller spreadsheets let you customize them in various ways to reflect your overall spending and daily account balances. You can access the spreadsheets through both Google Sheets and Microsoft Excel. Tiller is also great for couples. When you sign up for Tiller, you can link your and your partner's checking accounts to create shared spreadsheets. This setup allows you and your partner to stay in touch with each other's finances to work as a team.

>> **Goodbudget (`goodbudget.com`):** Goodbudget is based on the envelope budgeting method. It makes virtual envelopes for all your budget categories and can help you plan ahead and pay off your debt. If you're budgeting with a significant other, you can share and sync with your partner's categories and see each other's spending in real time, which means you're less likely to go over your budgeted amounts as a couple.

>> **PocketGuard (`pocketguard.com`):** Trying to figure out your finances for the first time can be challenging. That's why I love PocketGuard for college students. With this software, you can easily see how much money you have for whatever you need. PocketGuard negotiates your bills so you can save more money, which is an important life skill. I also love the fact that it's a way to budget with hashtags.

Looking at budgeting apps

If you don't have time for logging into software (see the preceding section), a budgeting app may be a great alternative. Every budgeting app is different, but they all have the same goal: to help you track your spending and save money. Budgeting apps are a convenient way for you to budget from anywhere. With real-time information, you can access your budget by tapping a few buttons on your phone.

Along with tracking your spending, each app has its own budgeting method. Different apps also allow you different ways to save money toward your financial goals. With some, you can set up automatic transfers into your checking account every time you make a purchase. Others find ways for you to cancel subscriptions and negotiate your bills. If you're finding it hard to remind yourself to transfer money into your savings account, these apps make it easy.

Apps can also pay your bills for you. Whether it's a push notification to pay your bills or being able to set up an automatic payment, an app can help you stay on track. This feature is great if you're new to budgeting or are forgetful. Paying your bills on time helps you avoid late fees or, even worse, service disconnection or disruption. (*Note:* You can link some apps to all your financial accounts, but others you can link to your checking account only.)

Another cool feature with budgeting apps is that they help you learn how to invest and give you opportunities to start investing. They're a great way for new investors to practice without spending much money. Investing is one of the key ways to grow your wealth, and the sooner you start, the better.

Here's a list of apps I believe are worth looking into. It isn't a complete list of available apps, but it's one to get you started. All these apps are available to download from Google Play and the Apple App Store.

>> **Simplifi by Quicken (www.quicken.com/simplifi):** If you like the idea of Quicken but don't like sitting down at your computer, don't worry. Simplifi by Quicken is an app that allows you to customize your budget and track your spending just like you can with the Quicken software I discuss in the preceding section. The app also finds subscriptions you don't use and helps you cancel them. With features to also help you track your savings goals, it's an easy way to budget.

>> **Fudget (www.fudget.com):** For a basic way to track your finances, Fudget can't be beaten. You don't have to create categories or eagle-eye your expenses. This app allows you just to keep track of your income and expenses so you can monitor cash flow. Monitoring your cash flow can be important when you use pay-yourself-first budgeting (which I cover in Chapter 6). Fudget is also available for from the Mac App Store and the Windows Store.

>> **Prism (www.prismmoney.com):** Prism is perfect for those who need additional help remembering to pay their bills and keep track of their spending, such as people with ADHD. You can easily link your bills to this app and get a notification when it's time to pay. When you're ready, simply hit the "pay" button, which takes care of everything on your behalf.

The following budgeting apps are great for couples:

» **Honeydue (www.honeydue.com):** Are you managing money for the first time as a couple? If you and your partner are just starting your money journey together, Honeydue may be for you. You can sync your checking accounts to review purchases with ease and also coordinate bills with your partner. And it's free!

» **Zeta (www.askzeta.com):** If you and your partner are busy people, Zeta is probably the budgeting app to use. Zeta is a bank that allows you and your partner to open a joint checking account. You can set up a budget and do a spending analysis to ensure you're both on the right track. Zeta can also automatically pay your bills for you and prevent overdraft fees by reminding you to transfer funds when your money runs low.

College students should try the following budgeting apps:

» **Qapital (www.qapital.com):** Qapital has two features to help you save money. One is *microsaving,* where the app rounds up your purchases and transfers the difference into a savings account. The second is an automatic transfer function that works whenever you spend. For example, if you grab a coffee to go, the app automatically transfers a dollar to your savings account.

» **Albert (albert.com):** Albert is technically a banking app, but the creators say it's more, and I can't disagree. This app allows you to ask a financial expert for advice directly at no additional cost. You also get cash back when you use the app for your daily spending. And if you're new to investing, Albert helps you start. You just need one dollar.

REMEMBER

Budgeting apps aren't magic. When your app notifies you of a spending trend, you still have to put in the work to reevaluate your allocations or dive deeper into your spending habits. But using an app as a tool can make navigating your finances easier than doing it on your own.

Picking the right app for you

Just because budgeting apps are an easy way to stay accountable doesn't mean you don't have to put some thought and effort into choosing one. You still have to do research to figure out the right budgeting tool for you. When selecting your app, here are a few things to consider:

» **Your needs and goals:** Different budgeting apps provide different things, so clarifying why you're using one in the first place is important. Is it to help you remember to pay your bills? Do you need push notifications telling you you're out of money? Figuring out this motivation can keep you from downloading multiple apps that lack the features you need.

>> **Style of budgeting:** You can find apps for every budgeting method, so don't feel you have to conform to zero-based budgeting if you're more interested in the pay-yourself-first method.

>> **Ease of use:** The app must be relatively easy to use, whatever that means to you. Some apps are more difficult and time-consuming than others. Some won't have enough involvement for your liking. The bottom line is that you're most likely to stick to something if it's easy to use, so keep it simple.

>> **Features and benefits:** Every app offers different features and benefits, like paying your bills or providing cash back. Decide which options are most important to you and your lifestyle. For example, if you're not using credit cards to reap rewards because you're using cash envelopes, consider apps that give rewards.

>> **New checking or savings accounts:** Although most budgeting apps allow you to sync to your existing checking account, some take it a step further by providing an opportunity to open a new account with them. Some of these accounts offer great perks, such as paying you interest like traditional high-yield savings accounts (HYSAs). Others allow you to open accounts with another person while using the app. Consider what ATMs these apps allow you to access for free or at least waive the fee for.

WARNING

If you open a new checking or savings account through an app, do your due diligence. Ensure the accounts are backed by the Federal Deposit Insurance Corporation (FDIC). Savings and checking accounts backed by the FDIC are insured up to at least $250,000 if something happens to the financial institution that the app is using. If an app's accounts aren't insured, proceed with caution.

>> **Pricing:** Many, but not all, apps are free. Some budgeting apps charge a monthly fee, while others waive a fee if you open a checking or savings account with them. If the benefits of a paid app outweigh those of a free one, consider it money well spent.

REMEMBER

You can use different apps at different stages in your life. I've been using an app that requires me to enter everything manually. Because I need my money to be tangible, this app keeps me from overspending. Next, I'll be looking for one that provides me with the option to open a new savings account. I hope the app will encourage me to save more to hit my new goals while taking advantage of interest on the money I deposit!

Taking the DIY approach

If software and apps aren't for you, you may want to try a more do-it-yourself approach to your budgeting. I mention the benefits of making money tangible in Chapter 5. By being as involved with your money as possible, you're more likely to take care of it.

One of the ways you can become more hands-on with your money is by writing your budget out in a notebook. You can list your income and then keep track of your expenses. Adding a category to each expense can help you keep an eye on your spending to ensure you stay under budget. Keeping a running ledger like a checkbook works best for me; you can see an example in Figure 7-1.

	October — Wells Fargo Account	
Date	Expense/Income with Amount Spent	Account Total (starting balance $537.80)
10/1	Netflix (−$14.99)	522.81
10/2	Spotify (−$17)	501.81
10/2	Paycheck (+$1,500)	2005.81
10/7	Starbucks (−$6.49)	1999.32
10/8	Target (−$75.67)	1923.65
10/8	Rent (−$975)	948.65
10/10	Venmo friend for takeout (−$20)	928.65
10/14	Sephora online order (−$36.45)	892.20
10/15	Uber (−$14.99)	877.21
10/15	Safeway (−$122.99)	754.22
10/16	Paycheck (+$1,500)	2254.22
10/20	Student loans (−$400)	1854.22
10/21	Electric company (−$79.55)	1774.67
10/22	Freelance payment (+$350)	2124.67
10/22	Starbucks (−$6.49)	2118.18
10/25	Internet (−$75)	2043.18
10/27	Amazon (Halloween costume) (−$59.33)	1983.85
10/28	Freelance payment (+$500)	2483.85
10/30	Hallow party supplies (−$43.67)	2440.18
10/30	Uber (−$35.66)	2404.52
10/31	Halloween candy (−$14.21)	2390.31
10/31	ITunes movie rental (−$5.99)	2384.32

FIGURE 7-1:
A sample page from a budgeting notebook.

If you want to be more creative, you can make a budget binder. You can find free printable PDF worksheets online for your spending, income, saving goals, financial account login information, and anything else you want to keep track of. I love the idea of being extra colorful by using various pens and highlighters. A lot of people find success when they use this creative approach.

Paper can come with a lot to keep track of, including clutter. If you still want DIY budget tracking but don't want a bunch of paper floating around, consider making a digital spreadsheet. You can download a budgeting spreadsheet from Google Sheets or Microsoft Excel (see Figure 7-2). Each spreadsheet has embedded math formulas that calculate how much money you have left to spend in each budget category. Spreadsheets can also keep your finances organized with hyperlinks to different financial accounts.

TIP

If you aren't a spreadsheet pro, don't worry! You can still use spreadsheets without knowing fancy formulas. Pop "free budget spreadsheet templates" into your favorite search engine, and thousands of options pop up. Some require you to sign up for a website's newsletter, but you can always unsubscribe after you get your spreadsheet. You can personalize the income sources and categories for easier use to make your money work for you.

Taking advantage of your accounts' resources

Many banks and credit cards offer a spender analysis tool already built into your account. This free resource can be the most accurate way to scrutinize your spending, particularly with specific merchants. It's also an easy way to flag billing errors or fraud in real time.

Simply log into your banking or credit account to see what's available in your account's dashboard. If you can't find anything online, reach out to customer service to see whether the company provides some sort of tool or, if not, what outside option it recommends.

Wells Fargo has a great example of such a tool. You can monitor not only your spending but also your cash flow and other items of your budget. This tool is great for visual learners because it formats your budget how you need to see it. Figure 7-3 shows you an example.

	A	B	C	D	E
1	**Net Income**	**$3,000**			
2					
3		**Budgeted Amount**			**Actual**
4		Dollars:	% of Income:	Dollars:	% of Income:
5	Rent	1200.00	40%	0.00	0%
6	Car loan	300.00	10%	0.00	0%
7	Utilities	250.00	8%	0.00	0%
8	Cellphone	90.00	3%	0.00	0%
9	Student loans	200.00	7%	0.00	0%
10	Transportation	100.00	3%	0.00	0%
11	Car Insurance	110.00	3%	0.00	0%
12	Groceries/Dining out	300.00	10%	0.00	0%
13	Entertainment	200.00	6%	0.00	0%
14	Personal spending	150.00	5%	0.00	0%
15	Miscellaneous	100.00	5%	0.00	0%
16	**Total**	**3000.00**	**100%**	**0**	**0%**
17				3000	100%

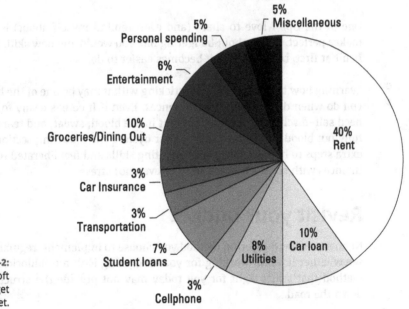

Recommended Budget

FIGURE 7-2:
A Microsoft
Excel budget
spreadsheet.

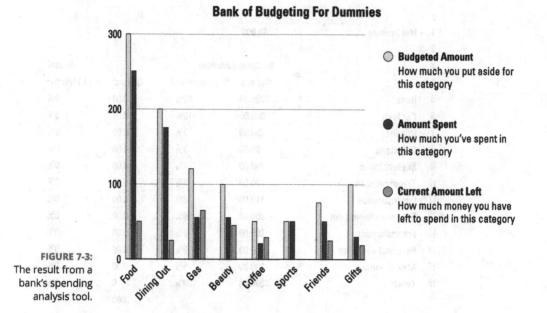

Bank of Budgeting For Dummies

○ **Budgeted Amount**
How much you put aside for this category

● **Amount Spent**
How much you've spent in this category

● **Current Amount Left**
How much money you have left to spend in this category

FIGURE 7-3:
The result from a bank's spending analysis tool.

Practicing Makes Perfect

One of the tips I love to share (and even remind myself about) is that practice makes perfect. Think about budgeting like you would any new skill. It may be difficult at first, but over time it becomes easier to do.

Learning how to budget and then sticking with it may be one of the hardest things you do when dealing with your finances. Even if it comes easily to you, you still need self-discipline. But after you put in the blood, sweat, and tears (well, hopefully not blood), the world can be your oyster. The following sections offer a few extra steps to help you ace your budgeting skills and feel liberated to take on your finances with confidence and less (or even no) stress.

Revisit your budget

No matter what budgeting method you choose to implement, regularly revisit it to see whether it's still working for you. Budgeting isn't a Goldilocks situation; the method that's just right for you today may not provide the structure you need down the road.

REMEMBER

Review your spending no less than once a month, even if you're staying within your percentages. This schedule is a way to see whether a bill or subscription price changed and make sure you don't have any erroneous or fraudulent charges.

Your regular budget review is also a great time to see how much progress you're making toward your financial goals. See whether you're on track to hit your target on time. If you're not, you can use this time to strategize to see where you can make a change. If you are making adequate progress, you can use this time to bask in your awesomeness.

Create a cash buffer

Another way you can keep your budget intact is by practicing maintaining a *cash buffer*, an amount of money set aside to cover any bills or purchases that weren't in the budget. Keeping a buffer in your everyday checking account can also help you cover expenses you didn't plan for during a budget cycle and prevent stresses to your budget. For example, if you overspend on your groceries by $50 or your kid forgets to tell you about a field trip, your buffer can soften the blow.

You may say, "Athena, isn't that what my emergency fund is for?" Well, no, not quite. Your emergency fund, which I talk more about in Chapter 8, is strictly for emergencies — events you couldn't have planned for. You got a hole in a tire on the way home? Emergency. Is the dog sick and needs to go to the vet? Emergency. You want to go to a last-minute birthday dinner for a friend? Not an emergency, even though you really want to go. This expense comes out of your cash buffer.

WARNING

You should keep your cash buffer and emergency fund in separate savings or checking accounts from each other. Having your emergency fund in the account you use for everyday spending makes tapping into it way too easy, especially for overspenders.

How much your cash buffer should be depends on your everyday spending. You want it to be sufficient to cover those random expenses without leaving you strapped for cash. If you live below your means, you may be able to get away with having $100 to $200. If you have a family or spend more in general, I recommend saving at least $500. As you get a feel for your budget and spending, you can adjust the amount as necessary.

You can also practice goal setting by making creating a buffer one of your first financial goals. Whether you designate an amount or a percentage of your income, having a guideline in place can motivate you to get that cash buffer setup taken care of. And because it's a smaller goal, accomplishing it first can build momentum for other goals you have lined up in the queue.

TIP

If you need to, start small. Dedicate $10 or $20 per paycheck toward creating a cash buffer. Even a small amount can be enough to keep you from incurring an insufficient funds fee or dipping into your emergency fund.

Look for ways to make your system easier to follow

The best expert on you is you. You know what makes you feel frustrated or overwhelmed, and you also know when a system feels manageable and satisfying.

One of the ways to make your budgeting system easy is to approach it like you would a work project. Being realistic with how you see things can help you find a budgeting method you can easily follow. If an overall picture is easier to visualize than a bunch of tiny steps, use the pay-yourself-first method. If you need a lot of structure in life, try the zero-based budgeting method.

TIP

Another way to make your budgeting system easy is to allow for fun money. When you have money to do whatever you want, sticking to saving the rest is easier. Even if you can't think of anything fun you want to do or buy, still allocate for fun in your budget. The time will come when you want to use it, and having it ready to go will make your heart happy. Chapter 16 has some great suggestions to help you budget for fun activities.

3
Taking Care of Your Priorities

IN THIS CHAPTER

» Discussing the basics of an
emergency fund

» Choosing the right place for you to
store your fund

» Creating an emergency fund

Chapter 8

Establishing an Emergency Fund

After you master the art of budgeting (or are at least trying a method out for size), you need to start working on your financial goals. One of the very first financial goals you should have is to build an emergency fund if you don't already have one. Used correctly, an emergency fund can protect your finances by helping you stay on budget and even stopping you from incurring additional debt.

If you're reading this book, chances are you've encountered a financial emergency. It may not have seemed like an emergency at the time, but whether you've had to pay for a sudden car repair or had the roof on your house spring a leak during a storm, you've encountered a financial bill you weren't prepared for or planning.

These unexpected expenses are why having an emergency fund is a critical part of your financial picture. Even if you don't spend your emergency fund, you'll still rest easier at night knowing it's there.

REMEMBER

Your emergency fund is different from your sinking fund. Emergency funds cover major unexpected expenses such as an immediate house repair, a car problem, or a vet bill. Sinking funds cover expenses you can plan for in advance for like gifts, clothing, or regular car maintenance.

DISCOVERING I NEED AN EMERGENCY FUND THE HARD WAY

My finances were problematic when I was younger. Robbing Peter to pay Paul was kind of my thing. (So was napping.) But that changed when I wanted to return to school.

My college career is a long and colorful one. I've always valued education, but getting caught up in my life outside the classroom was easy for me. As a result, I spent two years at a community college but didn't have a degree to show for it. After a break, I enrolled in a new college with two assumptions:

1. All my community college credits would transfer.

2. The new college's financial aid process was the same as my last school's.

However, only 15 of my 59 credits actually transferred, and the new school originally denied my financial aid. I was suddenly faced with having to pay for all my classes out of pocket. So I was starting over again with no way to even pay for it — great.

I hustled to come up with $800 in three weeks (and was successful!), but it's a situation I never want to experience again. Although scrambling to find the money included a lot of creativity that served me well — like becoming a nanny — it also included some embarrassment. For example, I sold my computer and ended up using the computer lab at school until I could save for another one. I had purchased that computer when I started my college career, and having to sell it caused shame. I felt like I had let myself down and vowed to try my hardest never to do that again. Now I keep an emergency fund so these unexpected financial wallops don't leave me fumbling to make it work.

Understanding Why You Need an Emergency Fund

An *emergency fund* is cash put aside for emergencies only. Emergency funds cover expenses that you're not expecting but that need to be addressed immediately before the situation becomes worse. An emergency fund can also help make you more comfortable when you're facing a rough situation, such as job loss or a medical emergency. By having an emergency fund, you can avoid having to take a step back in your finances. Recalculate your finances to cover the rest of your monthly expenses.

Emergency funds may seem a bit excessive if you've never had one. Who wants a giant pile of money sitting around if it can go toward a goal or your expenses? But even if you have the cash on hand to cover an emergency, that kind of unexpected expense can still derail your budget without a dedicated emergency fund.

In the following list, I provide a few reasons you may need an emergency fund:

>> **You want to prevent incurring more debt.** When you're first starting your budget journey, you're going to be focused on getting it right. You may not be able to recover from a blindsiding emergency without an emergency fund to prevent you from putting it on a credit card or taking out a loan.

>> **You've had health-related issues.** I found myself diagnosed with thyroid cancer when I was 31. I was extremely lucky to get diagnosed as quickly as I did and get in to see a surgeon who people travel in for. The only hiccup was that my health insurance provider considered him out of network, and if I wanted to book him, I had to come up with a $2,200 deposit upfront. Because I had an emergency fund that could bear that expense, I was able to get my cancer addressed quickly without blowing up my budget. This example may be extreme, but some emergencies can't wait.

>> **Your family won't or can't help.** Even if your family is as thick as thieves, your relatives may lack the financial resources to help each other in times of need. If your family doesn't have the means to provide you with financial assistance, having your own reserve of cash is important.

>> **You're a parent.** Children can be a blessing, but they also cost money. I personally know a lady whose child is accident-prone and, as a result, a frequent visitor to the ER. Your children don't have to break bones to cost you an arm and a leg, so having that emergency fund is essential.

>> **You have caregiver responsibilities.** Caregivers often lose out on wages because they have to take time off from work to care for their loved ones and/or cover their expenses such as food, clothing, and shelter. When my father had a stroke a few years ago, he was taken to a hospital over three hours away from his home. Although I loved that he was getting the best care 20 minutes away from me, he needed me to purchase clothing for him and later take him home, which meant travel expenses and time that I hadn't budgeted for elsewhere.

>> **You have pets.** My cat is the love of my life, but he's the most expensive pet on the planet. He even managed to rack up over $10,000 in medical bills over the course of two weeks due to a blocked bladder. I had to take out a personal loan to cover his medical care. If I'd had an adequate emergency fund at the time, I could've saved myself a lot of grief.

>> **You own a home.** If you're one of the lucky few homeowners who hasn't had to fix anything, all my friends are envious of you. One of my friends had to replace her washer and dryer at the same time. Another had to pay for a plumber to go under her house to fix a leak that caused mold in a wall. Being a homeowner can be as expensive as it is rewarding.

>> **You're in college.** Attending college is pricey (please see my financial aid fiasco in the nearby sidebar). Even with financial aid, you may need to cover additional expenses like fixing a broken laptop, finding out you need a textbook that wasn't on the syllabus, or paying increased parking fees. Saving extra money can mean having a little wiggle room so you can focus on studying.

>> **You're self-employed.** One of the hardest things about being self-employed is waiting to get paid. Your clients pay invoices or purchase items at different times, so predicting your cash flow can be tricky. If one client pays late, you can easily be scrambling to pay your bills if you don't have an emergency fund.

>> **You have a one-income family.** An emergency fund can also help if you're a one-income family and something happens to the breadwinner.

These are just a few reasons to have an emergency fund. Even if these situations don't pertain to you, something else will. By having adequate savings, you can keep your stress levels down.

Finding the Right Place to Stash Your Cash

The whole point of having an emergency fund is to help you be prepared for a financial emergency. For this reason alone, your money needs to be accessible. At the same time, that's a lot of cash to have just sitting around when it could also be working for you.

Your emergency fund can work for you if you place it into the right account. Depending on your risk tolerance and how fast you'll need to access the cash, you can consider a few different options outside your checking account.

Hitting up high-yield saving accounts

Traditional banks don't typically offer much interest on a savings account. Opening a savings account at the bank that holds your checking account is a convenient option for sure because your money is linked. But the rise of banks that operate entirely online without brick-and-mortar locations means more competition to get your attention, which is where high-yield savings accounts come in.

A *high-yield savings account* (HYSA) is a savings account that can offer typically 20 to 25 percent more interest than a traditional savings account. This interest is called *annual percentage yield*, or APY. For your reference: APY is the interest rate you get when you save, while APR (annual percentage rate) is the interest rate you're charged when you borrow.

Most HYSAs with higher interest rates (or APY) are offered through online banks. That's not to say you can't open an HYSA at a traditional bank, but finding a comparable rate there may be much more difficult. Table 8-1 shows various APY rates for a $10,000 deposit in a high-yield savings account.

TABLE 8-1 **APY Comparison on $10,000 Over a Year**

APY	Amount Over a Year
1.0%	$10,100
1.7%	$10,170
2.3%	$10,230
2.9%	$10,290
3.25%	$10,325
3.79%	$10,379

One of the hang-ups you may have with opening an HYSA through an online bank is that you may end up holding your savings account and checking account at different financial institutions. This situation can seem awkward when you can't immediately transfer the funds like you may be used to doing with traditional banking. Another factor that may prevent you from moving forward is that online banks with the highest APY typically only offer one financial product for you to take advantage of.

TIP

Many banks offer bonuses, such as those for new customers who deposit a certain amount or for keeping a specific balance in your account for a certain time. Bank bonuses are often a few hundred dollars, so take advantage of all the ones you can. And don't be afraid to switch banks if your current one is no longer working out for you.

Mulling money market accounts

A *money market account* is a savings account like an HYSA offered at traditional financial institutions. (You can read about HYSAs in the preceding section.) Like an HYSA, money market accounts offer the ability to collect a high APY on your money. But they come with restrictions, too. For instance, unlike most HYSAs, a money market account usually requires you to keep a minimum balance in your account. If your account dips below the minimum amount, you can be hit with fees.

Another major difference between a money market account and an HYSA is the type of access they provide. Money market accounts come with a checkbook and sometimes a debit card. HYSAs typically require an online funds transfer. Immediate access can come in handy when you're faced with an emergency, which depends on where your HYSA is held. If your HYSA is held at the same bank as your main checking account, then the transfer can be immediate; otherwise, transferring from a different bank may take two to three business days for it to clear.

Usually, money market accounts offer a higher APY than HYSAs. Because the APY a traditional bank offers can change at any time, having both a money market account and an HYSA may not be a bad idea.

WARNING

Even though money market accounts come with a debit card or checkbook to access your funds, don't use them as checking accounts. With a money market account, you not only have to keep a minimum balance of money in your account at all times but also are limited on how many transactions you can make in a month. Violating either of these parameters can cause you to incur fees you can otherwise avoid with a little preplanning.

Reviewing a Roth IRA

Roth IRAs are retirement savings vehicles for money you've already paid taxes on. For example, if you have a 401(k) with your employer, the money you invest is taken out of your paycheck along with other deductions such as health insurance. After these deductions are taken, you pay taxes on whatever income you have left over. Your 401(k) is funded with money that isn't taxed.

A Roth IRA is traditionally recommended as a savings vehicle for retirement. I discuss Roth IRAs in more depth in Chapter 9 to help you prepare for retirement. I bring them up here because they can be a great choice to keep your emergency fund if you're older than 59½. If you're older than 59½ and have held your account for 5 years, you can withdrawal funds without paying taxes or penalties.

Because a Roth IRA is funded with the income you receive after taxes, you can make early withdrawals from this type of investment account under certain situations. Circumstances that allow you to use this benefit are being a first-time home buyer, qualifying education expenses, and bringing a new child into your family through adoptions or birth. In order to make these early withdrawals, your Roth IRA must be less than 5 years old, and you cannot be older than age 59½.

CONSIDERING A CERTIFICATE OF DEPOSIT

A *certificate of deposit* (CD) is a savings vehicle that allows you to earn interest on one sum of money deposited at once. To collect the interest, you can't touch your CD over a predetermined time period (usually somewhere between 3 and 18 months depending on the account). CDs with the best APYs can lock you in for even longer — up to 36 months. There are four main types of CDs as shown in the accompanying figure:

- **Traditional CD:** A one time deposit that stays with your bank for a set period of time and earns a fixed interest rate.

- **Variable CD:** A one time deposit in which interest may fluctuate up or down. You'll still earn interest either way but could end up being less than if you had stuck with the fixed interest rate.

- **Bump-up CD:** A CD that has a set rate for the first year of the term than will allow you to "bump up" to a higher interest rate.

- **Liquid CD (no penalty):** The CD allows you to earn a set amount of interest like a traditional CD yet let you have early access to the money without a penalty.

If you need to access the money in your CD before the designated time frame ends, you may be subject to early withdrawal fees — fees that can eat up any interest you earned while your money was invested. That's why I don't like to recommend CDs for emergency funds. However, they're another alternative to help your emergency fund grow.

Although the APY can fluctuate on an HYSA or a money market account, CDs are locked in at a fixed rate for the term you pick. For example, if you purchase a 12-month-term CD at 3 percent, you're locked in at receiving only 3 percent on your investment. Always review rates to ensure you're getting the best return on your investment.

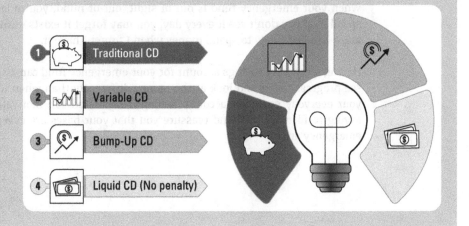

Whether you're under or above 59½, Roth IRAs can still be a good way to maintain an emergency fund and start contributing to retirement with the money you're going to save anyway. Remember that this money is still not as accessible as money in an HYSA or a money market account is.

WARNING

If you choose the Roth IRA route, ensure you have another retirement account you're not touching. Because you may have to take money in and out of the emergency fund Roth IRA, it's not a sustainable path to take care of your entire future needs. You can always utilize a 401(k) or another IRA for retirement.

Recognizing the importance of a separate emergency fund account

Even if you keep your emergency fund in a traditional savings account, make sure it's separate from your everyday checking account. You want to keep your money in a separate savings account to encourage yourself not to spend it on things that aren't emergencies.

REMEMBER

It's a fine line between keeping your emergency fund easily accessible and keeping it separate from your other finances. You want to be able to access it in case something happens. That's why you need it in the first place; it's like financial insurance. But if it's too accessible, you may be tempted to borrow from it. Raiding your emergency fund makes saving harder.

If you overspend one month outside of an actual emergency, you can easily borrow from a too-accessible emergency fund with the intention to pay it back later. This process can create a nasty cycle that can prevent you from saving your emergency fund and keeping it intact.

When your emergency fund is out of sight, out of mind, you're less tempted to spend it. If you don't see it every day, you may forget it exists until you need it. I know I'm less likely to spend money when I forget I have it.

Having a separate savings account for your emergency fund can also allow you to see progress faster and look at the money differently than when it's attached to your everyday spending account. Seeing it separated can motivate you to keep saving to hit your goal and reassure you that your bases are covered should an emergency arise.

Building an Emergency Fund from Scratch

Saving an emergency fund from scratch can be intimidating. It's a large amount of money, and your security is on the line. It takes some commitment, but if you start small and take actionable steps, you'll have your emergency fund saved in no time.

TIP

If you're a visual learner like me, consider using a budgeting app to keep track of your emergency fund. Many budgeting apps allow you to open a separate account with a competitive APY rate (which you can read about in the earlier section "Hitting up high-yield saving accounts"). You can set up automatic transfers every time you spend money as well as save additional money anytime with a quick swipe on your phone. Refer back to Chapter 7 for more on budgeting apps.

Decide your target amount to save

Deciding to save for an emergency fund can seem like a no-brainer. The real question, however, is figuring out how much money you need to save. If you don't have an emergency fund at all, you should be focusing on saving your first $1,000. If you've got that taken care of, your next goal is either $10,000 or three to six months of expenses. I discuss these options and some tips for figuring out what works for you in the following sections.

After you've decided on your targeted amount to save, you can figure out an actionable savings plan. If you need to, start small. You can always increase the amount over time. Start off with your emergency fund being a line item in your budget, and soon enough, you won't miss the money being deducted from your checking account.

REMEMBER

Whatever amount you choose to save is money you didn't have saved before. Even if all you can currently save is $25 a paycheck, that's $600 by the end of the year if you get paid twice a month. That $600 could take care of a car repair, a vet bill, or just some much-needed time off of work. Don't give up.

First option: $1,000

The first amount I recommend anyone save when starting an emergency fund is $1,000. Depending on your income and expenses, that amount may seem like a lot of money, or it may seem like a little. Either way, it's $1,000 you didn't have set aside before.

A Bankrate survey reports that 57 percent of Americans don't have the ability to cover a $1,000 expense. When you don't have a budget or your income can barely cover your expenses, saving for emergencies can be hard.

Even if $1,000 seems like a small amount, having it saved may keep you from having to put an emergency on a credit card or ask for a personal loan. These options can set you back financially and keep you from making progress.

Second option: $10,000

After you've saved $1,000 in an emergency fund, it's time to aim bigger. I'm talking about saving $10,000, baby. You may think, "Wow, Athena, that's a crap ton of money," and I agree. But $10,000 is an amount of money that can give you some options.

With an emergency fund of $10,000, you can purchase a used car when your car stops running. You can pay for a new HVAC that went out just before summer. You may even be able to take time off work to care for a loved one.

REMEMBER

This type of emergency fund works best for someone who has no dependents who rely on them financially. Because you have fewer expenses, this amount should see you through hardship. This number is also a great option if you have a steady income.

Third option: Three to six months of living expenses

Another way to approach your emergency fund is to save three to six months of living expenses. That high an amount may seem excessive or even impossible, but depending on where you are in your life, it may be the best fit for you and your finances.

With three to six months of expenses saved, you can pay your bills without worrying about where your (or your partner's) next paycheck comes from. I'd never wish a layoff on anyone, but they happen; companies change structures due to funding or management changes. On the flip side, you may be looking to leave your employer without having another job lined up or take time off for personal reasons.

REMEMBER

If you choose to save three to six months of your expenses as your emergency fund target, keep a couple of things in mind:

>> **You don't have to save all your expenses.** What I mean here is that an emergency fund is meant to cover only the necessities, such as shelter, food,

and transportation. If you think ahead and want to save enough for any other debt repayments or expenses you feel you need, go ahead and save for it. Your money works for you, and if you want to continue to live your lifestyle, do it. Just prepare wisely.

>> **Saving this type of emergency fund may take a lot longer than even the $10,000 option in the preceding section.** But if you have a family or other dependents relying on you to be a provider, this fund may be the one that works best. It's a large enough amount to keep your household running smoothly and pay for other emergencies, like car and household repairs.

Evaluating your circumstances

How do you decide which amount is best for you and your finances? If you're stuck or have decision fatigue, consider the following:

>> **Do you have regular income?** Having a steady income is a powerful thing, whether it's through your 9-to-5 job or retirement benefits. With a regular income, you can take more risks because you know that no matter what, you have more cash on its way. With regular cash flow you can count on, you may not need to save as much as someone whose income is more variable. However, you can also look at having regular income as an opportunity to put three to six months of expenses into your emergency fund should you experience a layoff or loss of income in the future.

>> **Can you get additional income from a part-time job?** You can dedicate an entirely new income source toward saving for your emergency fund. For example, if your goal is $1,000 and your income ends up being $250 per check, you'd put your first four payments to hit it. From there you can set a new goal. I discuss a few options for making additional income in the later section "Find ways to make extra money."

>> **Do you have a supportive network to help you financially?** At one point, I was having a hard time finding writing gigs to pay my bills. I debated asking my old job whether I could return, and one of my best friends, whom I consider a sister, told me not to. She said that if anything, she would lend me the money I needed so I could continue to focus on finding new clients. This extremely generous offer is one example of what having a supportive network can look like. If you don't have a supportive network that can help financially if needed, you should consider a larger amount for your emergency fund.

>> **Do you have lines of credit available?** Credit lines aren't the same as cash, but in a pinch or as a last resort, knowing you have the credit available can be a relief in certain instances.

Please don't mistake credit for an emergency fund. Putting emergencies on a credit card or taking out a loan subjects you to additional fees and money spent on interest over time. Some emergencies you must address may not even take a credit card as payment.

These questions are just a few things to consider when picking an amount to save. Your circumstances can change at any time, so try to be flexible. Today you may need only $5,000 for your living expenses, but later you may need $8,000.

Use financial windfalls

I love a good windfall. I appreciate every one I get, and I tell the universe thank you even if it's a small one, like a $5 gift card.

A *windfall* is anytime you receive a surprise sum of money you weren't counting on. In addition to gift cards, some examples of windfalls include the following:

>> A bonus from your day job or overtime you're offered

>> Cash back on a purchase

>> Money you receive as a gift

>> A tax return

>> Money received through a court settlement

>> An inheritance

>> Proceeds from the sale of a business

>> A return on an investment

Windfalls can help you build up your savings accounts without going above and beyond to find additional funds. When you utilize your windfalls, you can get ahead little by little. If I decide to put the $5 gift card toward getting $10 cat food, I'm now saving $5. That $5 can go into my savings account to help save toward my emergency fund.

Another example of using a windfall is saving the difference between what you'd planned to spend for service and the lower price you were actually charged. If you budgeted $50 for a haircut and only spent $40, that's $10 you can put into an emergency fund. Did you end up only being charged a $25 doctor co-pay rather than $50? Send that $25 to the emergency fund pronto.

TIP

Windfalls are usually associated with fun. Decide a percentage of your windfalls to save and then spend the rest. For example, if I make any extra income through my online store, 50 percent goes toward my savings goals, and the remaining 50 percent I let myself spend on something fun, like buying home decor. Allowing part of my windfall for fun helps me save the rest.

Take advantage of credit card rewards

If you get cash back through credit card rewards, transfer that cash to your savings account. If you're going to pay your credit card bill in full every month, you can earn these rewards without having to pay interest (see Chapter 15 for more information). Credit cards that offer cash back may also offer a cash bonus for signing up. Take the bonus and send it over to your emergency fund.

Consider automatic transfers into your emergency fund

A great way to help create an emergency fund is to deposit a portion of your income into a separate account regularly. As I explain earlier in the chapter, keeping your emergency fund in a different account from your everyday checking can prevent you from tapping into the emergency fund if you go over budget. Help create another layer of separation by simply having part of your paycheck transferred into your emergency fund automatically.

Grab a direct deposit slip for your new account and send the information to whoever does your payroll. If you work for yourself, figure out how to set up an automatic transfer that works for income that arrives intermittently. I assign different clients to different financial priorities. Each client is set up to go into a certain checking or savings account I have to help me hit my individual goals.

TECHNICAL STUFF

You can always set up an automatic transfer to your savings account. Every time I make a transaction with my debit card, one dollar automatically gets transferred into my savings account. I average about 25 to 30 transactions a month, which means $25 to $30 gets transferred without my having to think about it. This approach can add up to $300 to $360 in additional savings without any effort from me.

Find ways to make extra money

If you're still looking for ways to fund your emergency savings, consider finding a way to make extra money. Because of the rising cost of living, having more than one income stream coming in is important now more than ever. Many people can't afford to live off one income, and even those who can may not have much leftover for audacious financial goals. The following are some money-making options you may want to consider.

Try out the gig economy

If you prefer to work on your own schedule, consider finding a job in the gig economy. Jobs in the gig economy — known as a *side gig* — are an easy way to make money on your own terms. You have control over your own work schedule; when and how many hours you want work are up to you.

How the *gig economy* works is that a company lists available tasks or "jobs" for someone to complete. If you choose a task, you're paid after you complete the work. Some tasks are one-time requests, while others may be spread out over a few days or several months. You can then choose whether to complete another one. For example, when I was an Uber Eats driver, I set a daily goal for myself to earn $50. After I hit my daily goal, I turned off my app and went home.

Check out the following list for a few examples of gig work:

>> Uber (rideshare) www.uber.com

>> Lyft (rideshare) www.lyft.com/driver

>> Turo (turn your car into a car rental service) turo.com/us/en/list-your-car

>> Uber Eats (food delivery) www.ubereats.com

>> Door Dash (food delivery) dasher.doordash.com/en-us

>> Rover (dog walking and pet sitting) www.rover.com

>> Wag (dog walking and pet sitting) wagwalking.com/dog-walker

>> Meowtel (cat sitting only) meowtel.com

>> Instacart (personal grocery shopper) shoppers.instacart.com

>> Shipt (personal shopper) www.shipt.com/be-a-shopper

>> Amazon Flex (deliver for Amazon) flex.amazon.com

>> Bellhop (help others move) www.getbellhops.com/being-a-bellhop

>> Neighbor (store other people's items) www.neighbor.com

>> HouseSit Match (house and pet sitting) www.housesitmatch.com

- » AirBnB (host others in your home) www.airbnb.com
- » Couchsurfing (host others in your home) www.couchsurfing.com
- » Amazon Mechanical Turk (online tasks for others) www.mturk.com
- » Scribie (transcription for others) scribie.com
- » VIP Kid Global (teach English as a second language) www.vipkid.com/en-us
- » Etsy (sell your crafts and templates) www.etsy.com
- » Care.com (child and senior care) www.care.com

Now, let's take a closer look at some of these job options:

- » **Become a rideshare driver or a personal shopper:** Some tasks can include shopping for and delivering customers' items, like food or groceries, to a private residence. If you prefer to be on the move, you can consider becoming a rideshare driver. Rideshare drivers can easily make $100 a day, and many companies offer weekly bonuses based on performance. For example, if you complete ten rides within five days, you get an extra $50.

  Certain companies allow you to cash out every day, while the majority allow you a weekly payment. Both options can help you speed up your savings rate on your own terms.

- » **Become a caregiver:** Websites such as Care.com let people place ads looking for extra help to care for a loved one. Nannies, babysitters, and careers for seniors are typical examples. When I was in college, I regularly was a nanny on the weekends to help pay for my associate's degree. It was an easy gig that helped me prepare for my education career and also paid quite well. With my income as a nanny, I could subsidize my part-time income while earning my degree.

- » **Offer a pet sitting or walking service:** If you love animals more than you do people, consider pet sitting. After you create a profile with a service such as Rover or Wag, friends can fill out referrals for you based on your experience with animals. The more reviews you have, the more likely pet owners are to select you.

  If pet sitting doesn't seem like the right fit, look into becoming a dog walker. You can get paid per hour to get your steps in while walking your new four-legged friend. Some dog walkers also spend time during the day providing companionship to older animals who need special care.

>> **Provide freelance services:** If you already have a specific skill set like editing or graphic design, consider freelancing as an option to make more income. As a freelancer, you can charge for projects independently or become a contracted employee. After you build a portfolio, you can sign up for different platforms to bid on projects. You can also pitch potential clients for work.

Sell stuff around your home

Do you have a lot of extra junk — um, I mean stuff — lying around your house? Sell it! If you have high-end clothes or accessories (or that jewelry your ex gave you), you can sell them on a consignment website or take them to a consignment store.

You can also sell just about anything on eBay. I've seen everything there, from clothes to car parts to beauty products to pet gear. I've even seen people sell items like unopened vitamins out of subscription boxes. eBay is also a great place to sell all those knickknacks you have from Grandma that are just collecting dust.

Consider renting a room

If you have extra space and don't mind being around people, consider renting a room to someone. I rented a room from my old roommate, and she made a few thousand dollars from someone she hardly saw around the house. Not all roommates are gone 24/7, but you can find a roommate compatible with your lifestyle. You can also give yourself a timeline on how long you'll have a roommate so you know that there's light at the end of your money-making tunnel.

Another way people earn this type of income is by renting their residences as short-term vacation rentals. With websites such as Airbnb and VRBO, renting a room in your home or the entire house for a nightly fee is easy. One of my best friends used to rent a bedroom in her house a few days out of the month and made, on average, close to $1,000. She used the funds to help pay for pet-associated costs such as dog training.

Look into other part-time employment

If the gig economy isn't your thing, or your local area doesn't offer these types of opportunities, you can always look into getting a regular part-time job. Many part-time jobs don't come with benefits, but some employers, such as Starbucks and UPS, offer not only health insurance but also tuition reimbursement for part-time employees.

Many businesses happily employ people who want to work only a few shifts a week, especially on weekends. If you worked just one part-time shift a week and made $100, you'd have earned an additional $5,200 over an entire year. If you bumped it up to two shifts, you'd save $10,400.

Learn a new skill

TIP

Another option to make additional income is to pick up a new marketable skill. The Internet has made learning new skills at no additional cost and accessing classes through your local library or websites like Coursera (www.coursera.org) and LinkedIn Learning (www.linkedin.com/learning) easy. New skills that are in demand can help you negotiate a raise with your full-time employer and/or potentially pivot your career toward a more lucrative field.

Chapter **9**

Saving for Your Retirement

'll never forget the first time an employer sat me down to discuss retirement options. I was approaching the end of my 90-day probation period at a new job. Things were going pretty well, so naturally I was worried when the human resources manager wanted to meet with me before my shift. Imagine my surprise when she handed me an envelope stuffed with retirement options she wanted to go over. Retirement options? As a part-time employee? But she was right; I should have been thinking about my financial future even then.

With so many people living paycheck to paycheck, saving for future goals such as retirement can seem impossible. United States Census Bureau surveys indicate that a surprising number of people age 55 to 66 have nothing saved for retirement.

So if you're currently at zero, don't feel bad. It's not just a "you" problem. That's why sticking to whatever budgeting method you choose helps tremendously when you're saving for your retirement — every little bit helps. That's why when you have the opportunity to earn free money, such as an employer-matched retirement fund, you don't want to leave it on the table. By paying attention, you can jump on every chance that comes your way. I explain a few options in this chapter.

REMEMBER

All the budgeting methods I discuss in Part 2 not only encourage saving for retirement but also show you how to do it. Also, avoid early withdrawals from your retirements accounts to receive the maximum benefits. See Chapter 16 for more information.

Accessing Employer-Matched Retirement

Before you start to review your retirement plan, you need to know what type of plan is offered through your employer: for-profit companies may have a 401(k) and nonprofits or government agencies may offer a 403(b). While not as common for 403(b) plans, employers sometimes offer a matching 401(k) retirement contribution as part of their benefits packages. An employer who offers to match your retirement is willing to give you additional money to save for your future; it's a sign your employer is invested in you and your future.

TECHNICAL STUFF

Take advantage of all employee benefits you can. For example, some employers reward you with a gift card if you get your annual physical. My fiancé, who works at a tech start-up, gets a lot of discounts at places like Disney World and Lenovo. I was able to use his discount to purchase the laptop I'm using right now for 50 percent off!

Cashing in on any free money your employer offers you is a no-brainer. Free money from an employer contribution match can help you grow your retirement faster. Every dollar you contribute, even without an employer match, gets you one step closer to being able to live comfortably when you're older.

Companies offer different types of employer retirement match contributions, which I outline in the following sections. You can use all of them to your benefit, but some may work better for you than others.

WARNING

If your employer is offering a retirement match, it's most likely doing so under the agreement of a vesting schedule. A *vesting schedule* is a contractual agreement between you and your employer that states you must fulfill a term of employment before you fully own the company's contributions to your retirement account. Your employer is interested in keeping you as an employee for as long as possible if it's contributing to your retirement. Make sure you understand whether your company has a vesting schedule. If you change jobs before the vesting schedule is over, you lose some or even all of the contributions your employer made.

Partial matching

If your employer does a *partial match*, it contributes a certain percentage of the income you've saved on your own. If you make $2,500 every two weeks and contribute 4 percent of your income to your 401(k), you're saving $100 every paycheck, for a total of $2,600 a year. If your company offers a partial match of 50 percent, it's contributing an additional $50 to your 401(k) each pay period. That's an additional $1,300 on top of your contribution, for a total of $3,900 saved.

Dollar-for-dollar matching

Employers that offer *dollar-for-dollar matching* contribute the same percentage of your income as you do up to a certain amount. So if you deposit 4 percent of your $2,500 paycheck, your employer contributes an additional 4 percent on your behalf. In this case, that's a total of $5,200 saved ($2,600 each from you and your employer).

REMEMBER

You can always contribute more money than your employer is willing to match. Say your company caps retirement matching at 5 percent, but you choose to save 6 percent of your income ($150 per paycheck using the previous example). Even though you're using dollar-for-dollar matching, the company would only contribute $125 per check because your deposit goes over the limit.

Tiered matching

Tiered matching allows a company to match a certain percentage dollar per dollar and then partially match the next percentage you save.

Say your employer matches your contributions dollar for dollar up to 4 percent and then provides a 50 percent match after that. You get $100 for every $100 you save from your $2,500 income, up to $2,600. If you decide to save an additional 2 percent so you can get the partial match, your extra contribution is $50. For this $50 you save, your employer contributes only $25. So your contributions at the end of the year would look something like this:

$2,600 + $2,600 (dollar-for-dollar match on 4 percent) = $5,200

$1,300 + $650 (50 percent partial match on 2 percent) = $1,950

$5,200 + $1,950 = $7,150 total retirement contributions

Making Your Money Work for You

The more opportunities you take advantage of to help you max out your retirement savings, the more likely you'll have a padded retirement fund. Your retirement contributions can ensure you have access to resources for long-term care if needed and help supplement your Social Security income when you retire.

REMEMBER

Social Security benefits may not be enough to live on depending on your situation and location. According to the Social Security Administration's statistical data for December 2022, retired workers received only $1,825 in monthly Social Security benefits. In Phoenix, Arizona, the average monthly rent is $1,590. A retired person there relying only on Social Security would have less than $300 to pay for all their other living expenses.

Set a retirement savings goal

When considering retirement, you need to establish a target savings goal. You have to know exactly how much you're saving so you can set actionable steps to get you there. Telling yourself just to save as much as possible to be comfortable when you're ready to retire is easy, but you can get to the point where balancing the need to save with the need to live a quality life now is challenging.

REMEMBER

Recognize the difference between living frugally and cutting enough costs to the point that you're miserable. You can live frugally by cutting coupons or using a rebate app when shopping, but not allowing yourself to shower at home so you can save money on the water bill is cutting expenses to the extreme. Making yourself miserable when you don't have to can keep you from wanting to budget and save at all.

TIP

If you're having trouble finding the right amount to save, use a retirement calculator. Retirement calculators help you predict how much money you need by using your age, your current income, your current savings, and your current monthly contribution to give you an estimate and help you find a savings deficit. It can also give you steps to get on the right path if you aren't already. Merrill Lynch has a great calculator you can take advantage of (www.merrilledge.com/retirement/personal-retirement-calculator).

Max out your retirement contributions

Saving money before you have to pay taxes on it means you have to pay fewer taxes on your money. It sounds counterintuitive, but every dollar you save pretax is one fewer dollar that you're paying taxes on. Say you earn $500 and have a tax rate of 20 percent. If you didn't save anything, you'd be paying $100 in taxes, leaving you with $400. If you saved $100, you'd only pay tax on $400. As a result, you'd pay $80.

TIP

Always be sure to check the IRS limits on 401(k) contributions so you can save as much as possible. Every year the IRS determines how much you can contribute to your 401(k) or 403(b) for that fiscal year; For 2023, at the time of this writing, the maximum amount you can save in your 401(k) or 403(b) is $22,500 for a traditional 402(k) and $19,500 for a SIMPLE 401(k).

Consider more than one retirement account

Regardless of whether your employer offers a 401(k) or 403(b), you can still save for retirement in other investment vehicles. By saving for your retirement in different accounts, your portfolio becomes more diverse. You know what they say: Don't keep all your retirement in one basket (or something like that).

A *Roth IRA* is a retirement savings account you fund with money that's already been taxed. So although you're not getting the same benefit of investing money without paying taxes (as I explain in the preceding section), it's still a way to save. Under certain situations, you can make withdrawals from this type of investment account. Circumstances that allow you to use this benefit are being a first-time home buyer, qualifying education expenses, and bringing a new child into your family through adoption or birth. In order to make these withdrawals, your Roth IRA must be less than 5 years old, and you cannot be older than age 59½. If you're older than 59½ and have held your account for 5 years, you can withdraw funds without paying taxes or penalties. So it's a cool way to keep the money you're earning while having access to your cash if needed before age 59½.

WARNING

Portfolio income from investing is for the long haul. The market cycles between a *bull market* (when stock prices are going up) and a *bear market* (when stock prices are going down). Investments grow over time, and you need to remember that investing isn't a get-quick-rich scheme. Make sure to consult a professional when building out your retirement portfolio. There may be an investing opportunity you overlooked that would work in your favor.

Keep your cost of living low

After you figure out your life on a budget, don't raise your expenses unless you absolutely have to. If you can keep your expenses low, you can save money much more easily as it comes in. Every time you get a raise, you can funnel that money into your retirement account without feeling the strain on your cash flow. This approach is an easy way to make your money work for you without feeling like you're sacrificing.

Every six months, review your expenses to see whether you can cut anything. Call your service providers and ask about negotiating your rate. By doing so, you're keeping your overall expenses low so that if you do have to spend more on something like groceries, your cash flow isn't as affected. This balance allows you to keep saving.

Using a budgeting app is an efficient and easy way to cut your expenses without much effort. Some apps analyze your spending to remind you about subscriptions you can cut and negotiate your bills with your providers on your behalf. This feature saves time and money, both resources you don't want to waste.

Use catch-up contributions if they're needed

If you're 50 or older, you can take advantage of what's known as *catch-up retirement contributions*. At the time of this writing, you can contribute up to an additional $7,500 dollars to your 401(k) and IRA accounts. Catch-up retirement contributions can help you increase your accounts and give you additional income in retirement. This concept can help tremendously if you're late to the retirement savings game.

Chapter **10**

Eliminating Debt

I hate having debt — *hate it!*. As much as I like to think I'm the perfect financial guru (hello, personal finance columnist!), I'm just human like everyone else. I've been in debt since I was 19 and took out my first student loans. I've also taken out auto and personal loans and used credit cards to my advantage. The point is that 99 percent of the population just can't feasibly make a significant purchase or tackle a crisis without taking on some kind of debt.

In this chapter, I look at the different types of debt to help you create a budget for paying debt off. I discuss how to rank the importance of each debt so you can create a payoff plan that works with your budget, and I share tips anyone can use to keep themselves from accumulating more debt. It's all fun and games when you come home with something shiny until you have to pay it back.

REMEMBER

The illusion that you're a terrible person if you have debt is a common misconception. In fact, many personal finance gurus even suggest that if you have debt, you shouldn't enjoy your life until you pay that debt off in full. Ignore them. Debt happens to everyone at one time or another, and you don't deserve a lower quality of life than the person down the street.

Looking at the Different Types of Debt

You acquire *debt* when you borrow a certain amount of money intending to pay it back. People can take on debt, but so can companies, corporations, and even countries. Heck, as of this writing, the United States is more than $31.2 trillion in the hole, according to U.S. Debt Clock.org.

Different types of debt affect your credit score in different ways, which you can read more about in Chapter 15. You want different types of debt paid off in full on your credit report so lenders can see that you're a trustworthy applicant capable of paying off a loan. You *do not* want open or delinquent accounts all over the place. In the following sections, I review the different types of debt so you can get organized and pay these monsters off.

REMEMBER

You often see people refer to debt as being "good" debt or "bad" debt. *Good debt* typically provides a return on your investment. Student loans are considered good debt because you're using them to secure a college degree, which helps increase your earning potential. Another example of good debt is home loan because your home can appreciate in value over time, allowing you to sell for a profit. *Bad debt* is anything you've borrowed that doesn't further your finances; I think of bad debt as anything that decreases your net worth over time, usually with depreciating assets. This type of debt includes auto loans (because cars lose their value) and credit cards.

Student loans

Student loan debt is money you borrow for costs associated with higher education, such as tuition, textbooks, laptops, and living expenses. If you attend a trade school, additional expenses can apply. For example, you may need specific tools if you go into automotive repair or a stethoscope if you're a medical assistant. I used a student loan to help with my transportation and lodging when I studied abroad. (If anyone asks, I really do have a certificate in counterterrorism. What I do with it must be mentioned in a different book. *Shhh!*)

These types of debts are considered *unsecured installment loans*. When a debt is *unsecured*, you aren't providing any collateral to the financial institution (or lender). An *installment loan* means that you'll pay back the loan at regular intervals, but the payment amount may change based on the type of interest rate you have (that is, a fixed rate versus an adjustable rate). Student loan debt can be recalculated depending on the type of loan and repayment plan. The interest rates on a student loan can be fixed or graduated (the rate increases as income increases). The lender determines the frequency of payments, which can vary but usually occur once a month over several years. Repayment starts six months after graduation, a span known as a *grace period*.

You can receive either a federal loan from the U.S Department of Education or a private loan through a bank or alternative lender. Private loans are much harder for a younger student to obtain because these loans are typically based on your credit score and credit history. Federal loans, on the other hand, require you to complete the Free Application for Federal Student Aid (FAFSA). Each of these types of loans has different requirements as well as pros and cons, such as income-based repayment options or the ability to refinance at a lower rate.

TIP

I highly encourage everyone who hasn't started their higher ed journey yet to at least fill out the FAFSA. A lot of schools award grants and scholarships based on the information you provide. You can find the online application at studentaid. gov. See Chapter 12 for more information.

Credit cards

Credit card debt is money you borrow from a financial institution or company through a line of credit. A *line of credit* is a preselected amount of money you can access at any time as long as you don't exceed the available funds. The length of time to pay back the money is typically a month. After the month is over, the funds you borrowed acquire interest, which means you have to pay back more than what you had initially borrowed in the first place.

Credit cards, like student loans (see the preceding section), may be unsecured. If a credit card is secured, the lender wants you to put some skin in the game by providing some collateral such as paying a hefty fee or providing a cash deposit when you open the account. The lender doesn't keep the collateral forever — usually a year, sort of like a deposit. After you've established a history of making your payments on time, it refunds your collateral and moves you to an unsecured line of credit.

Along with being unsecured or secured, credit cards are also known as revolving debt. *Revolving debt* allows you to borrow money and pay it back, only to repeat the cycle again and again with no end date. Credit cards can also come with perks such as free travel, cash back, and discounts meant to keep you using your credit card again and again. When you use credit cards responsibly, you can take advantage of these perks without spending additional money if you pay your card off in full every month. I know many travel bloggers who haven't paid for a room or flight in years!

Home and auto loans

Unlike the student loan and credit card debt in the preceding sections, which can slowly creep up on you, purchasing a home or automobile can cause you to acquire a large amount of debt at one time. New cars can start at $20,000 and go up from there. Homes typically go for hundreds of thousands of dollars and, depending on the location, sometimes even more! I don't have that type of cash laying around, and I'm going to assume you probably don't either.

Home loans

Mortgages, like student loans, are considered installment debt. When you're approved for a mortgage, the bank that has approved your financing sets up an arrangement with you to pay back the loan over time — usually 15 or 30 years. Still, the exact arrangement depends on your lender and other factors, such as what type of loan you're approved for, interest rates, and whether you have a down payment.

Mortgages are considered secured debt. A lender knows it's getting its money back no matter what when helping you finance a home. So if you end up short one month and can't pay your mortgage, no sweat — to the lender, not you. You'll have to pay when it shows up on your credit report. However, after you're 120 days late, the lender will start the foreclosure process and take the house back. Sure, it would've made more money if you had fulfilled the loan's terms, but it's still getting something out of the deal.

WARNING

I discuss how to prioritize your debt within your budget later in this chapter, but please pay your mortgage. You don't want a foreclosure on your credit report! Foreclosures can prevent you from finding a new place to live, even when you're just looking to rent. This costly mistake can cost you thousands of dollars for years to come.

Auto loans

If you don't have enough cash to purchase a vehicle outright, you need a bank or credit union to finance you with an auto loan. Suppose you're buying a car through a dealership. In that case, its finance department reviews options with you based on your credit history and whether you're providing a down payment or a trade-in. Dealerships usually have preferred lenders they work with. You can choose to finance with them or look at your bank for finance options.

Auto loans are secured loans you pay off in installments. Because it's an installment loan, you make monthly payments over a timeline, usually no more than six years. Six-year loans are more common when you're purchasing a brand-new car versus an older model because the loan amount tends to be more significant. Auto loans also come with collateral, which is why they're secured. If you don't make your payments, the lender can take the vehicle in a process called *repossession*. It finds someone else to buy your car and then sticks you with the difference of what's still left on your loan. This process happens in a much shorter time frame than a home foreclosure (see the preceding section), but can you imagine? You're getting up to get a coffee one day, and then *bam!* Your car is gone!

This actually happened to me when I was at work (I know!). I was 21 years old and living high on the hog, also known as not on a budget. Living my best life, I hadn't made a car payment in full for a while. While walking out of work one day, I couldn't find my car. I ran home to ask my dad for advice. He asked whether it had been repossessed, and I called my bank to find out that, yes, the car was being held hostage at a secret location. Good thing I hadn't filed a police report — *ugh!*

Miscellaneous debt

If you've read the preceding sections, you may be thinking, "Athena, I owe someone money, but you haven't even mentioned it yet!" Never fear, for this section talks about other types of debt you may need to include in your budget.

Government agencies

Child support, outstanding taxes, any debt owed to agencies besides the IRS, and any excess unemployment payments are all debt that falls into this category. Debt owed to the government is serious business. In fact, unpaid debt can lead to many repercussions, such as having your paycheck garnished or, in some cases, losing your driver's license.

The United States Department of Treasury's Financial Management Service operates the Treasury Offset Program, also known as the TOP. The TOP allows federal and state agencies to collect money however they see fit, such as by garnishing your wages through your employer or taking the money out of your tax refund. Your employer has no choice but to abide, which means a relatively smaller paycheck.

WARNING

Don't forget your property taxes. This bill is just as important as paying your mortgage. When your property taxes become delinquent, the state where the property is located can sell your property even if you own the home that's located on it. If you need assistance, ask your mortgage lender if you can open an escrow account.

Court-ordered debt

Specific crimes like unpaid parking tickets, breaking traffic laws, and more severe ones like misdemeanors and felonies carry a fine. Fines cost money and hopefully discourage you from committing the crime again. You usually pay this type of debt to the court, where a judge presides over your case. You may also be asked to pay court fees and, if applicable, restitution toward a victim.

Overdue bills turned over to collection agencies

Unpaid bills that go to a collection agency show up on your credit report to haunt you. Evictions, utility bills, and outstanding lines of credit from places like department stores all fall in this bucket. Once I forgot to pay an Internet bill. I was 19 and was experiencing financial abuse from a relative. My friend and I moved me out one afternoon when everyone was at work.

I was so flustered that I forgot about the bill until I received a disconnection notice at my new place. I had forgotten to cancel the service, and it was left on for three months with no payment. I was so angry at the situation I threw the bill in a junk drawer. Take that, Internet provider! (Mature was definitely my middle name back then.) The consequences, such as not being approved for a cellphone I wanted a year later, didn't occur to me, and the unpaid bill left a wound on my credit report.

REMEMBER

Bills you'd rather ignore don't go away, as much as you want them to, which is why your budget helps you figure out where the money to pay them comes from.

Medical bills

Recently, the Consumer Financial Protection Bureau reported that consumers collectively had $88 billion of medical debt. *Medical debt* includes any services you receive from your provider, testing, bloodwork, and hospital stays. It can even include medication and transportation to receiving medical care, like a ride in an ambulance. Many insurance companies charge high premiums, and despite the 2010 passage of the Affordable Care Act (or ACA), many Americans still struggle to afford healthcare coverage. Some employers cover part of the insurance premiums, but others don't. Even if you have health insurance, you're expected to pay what's known as a deductible before your health insurance provider covers any of the bill.

Personal loans

You can also take out what's known as a personal loan from a bank or another financial institution. *Personal loans* are unsecured loans from a lender that you pay back in monthly payment or installments. Weddings, trips, and holidays are some reasons I've seen people take out personal loans.

Loans from friends or family

Sometimes loans don't come from a bank but from a friend or family member. These loans typically have no interest rate or payment schedule because the lender provides the money in good faith that you'll eventually pay them back. I had a loan from an ex-boyfriend when the love of my life, a polydactyl cat named Harrison George, needed emergency surgery. I'm glad to say Harrison is doing well and meowing at me as I write this very chapter.

Paying Off Your Debt

Your debt may seem overwhelming, and you may wonder what the purpose of creating a budget is when you have so many other bills to pay. But a budget is a money plan that tells your money where to go, not the other way around. If paying off debt is going to be a part of your budget, pull up a seat. In the following sections, I discuss how to pay off your debt so you can eventually start putting your money toward your other financial goals.

REMEMBER

There's no right way to pay off your debt. Just like everything else about you, your debt is unique. You have different financial responsibilities than I do and vice versa. Your debt repayment plan will be different if you have kids or take care of an older family member. It will also look different based on your income and current expenses. That's why mapping out where your money goes, as I explain in Chapter 2, is so important. After you've aced that step, you can strategize toward making your debt repayment plan.

Compiling a list of your debt

The first step to tackling debt repayment is to compile a debt assessment by making a list of the different types of debt you currently have. You need to see all this information in front of you so you aren't forgetting anyone you owe money to. You can include an amount as small as owing your spouse $5 for a coffee or as large as your mortgage. For each debt, I want you to log into your account online to make a note of the following things:

>> **The company the debt is owed to, the amount owed, and the due date for payment:** If you haven't made payment arrangements, make a note of that, too.

>> **Type of debt:** Is this debt your mortgage, car loan, or an unpaid bill? Look over the list in the earlier section "Looking at the Different Types of Debt" if you're unsure how to categorize it. You can also leave a reminder to ask someone or even call the company to which you owe the debt.

>> **Secured or unsecured debt:** Both can be harmful to your credit report if you don't pay, but this information is important because secured debt usually means that you have some type of collateral the lender can confiscate if you don't pay the debt on time. The collateral can be vital to your and your family's survival if it's an auto or home loan. Unsecured debt has no collateral at stake.

>> **Revolving loan or installment loan:** With an installment loan, you already have a payment arrangement in place. After you've paid off revolving debt, you can always borrow more.

>> **Any pressing circumstances related to the debt:** A pressing circumstance may be a garnished paycheck or the threat of a suspended driver's license. I'd even go so far as to say that any tension between you and a friend or family member over a loan is a pressing issue.

Next, you should reorganize the information in either a spreadsheet or in a notebook. First, list the name of the creditor, the type of debt, the payment amount, the due date, the interest rate or APR (annual percentage rate), and the total amount still owed. If an account has a payoff amount listed anywhere, you can add it as a note. Figures 10-1 and 10-2 are two formatting examples of a debt assessment.

	A	B	C	D	E	F
1	Creditor	Type of Debt	Payment Amount	Due Date	APR	Amount Still Owed
2	Bank of America	Mortgage	$1,978.55	1st of every month	4.50%	$345,231
3	Credit Union	Personal Loan	$150	5th of every month	3%	$2,450
4	Credit Union	Auto Loan	$497	10th of every month	3%	$16,679
5	SoFi	Student Loan	$358	15th of every month	7%	$28,766
6	Capital One	Credit Cards	$179	20th of every month	19%	$2,023
7	American Express	Credit Cards	$67.44	25th of every month	15%	$786
8	Mastercard	Credit Cards	$97	30th of every month	18%	$877
9	Dr. Smith	Medical Bill	$50	30th of every month	0%	$350

FIGURE 10-1: A debt assessment spreadsheet.

Debt Total, January		
Creditor (Debt Type)	Payment Amount / Due Date / APR	Amount Still Owed
BOA (Mortgage)	$1,978.55 / 1st every month / 4.50%	$345,231
Credit Union (Personal)	$150 / 5th every month / 3%	$2,450
Credit Union (Car)	$497 / 10th every month / 3%	$16,679
SoFi (Student)	$358 / 15th every month / 7%	$28,766
Capital One (CC)	$179 / 20th every month / 19%	$2,023
Amex (CC)	$67.44 / 25th every month / 15%	$786
Mastercard (CC)	$97 / 30th every month / 18%	$877
Dr. Smith (Medical)	$50 / 30th every month / 0%	$350

FIGURE 10-2: A debt assessment compiled on a notebook page.

Considering different payoff methods

What does a debt payoff plan even look like? Well, you can keep doing what you're doing now and pay your monthly payments. Or you can try one of these three main debt payoff methods:

>> The snowball method

>> The avalanche method

>> The fireball method

REMEMBER

If making the minimum payments is where you are right now in your money journey, that's okay. You'll eventually work your way to where your financial goals allow you to pay off more of your debt. I pay my monthly car payment without trying to pay it off because I have other priorities. I'm not a bad person for not wanting to pay off my debt faster than I have to, and neither are you.

The snowball method

My absolute favorite way to pay off debt is the debt snowball method. The *snowball method* works like this: You pay your regular debt payments, and then anything extra you can come up with to pay on your debt goes toward the smallest one first. You then continue this process until your smallest debt is paid off. The goal of the snowball method is to keep you consistent with your debt repayment by motivating you with small wins. When you continually succeed in any area of your life, it's easier to stay on track consistently. Consistency is what's going to enable you to achieve your goals.

Using your debt assessment from the previous section, arrange your debts from smallest amount owed to largest amount owed. It may look like Figure 10-3 or Figure 10-4.

For example, say your first smallest debt is a bill you owe the dentist. It's $350, and you're currently paying $50 a month. Your next smallest bill is a credit card for $786, and you're paying $50 on this one as well.

You're able to cut some expenses in your budget, which frees up $100 per month (good job!), and you've decided to put this money toward debt. Throw the extra $100 on top of the regular $50 payment and pay the dentist bill in full within two months.

	A	B	C	D	E	F
1	**Creditor**	**Type of Debt**	**Payment Amount**	**Due Date**	**APR**	**Amount Still Owed**
2	Dr. Smith	Medical Bill	$50	30th of every month	0%	$350
3	American Express	Credit Cards	$67.44	25th of every month	15%	$786
4	Mastercard	Credit Cards	$97	30th of every month	18%	$877
5	Credit Union	Personal Loan	$150	5th of every month	3%	$2,450
6	Capital One	Credit Cards	$179	20th of every month	19%	$2,023
7	SoFi	Student Loan	$358	15th of every month	7%	$28,766
8	Credit Union	Auto Loan	$497	10th of every month	3%	$16,679
9	Bank of America	Mortgage	$1,978.55	1st of every month	4.50%	$345,231

FIGURE 10-3: A debt spreadsheet organized by the amounts still owed.

Debt Total, January

Creditor (Debt Type)	Payment Amount / Due Date / APR	Amount Still Owed
Dr. Smith (Medical)	$50 / 30th every month / 0%	$350
Amex (CC)	$67.44 / 25th every month / 15%	$786
Mastercard (CC)	$97 / 30th every month / 18%	$877
Credit Union (Personal)	$150 / 5th every month / 3%	$2,450
Capital One (CC)	$179 / 20th every month / 19%	$2,023
SoFi (Student)	$358 / 15th every month / 7%	$28,766
Credit Union (Car)	$497 / 10th every month / 3%	$16,679
BOA (Mortgage)	$1,978.55 / 1st every month / 4.50%	$345,231

FIGURE 10-4: Debt compiled on a notebook page, organized by the amount still owed.

Now you have an extra $150 a month in your budget to use toward debt repayment (the $100 you freed up in expenses, plus the $50 you were putting toward that dentist's bill). You can apply this $150 toward your next smallest debt, your credit card. When your next payment is due, you pay $200 rather than the regular payment of $50. You've snowballed your old debt payment amount toward another debt payment amount. This approach is going to enable you to pay off this debt faster, too.

The one con with this debt repayment strategy is that you pay more interest over time. Paying more in interest and other fees means you're paying more money in the long run than you would with something like the avalanche method, which I discuss in the following section. But if using the snowball method means you're motivated to actually stick to your debt repayment strategy, that trade-off may be okay for you.

The avalanche method

If you'd rather save money and possibly get out of debt faster, then the avalanche method may be a better fit for you than the other methods I'm sharing. The *avalanche method* requires you to focus on paying down your debt by homing in on your interest rather than the amount owed. The longer you take to pay a creditor back, the more interest your loan accrues. Depending on the type of debt you have, the interest can fluctuate and collect on different amounts of money at different times.

Using your debt assessment from earlier in the chapter, organize your creditors from the highest to lowest interest. Figures 10-5 and 10-6 show two formatting examples that use the avalanche method.

	A	B	C	D	E	F
1	**Creditor**	**Type of Debt**	**Payment Amount**	**Due Date**	**APR**	**Amount Still Owed**
2	Capital One	Credit Cards	$179	20th of every month	19%	$2,023
3	Mastercard	Credit Cards	$97	30th of every month	18%	$877
4	American Express	Credit Cards	$67.44	25th of every month	15%	$786
5	SoFi	Student Loan	$358	15th of every month	7%	$28,766
6	Bank of America	Mortgage	$1,978.55	1st of every month	4.50%	$345,231
7	Credit Union	Personal Loan	$150	5th of every month	3%	$2,450
8	Credit Union	Auto Loan	$497	10th of every month	3%	$16,679
9	Dr. Smith	Medical Bill	$50	30th of every month	0%	$350

FIGURE 10-5: A debt spreadsheet organized by APR.

Debt Total, January		
Creditor (Debt Type)	**Payment Amount / Due Date / APR**	**Amount Still Owed**
Capital One (CC)	$179 / 20th every month / 19%	$2,023
Mastercard (CC)	$97 / 30th every month / 18%	$877
Amex (CC)	$67.44 / 25th every month / 15%	$786
SoFi (Student)	$358 / 15th every month / 7%	$28,766
BOA (Mortgage)	$1,978.55 / 1st every month / 4.50%	$345,231
Credit Union (Personal)	$150 / 5th every month / 3%	$2,450
Credit Union (Car)	$497 / 10th every month / 3%	$16,679
Dr. Smith (Medical)	$50 / 30th every month / 0%	$350

FIGURE 10-6: Debt organized by APR on a notebook page.

Let's look at the creditors with the highest interest rates, which looks like this:

1. Credit card 1 at 19 percent with a $179 monthly payment

2. Credit card 2 at 18 percent with a $97 monthly payment

3. Credit card 3 at 15 percent with a monthly payment of $67.44

You've cleared up an extra $100 in your budget for debt repayment. Because you're paying the most interest on your credit card, you focus on that bill first. Rather than paying $179 on credit card 1, you're now paying $279. After you pay off that credit card, you then move onto the next credit card. You take that $279 and apply it to the monthly credit card payment until that debt is gone. Then you continue onto your student loan and so on until you've paid everything off.

If you don't have a problem with consistency, this payoff method may work for you. You're paying off your debt at a much faster rate than before while also paying less money overall. Depending on the type and amount of loan, you don't always have small wins along the way, so this debt payoff method requires you to be patient. But saving money is always a win because you can then apply that cash to your budget somewhere else.

The fireball method

Though debt is still debt at the end of the day, the fireball method, coined by SoFi, allows you to categorize your debt to pay it off on a timeline that works for you. This method plays off the snowball method I cover earlier in the chapter.

First, refer to your debt assessment from earlier in the chapter and categorize your debt as either good or bad. (Check out the earlier section "Looking at the Different Types of Debt" for more on this distinction.)

Figures 10-7 and 10-8 show the two formatting examples to categorize good and bad debt.

Then arrange each list debt from smallest amount owed to the largest amount owed. Figures 10-9 and 10-10 show two formatting examples that use the fireball method.

Now focus on your bad debt, paying off your smallest loan first. Like the snowball method, you'll still be making your minimum payments, but any extra money goes toward eliminating your smallest debt first. After you pay it off, you apply that payment amount to your next highest debt. Unlike the snowball method, you're focused on only your bad debt for now.

FIGURE 10-7:
A spreadsheet separating good and bad debt.

	A	B	C	D	E	F
1	**Good Debt**					
2	**Creditor**	**Type of Debt**	**Payment Amount**	**Due Date**	**APR**	**Amount Still Owed**
3	SoFi	Student Loan	$358	15th of every month	7%	$28,766
4	Credit Union	Auto Loan	$497	10th of every month	3%	$16,679
5	Bank of America	Mortgage	$1,978.55	1st of every month	4.50%	$345,231
6						
7	**Bad Debt**					
8	**Creditor**	**Type of Debt**	**Payment Amount**	**Due Date**	**APR**	**Amount Still Owed**
9	Capital One	Credit Cards	$179	20th of every month	19%	$2,023
10	Mastercard	Credit Cards	$97	30th of every month	18%	$877
11	American Express	Credit Cards	$67.44	25th of every month	15%	$786
12	Credit Union	Personal Loan	$150	5th of every month	3%	$2,450
13	Dr. Smith	Medical Bill	$50	30th of every month	0%	$350

Debt Total, January - Good

Creditor (Debt Type)	Payment Amount / Due Date / APR	Amount Still Owed
Credit Union (Car)	$497 / 10th every month / 3%	$16,679
SoFI (Student)	$358 / 15th every month / 7%	$28,766
BOA (Mortgage)	$1,978.55 / 1st every month / 4.50%	$345,231

Debt Total, January - Bad

Creditor (Debt Type)	Payment Amount / Due Date / APR	Amount Still Owed
Dr. Smith (Medical)	$50 / 30th every month / 0%	$350
Credit Union (Personal)	$150 / 5th every month / 3%	$2,450
Capital One (CC)	$179 / 20th every month / 19%	$2,023
Mastercard (CC)	$97 / 30th every month / 18%	$877
Amex (CC)	$67.44 / 25th every month / 15%	$786

FIGURE 10-8:
A written list separating good and bad debt.

	A	B	C	D	E	F
1	**Good Debt**					
2	**Creditor**	**Type of Debt**	**Payment Amount**	**Due Date**	**APR**	**Amount Still Owed**
3	Credit Union	Auto Loan	$497	10th of every month	3%	$16,679
4	SoFi	Student Loan	$358	15th of every month	7%	$28,766
5	Bank of America	Mortgage	$1,978.55	1st of every month	4.50%	$345,231
6						
7	**Bad Debt**					
8	**Creditor**	**Type of Debt**	**Payment Amount**	**Due Date**	**APR**	**Amount Still Owed**
9	Dr. Smith	Medical Bill	$50	30th of every month	0%	$350
10	American Express	Credit Cards	$67.44	25th of every month	15%	$786
11	Mastercard	Credit Cards	$97	30th of every month	18%	$877
12	Capital One	Credit Cards	$179	20th of every month	19%	$2,023
13	Credit Union	Personal Loan	$150	5th of every month	3%	$2,450

FIGURE 10-9: A spreadsheet arranging bad and good debt by amount owed.

Debt Total, January - Good

Creditor (Debt Type)	Payment Amount / Due Date / APR	Amount Still Owed
Credit Union (Car)	$497 / 10th every month / 3%	$16,679
SoFi (Student)	$358 / 15th every month / 7%	$28,766
BOA (Mortgage)	$1,978.55 / 1st every month / 4.50%	$345,231

Debt Total, January - Bad

Creditor (Debt Type)	Payment Amount / Due Date / APR	Amount Still Owed
Dr. Smith (Medical)	$50 / 30th every month / 0%	$350
Amex (CC)	$67.44 / 25th every month / 15%	$786
Credit Union (Personal)	$150 / 5th every month / 3%	$2,450
Mastercard (CC)	$97 / 30th every month / 18%	$877
Capital One (CC)	$179 / 20th every month / 19%	$2,023

FIGURE 10-10: A written list arranging bad and good debt by amount owed.

After you've taken care of the bad debt, you then turn to your good debt. But instead of throwing all the money you were applying toward your bad debt to the good debt, you put it toward your savings goals, such as paying for a down payment on a house. Essentially, you're starting a new snowball for your good debt. Because you're still paying off your good debt, this method encourages you to work on your other goals simultaneously. Most people take advantage of this time to work on catching up on retirement. Wherever you put the money, this method can help you determine what debt you should take care of first while motivating you with small wins.

REMEMBER

The only issue I have with this method is the significance of designating something as good or bad. People often associate the word *bad* with shame, and personal finance shouldn't be shameful. You don't always choose to take out bad debt; sometimes things happen, like medical emergencies, car repairs, and sick pets.

THE DEBT CONSOLIDATION METHOD

I don't actually recommend the debt consolidation method, but I feel you as a consumer deserve to know all your options to make the best choice for you.

Debt consolidation is when you combine multiple debt repayments into one. So instead of paying everything to multiple creditors separately, you only have one to pay. Many debt consolidation companies allow you to consolidate only lines of unsecured debt.

You find three different types of debt consolidation:

- **Credit counseling:** Various nonprofits offer credit counseling services as well as debt consolidation programs. These outfits are strictly regulated by law in what they can and can't do when serving you. Because they must act in your best interest, that means providing you with financial education and discussing what your debt relief options are, including debt consolidation or bankruptcy. It also means debt relief options that are free or low-cost.

- **Debt relief or settlement companies:** Instead of looking at your individual situation to provide you with helpful and productive solutions, a debt relief or settlement company offers to negotiate with your creditors when you enroll in a debt management plan through its organization. Along with requiring additional fees on top of your monthly payment, it directs you to stop paying your creditors so it can negotiate a better rate on your behalf.

  Not paying your creditors does more harm than good. Being delinquent on one account can harm your credit score, but being delinquent on several is truly bad

(continued)

(continued)

news. This type of debt consolidation can prey on you as a consumer and ruin your credit score without your knowledge. Ruining your credit score can make your financial situation even worse.

- **Debt consolidation loans:** A debt consolidation loan through a financial institution allows you to borrow an amount of money that covers the amount you owe your creditors for your current debt. If approved for the loan, you may receive the funds to pay off your creditors, or the financial institution may offer to pay them off directly. You then get a monthly payment plan to repay the loan with a fixed interest rate.

You can do a lot of the work that debt relief management companies charge you for. This approach allows you to save money and also your credit score. You don't have to sign up for a debt repayment plan, because you can pay the debt independently. Companies just want you to think that you can't.

The idea of one monthly payment can sound tempting, especially if you have tons of debt to pay. And I think you can make debt consolidation loans work if you use them appropriately. But I also think debt consolidation loans aren't a quick fix.

If you choose this route, you may not be addressing the root issue of your debt. You can also get into more debt because you're making your credit cards and other lines of credit available again. Telling yourself you'll just use the card once and pay it back, only to find yourself right where you started, is so easy.

Applying additional strategies

You can implement a variety of other strategies to help pay your debt off even faster.

Make a debt payoff settlement

One of the ways I was able to pay off debt while working part-time was by learning how to negotiate with debt collectors.

When you fall behind while paying your debt, you become delinquent. Your creditor may work with you to get back on track, but if it sees no progress, it eventually gives up and, in the case of unsecured debt, sells your debt to a collection agency.

Debt sold to collection agencies shows up on your credit report, so you want to avoid this scenario as much as possible. But if you're stuck with a collections bill, call the agency and see whether you can settle for less than the amount you owe.

Collection agencies don't really have people banging down their doors to pay their debt, so they're more likely to work with you and accept an amount less than you owe.

A collection agency will most likely accept half of what you owe. Say you have a creditor $500 debt in collections. When you have $250 to part with, call the agency and ask to speak to someone about a settlement offer. First, kindly thank them for taking your call and for being patient with you while you get your financial affairs in order. Next, acknowledge the fact that you do owe them money and ask whether they'd be willing to settle your account today if you could make a cash payment.

If they say yes, great! Ask them for an amount they're willing to accept and then go from there. *Tip*: You always ask what they can do first because they may come back with a lower amount than you had originally thought to offer. After you agree on a payoff amount, ask to receive it in writing via email so you can pay while still on the phone.

After you've received confirmation in writing, go ahead and make your payment. Make sure to ask for a receipt via email and also by mail. Keeping detailed records of payment is important; selling someone's debt from collection agency to collection agency is a common practice, and you don't want to have to pay for the same debt mistake twice.

Negotiate with creditors

You don't have to wait for your debt to end up being turned over to collections to negotiate with your creditors. If you have a bill like medical debt, call the medical provider to see what it can do. A lot of doctor's offices will allow you to settle your bill for an agreed-upon portion because getting a small guaranteed payment is better than never receiving any payment.

Some medical providers, like hospitals, have financial relief departments. The financial relief department assigns a case worker to look over your medical bills along with your finances to see whether you qualify for assistance. Depending on the amount, they may agree to put you on a payment plan or waive the debt entirely. I was able to take care of a program offered through a hospital for one of my annual trips to the emergency room. (Thanks, chronic asthma!)

TIP

To find a nonprofit hospital located closest to you, type "nonprofit hospital (city you're currently located)" into an online search engine. You can then filter results to find one that meets your needs.

When you have medical emergencies, try to seek medical care at a nonprofit hospital. By law, nonprofit hospitals must offer financial assistance programs. You can also call your local community resource center to see whether any other organizations in your area can help with medical assistance.

Ask about hardship programs

If you have credit card debt that you need assistance with, ask your creditor whether it offers any payment assistance. Some credit card companies have hardship programs that can allow you to go on a monthly repayment plan with more affordable payments. They may also lower any fees or interest you currently pay for a few months. Circumstances that can qualify for hardship include but aren't limited to divorce, death of a loved one, loss of job, or health issues.

TIP

Your other creditors may offer financial assistance programs as well. Some creditors offer a pause on payments by extending the length of your loan. Other options can include moving your payment due date into the future to give you some time to catch up.

REMEMBER

Asking for help can hurt your pride. But you know what? It shouldn't. Instead of being sad or ashamed you had to ask for help, be proud. It takes a strong person to know when they need help, and it takes an even stronger person to ask out loud. Needing help is okay, and your finances will be better off too!

Use balance transfers

Another strategy you can look into is opening a new credit card for a balance transfer. A *balance transfer* is when you move your debt from one creditor to a new creditor for a lower interest rate. Sometimes the interest rate on a balance transfer is as low as 0 percent. The goal of the balance transfer is to save you money in finance fees by offering you a low rate for a predetermined time period. You may also be able to move other types of debt with the balance transfer, such as an auto or personal loan.

To apply for a credit card that offers a balance transfer, you most likely need to have a credit score of 670 or above. I talk more in-depth about your credit score in Chapter 15, but for now, know your credit score can range from 300 to 850. The higher the credit score you have, the better.

WARNING

Make sure you're aware of the terms and conditions of your new balance transfer credit card. With balance transfers, your 0 percent APR typically only lasts 12 to 18 months. After that, your credit card balance starts collecting interest on the debt you've transferred over. The whole point of a balance transfer is to save money on fees and interest, so take advantage of it as much as possible. Also, make sure you know what if any circumstances, such as making a late payment, may cause you to lose your 0 percent interest rate.

If you're approved, double-check how the debt will be transferred over. A creditor may contact the other creditors directly on your behalf to pay your debt off, or it may expect you to take care of it on your own. Make sure to transfer the debt incurring the highest interest rate first so you can take advantage of the lower interest rate as much as you can.

Make extra payments

If, after creating your budget, you find yourself with extra money, consider using it to make extra payments on your debt. One way to approach this strategy is by making a payment that's applied to the loan principal, such as on a mortgage.

When you pay extra on your mortgage, you can ask your loan provider to apply the money to your loan principal. Every time you pay additional money to your loan principal, you're paying less interest. By lowering the amount you owe directly, you lower the amount you pay over time in financing fees. You can even accomplish this goal by splitting up your monthly mortgage payment and applying half every two weeks. By using this tactic, you're making 13 payments a year rather than 12. *Note:* Not all creditors allow extra payments to go to the loan principal, so always research the terms of your loan.

TECHNICAL STUFF

If you're interested in seeing how you can apply this strategy to your situation, check out the extra payments calculator from Freddie Mac. This calculator allows you to input different payment amounts across different scenarios. I love it because it allows you to see that even small additional payments here and there can add up over time. Find the calculator at myhome.freddiemac.com/resources/calculators/extra-payments.

Use financial windfalls

Using any *windfalls* (unexpected money) you receive can help you get out of debt faster. Because you've already covered your expenses, put that extra money to work. If you get a bonus or overtime pay, put it on your car loan. Taking advantage of extra money you weren't expecting can help get you ahead farther than you think.

TIP

If you feel the urge to use that windfall to treat yourself, consider the 80-20 rule. Apply 80 percent of your windfall toward your debt and then keep the remaining 20 percent for fun. I love this approach because you're taking care of business, but you're still making fun a priority. Prioritizing fun is one way to keep you motivated on your debt journey.

Avoiding Accumulating More Debt

Paying your debt off is important, but so is keeping yourself from getting into more debt. Incurring more debt is easy to do and can happen quickly. However, you can be proactive while keeping your budget intact.

Here are a few tips to keep in mind when you're reviewing your debt and debt repayment:

>> **Know your rights.** Before you speak to any debt collector or creditor, be aware of the questions they can and can't ask. Also beware of illegal debt collection practices, such as contacting you by phone after you've asked them to stop. Check out the Fair Debt Collection Practices Act for more information: www.federalreserve.gov/boarddocs/supmanual/cch/fairdebt.pdf.

>> **Check your budget to ensure the amount you can pay toward your debt.** Don't promise an amount you can't pay.

>> **Make a list of debts you want to negotiate.** Refer to the section "Considering different payoff methods" earlier in this chapter for information on compiling a debt assessment.

>> **Call your collector.** Use the following phone script for reference:

"My name is [insert your name], and I am calling to discuss my current account status. I know I'm late, but I am currently facing an unforeseen financial hardship that has affected my finances, including this account. I would like to see what we can do to help bring my account to good standing. Can we discuss what my options are? Is it possible to arrange a payment plan?"

Note: If you are arranging a payment plan, always be sure to get it in writing and do not offer to pay more than you can realistically afford based on your current budget.

>> **Make sure you get the settlement agreement in writing.** Before you hand over the case, ensure you've received the debt repayment agreement in writing, even if that's email, from the debt collector. Also document what time your phone call took place and to whom you spoke.

>> **Stick to the repayment plan.** Follow through with your end of the agreement. If you don't, the collector can then decide that you must pay the full amount, and it probably won't be willing to work with you on a settlement again.

NEGOTIATE PRICES AND INTEREST RATES

One skill that will take you places in your money journey is negotiation. You can negotiate not only pricing on large ticket items but also lower interest rates with your creditors. By negotiating your rates, you save money by paying less in finance fees. Negotiating can be scary, but the worst someone can do is tell you no.

Case in point? My experience at the car dealership. I was in and out with a brand-new car in less than three hours. After I'd owned my old Hyundai Accent for almost ten years, the air conditioner went out. I had put so much money into this car leading up to this incident that my mechanic refused to fix it. He told me my money would be better spent toward a new car and then showed me how much I had spent in car repairs in the past two years.

I introduced myself to a salesman and told him politely yet firmly how much money I could put toward a down payment, including my car, and how much I'd pay monthly to finance a car. Because I was upfront, he showed me what I could qualify for so neither of us wasted time. After I selected the car I wanted, however, the finance department notified me that my car payment would be more than what I'd specified to the salesman. I explained again that I wanted to stick to a certain amount, and they told me it wouldn't be possible. At this point, I knew I had been approved for financing, so I confidently asked for my key back. I ended up securing a loan that fit my terms, but if I hadn't, I wasn't afraid to walk away.

Look into refinancing options

If your student, auto, or mortgage loan has a high interest rate, consider refinancing to save money. When you *refinance* a loan, you take out a newer loan with better terms and conditions to pay off an old loan. By refinancing a loan, you can have smaller monthly payments while paying less money overall with a better interest rate. This option is great if you have a good credit score.

TIP

If you don't have a high credit score, look to see what you can do to improve your rating. Make sure you pay your debt on time and work hard to lower your *credit utilization rate* (how much of your available credit you're using).

As you improve your credit score, more financial products become available. Eventually, you'll be able to find a loan with better terms than what you're currently paying.

Save an emergency fund

Emergency funds are crucial to keeping you out of debt. When people don't have the money to cover a financial emergency, they often charge it to a credit card or take out a loan. This scenario can turn into a nasty cycle of endless debt repayment that keeps you from achieving your financial goals. Having an emergency fund allows you to have the money available to keep emergencies from derailing your budget.

You can also avoid some emergencies if you plan ahead in your budget and take time for regular maintenance and screenings. Go to Chapter 8 for a more in-depth discussion about how to prepare and utilize your money for emergencies.

Say no to credit card offers

When I briefly worked for a department store as a makeup artist, part of my training was on how to convince people to open a store credit card. I received bonuses for every credit card I got someone to open and for hitting certain target amounts within a monthly period. I was 21, and I didn't think about what I could be getting someone into by pressing a credit card on them in the name of saving money.

REMEMBER

If you're trying to pay off debt, stay away from store credit cards and other in-house financing options. This type of consumer financing can keep you stuck in the cycle of charging for an item you don't need because you're "saving" money. If saving money is what you're after, look up discount codes on the Internet. I swear you can find a coupon for just about everything out there if you search hard enough.

Another great way to stay away from credit when working on debt repayment is to pay in cash from your bank account. Instead of using your credit card, pay with your debit card, which is deducted from your account. Go through any online retailers you use and update your payment information. This step ensures you're using your budget to pay for your purchases and not relying on credit. Please keep in mind that there is a higher fraud risk when using your debit card. Banks can only offer so much in terms of fraud protection, unlike credit card companies.

Invest in the right insurance

One way to keep yourself out of debt is to have adequate insurance for your health, car, and home. Insurance is an important tool for protecting both you and your finances. Instead of your having to take care of a financial emergency all on your own, an insurance policy can help you weather the cost (after you pay a deductible or co-pay). Insurance doesn't have to be expensive, either. Both online and in-person insurance brokers can offer you great deals and rates.

Health insurance is expensive, but going without insurance can cost more. Medical bills are one of the main reasons people declare bankruptcy. If you don't have health insurance and need major surgery, you can be hundreds of thousands of dollars in debt before you even know it. A lack of health insurance can also cost you your quality of life. Without health insurance, you may not have adequate preventive care — care that can help you avoid having serious medical issues in the future — or be able to fill the prescriptions you need.

REMEMBER

You should also consider life insurance, short-term and long-term disability insurance, and long-term care if you're close to or in retirement.

TIP

Don't forget Fido. If you're a pet owner, you need pet insurance. My cat's health emergencies have cost me, to the tune of almost $20,000. I could've avoided this spending if I had gotten pet insurance early on. Though he would've still had his health issues, I would've paid a fraction of what I've forked out. Pet insurance could have also helped with the prescriptions he has to take for the rest of his life. Cats live a long time, and we're only at age 9.

4

Budgeting in Action

Figure out ways to beat inflation, decrease job-related expenses, and examine how to manage a budget with irregular pay.

Know how to budget as a college student, couple, parent, or retiree.

Use your budget to save for your dream home, purchase a car, and navigate spending for other life events.

Chapter **11**

Budgeting in a Tough Economy

You may be saving for a rainy day, paying off debt, and living your best life within your budget, but what happens when things go rogue? If you lose your job, will you be able to survive on your savings and bounce back? Or will you end up putting your living expenses on credit cards? Budgeting in any economy means you must be ready to take on different situations and put your resources to good use. In this chapter, I show you how to prepare for economic changes that are out of your control. So lace up those boxing gloves and get ready to be thrown into the ring.

Keeping Your Head through the Ups and Downs of Inflation

Inflation is an economic situation marked by increased price levels and decreased purchasing power. In inflated markets, items no longer cost what you're used to or even what they should. So many factors go into inflation rates that everyday consumers have no control over. Even without control over the inflation rate, however, you can do your best to make your budget work for you. I offer some suggestions in the following sections.

Comparison shop to find the best deals

One of the ways you can make your money stretch no matter the current state of inflation is by *comparison shopping* — checking different stores' prices for a specific item. By doing so, you sometimes can secure an item for much cheaper than you would at your usual first choice store. You can also compare shops to see the price difference in total purchases, such as groceries. In the following sections, I offer some options to help you find the best deals.

Use online tools

The easiest way to start comparison shopping is right in the comfort of your own home. A ton of tools can do the heavy lifting for you when you shop online. For example, you can add an extension on your web browser for Honey (www. joinhoney.com).

Honey works in the background by searching for coupon codes (while you shop) that you can apply to your online purchase. If the store you're browsing doesn't offer a coupon code for your item, Honey alerts you to a retailer that does. It also allows you to save an item you want to buy and then pings you when the price drops.

Another web browser extension you can check is Capital One Shopping (capital oneshopping.com). This tool is a part of the financial institution Capital One, but you don't need to be a current customer to use it. Capital One Shopping works almost exactly like Honey, but it steps things up by allowing you to access its online platform that specifically tells you what retailers it's currently partnering with to help you take advantage of cash back and sales. You can type an item directly into its search engine instead of sifting through retailers.

Apps to help you find deals

You don't have to rely on shopping through your laptop browser to snag the best deals (see the preceding section). Apps for your phone can do the same thing. The apps are easy to navigate, but they usually require you to earn a minimum in points or cash to redeem your benefits. Here are some of my favorites.

>> **Ibotta:** You can use Ibotta both on your phone and with an online browser, but I prefer the app for easier access. Ibotta allows you to get cash back when you purchase certain items from participating stores. Many national retailers are on Ibotta, so you can likely find the one you shop at the most. The eligible items change weekly, but some are consistent, like bananas and milk. After you hit $20 in accumulated rewards, you can withdraw the cash to use as you like.

- **Fetch:** Unlike Ibotta, Fetch doesn't allow you to earn cash back, but it does reward you with a points system. After you buy from any retailer, you simply scan your receipt to earn points that you can later redeem for a gift card to a participating store. Like Ibotta, you can receive additional points by shopping at specific stores and buying participating brands.

- **Rakuten:** Rakuten is an app and web browser extension that offers cash back when you shop at a participating retailer. Simply look through the app to see what stores currently offer cash back and then shop through the app's link. After you've made a qualifying purchase, Rakuten deposits your cash back into your Rakuten account. You can redeem your cash every three months by check or PayPal. If you're using Rakuten consistently, your cash back can add up fast.

WARNING

When comparison shopping, be careful to check the quality of the item in question. Buying the cheapest option can be tempting, but if it breaks within a month, you're back where you started. Always check the ratings and the reviews from customers so you can make an informed choice.

TIP

Don't let the lack of a receipt keep you from making a return. A lot of retailers now have the ability to look up your transactions through the credit or debit card you used for the purchase. They may only offer you credit in the form of a gift card, but you can spend that money on something that works for you.

Adjust spending categories and goals

When times are tight during inflation, being as realistic as possible with yourself is important. That doesn't mean you don't need to have financial goals for yourself. On the contrary, it means you need to be living like a lean, mean, money-saving machine.

Go over your spending and make sure everything you have in your budget is serving a purpose in your life. If it's not, get rid of it. Check to see whether you have any subscriptions or services you aren't using and hit the cancellation button. Spending your money on things that aren't serving you is a waste.

Don't forget your emergency fund

If you don't have an emergency fund, start saving one. An emergency fund is what keeps you afloat during tough times such as periods of inflation. Chapter 8 has more details on the significance and mechanics of an emergency fund.

If you're working on an emergency fund, you can find lots of ways to save additional money to hit your goal faster. Consider cutting back on your budget by a few dollars here and there. Here are a few examples specific to some of the budgeting methods I discuss in Part 2:

>> **Zero-based budgeting (Chapter 3):** Try to spend less than the allowed amount. For example, if you've given yourself $220 dollars to spend on groceries, see whether you can slide in at $200 and save $20 toward your emergency fund.

>> **50/30/20 budgeting (Chapter 4):** Reduce your wants and needs by 5 percent and then allocate that savings to your emergency fund.

>> **Pay-yourself-first budgeting (Chapter 6):** Increase the percentage you save toward your goals and put the extra in your emergency fund. If you put 10 percent toward your goals, up that to 15 percent and live off 85 percent rather than 90 percent.

TIP
Putting your emergency fund in an account that offers a competitive annual percentage rate (APR), such as a high-yield savings account (HYSA), is an especially good idea during times of inflation because that extra interest can really make a difference.

Another way to add more to your emergency fund if you don't have adequate savings is to cut back on debt repayment. I'm not suggesting you stop making debt payments altogether, just that you don't pay more than your minimum payment. Normally I preach about interest rates costing you thousands of dollars. But when inflation rears its ugly head, having an extra thousand dollars in your emergency fund will serve you more than making an additional debt payment if you get laid off.

Look into additional income streams

Another way to achieve financial stability in times of inflation is to look into expanding your streams of income. You should look at three different types of income:

>> Active income

>> Passive income

>> Portfolio income

Active income

Active income is exactly what it sounds like: You need to be actively doing something to receive it. The most likely source of active income you have is your day job. Whether you're a company employee or working for yourself, you're actively exchanging your skills and labor for a paycheck.

Here are a few examples of active income:

>> Salary from a full-time job

>> Hourly wages from a full- or part-time job

>> Sales commission

>> Bonuses

>> Tips

>> Side-gig earnings (from ridesharing, pet sitting, and so on)

>> Freelancing or consulting

You also earn active income whenever a friend or family member pays you for a task, such as helping them clean their home or babysitting.

Passive income

If taking on another job isn't feasible or not something you want to do, then the next type of income stream is for you. *Passive income* is income you're not actively pursuing or working to earn. You typically have to do some work initially, such as creating some sort of product, but you continue to earn income off that work after it's completed. For example, one of the ways I earn passive income is by selling printables in my Etsy store. Creating the printable took me a few hours, but I can now sell it as-is without having to worry about reproduction costs.

Here are a few examples of passive income:

>> Renting a room or extra storage space in your home or a parking space

>> Receiving royalties from songwriting, writing and publishing a book, and so on

>> Building a website that generates affiliate income

>> Creating a blog or social media channel to advertise products

>> Receiving revenue from paid downloads of an app you created

>> Making an online course in something you know well and selling it on a platform such as Teachable

>> Creating and selling designs, PDFs, or spreadsheets on Etsy

>> Selling stock photography online

Portfolio income

Portfolio income is generated from financial assets you've already invested money into. In some cases, portfolio income can even include items you've purchased. Here are a few examples of portfolio income:

>> **Earned interest:** An example of portfolio income is when a financial institution pays you interest if you've opened certain accounts and investment tools. Savings vehicles such as HYSAs, money market accounts, and certificates of deposit (CD) earn interest. When you invest in mutual funds, index funds, and exchange-traded funds (ETFs), you loan money to a company that pays you back through interest.

>> **Bonds.**

>> **Real estate.**

>> **Dividends:** When you purchase stocks, you own a share of a company. If that company pays investors *dividends,* you have the opportunity to share its profits.

>> **Annuities.**

You can also earn money by selling real estate, a rare painting, or any item that appreciates over time at a higher price than what you paid.

Plan ahead as much as possible

One of the top ways you can save money is by planning ahead. When I was going to college and working full-time, I was constantly going through the drive-through rather than cooking for myself. Not only did I gain weight, but I also felt like crap. The next semester, I worked on meal prepping and carrying snacks in my handbag. My eating wasn't perfect, but I was at least staying out of the drive-through.

Wasting money on convenience like fast food can have you spending money you don't need to. If you haven't already done so, start using a physical planner or a planning app to get organized. When you know in advance you'll have a busy day or week, you can make sure to cook ahead so you're not relying on delivery.

You can also plan ahead by using leftover funds in on of your monthly, or weekly, budget categories. For example, I have a list of events I'd like to attend in the future. I put whatever cash I have leftover toward the event. This helps me pay for something without having to make it a budget item when the time comes.

You can also plan ahead by utilizing your sinking fund(s). When you make saving money for future purposes a habit, you and your budget aren't caught off guard.

By being aware of how much I realistically have to spend on gifts, I can take advantage of sales and cash-back programs so I can purchase them for the lowest amount possible. By shopping ahead, you can find a meaningful gift without breaking the bank.

Consider living frugally

Listen, I refuse to encourage anyone to do unnecessary suffering to hit their financial goals. But I admit that sometimes you may need to live like a pauper to make it work, depending on the situation. Luckily, living frugally doesn't mean you're living off beans and rice like some other financial gurus would have you believe. Instead, I suggest working the budget smarter, not harder, by doing things like the following:

>> **Enjoy what you currently have as much as possible.** You may even decide to start using the supplies you have on hand for an old hobby or get rid of stuff you don't need.

A lot of people who live frugally are minimalists. I am not a minimalist *by any means*. I love me a good cat knickknack as much as anyone. However, I do try not to buy stuff if I don't need it. This guideline means I lay off buying home decor, excess snack options for the cupboard, and expansion packs for my favorite video game.

>> **Look for quality.** Manufacturers use different materials to help make items that fit everyone's price point. The higher a cost of an item, the more durable it tends to be, meaning that even though you may be shelling out more upfront, you're being frugal in the long run because you don't have to keep replacing the item. *Tip:* You can grab great items in consignment stores in your local neighborhood and online. This strategy is how I never pay over $60 for a pair of designer sunglasses.

>> **Be strategic about presentation.** When you purchase quality items, make them stand-alone pieces to focus on. If you have a nice vase, use it as a table centerpiece while keeping the rest of the table bare. Visitors will be drawn to the nice vase instead of looking everywhere else.

TIP

>> **Sign up for store loyalty programs**. Stores send you coupons and special sales after they have your email address. This method is how I stock up on home essentials.

If you don't want your regular email address getting sales emails, sign up for a new one instead. This way, you're not missing important emails and other notifications you're looking out for.

>> **Purchase gift cards through online discounted gift card sites.** When people have gift cards they know they'll never use, they can sell them to websites like Raise (www.raise.com). After Raise verifies the gift card amount, it buys the card and then resells it to someone else for a discount. Some gift cards are harder to find than others, but discounted gift cards are always a great way to purchase an item you were going to buy anyway for significantly less. I was able to get a $200 Southwest gift card through Raise for only $180.

Evaluating Your Job and Its Related Expenses

Your earning potential, or lack thereof, can keep you from creating wealth. Even if you have the most kick-ass budget out there, you can't save what you don't earn. Let me repeat that: You can't save what you don't earn. So you must give yourself a head start by routinely evaluating your job and its related expenses.

Discuss your options for alternative work environments

If the COVID-19 pandemic taught employers anything, it's that people can work remotely from home and still be productive. Working from home can provide many benefits that don't even include your paycheck.

Some people gain hours of their time back when they stop having to commute, which also improves their overall quality of life. Working from home can help you save on transportation costs and meals out — two areas people go over most in their budget — as well as on childcare over time because you can reduce the hours you need help.

If you're not working remotely, ask for a meeting with your manager to present your case. Don't forget to share any work highlights you've accomplished lately. Also be ready to explain how you'd benefit from working from home. Your manager wants you to be as productive as possible, and if working alone all day is what will help, they'll most likely consider it as long as you can be accountable.

Analyze your compensation package

If you aren't being properly compensated, either in money or benefits, your salary isn't keeping up with inflation and the rising cost of living. One of the reasons I left my day job was that I simply couldn't pay my bills without taking on other jobs, which left me exhausted. I loved the work we did, but I simply couldn't afford to do it anymore.

Even if you've recently increased your income, double-checking your overall compensation from your employer doesn't hurt. You need to ensure your health insurance is affordable and you have adequate paid time off. If your employer offers an option to open a retirement account through it specifically (and not all do), make sure you're taking advantage and saving for your future. You can read more about maximizing employer retirement accounts in Chapter 9. Some employers even offer additional perks outside of traditional compensation, such as discounts on phone service and hotel stays.

If a raise isn't in your employer's budget, you can still negotiate for other perks. Ask for more time off or even flexible hours.

Assess work-related costs

It costs money to make money, and your job isn't an exception. Working at a place that isn't fairly compensating you financially — or that's costing you a fortune to work at — doesn't make sense.

Unless you live in a city with a rockin' public transportation system, you're probably spending more time and money than you want to get to work. If your transportation costs are taking a significant chunk of your paycheck and working remotely isn't possible, you may consider finding a new job closer to your home or moving closer to work. These options may not be feasible right now but can be on your radar for the future.

If this situation sounds like yours, look into companies hiring remotely. LinkedIn (www.linkedin.com) is a social media platform for professional networking. After you create a profile, LinkedIn makes finding jobs through its platform easy and even offers certificates to help up your professional game. You're also able to connect with people in your professional network as well as meet others. Even if you're not currently looking for employment, make sure you create a profile anyway. You never know when an opportunity may pop up!

If you have young children, odds are that paying for childcare is part of your job-related expenses. If you're part of a two-income household, run the numbers to make sure childcare isn't taking away most of your or your partner's individual salary. Having a serious conversation about childcare arrangements may be necessary, even though leaving the workforce is a serious decision that can affect your earning potential.

Budgeting with Irregular Income

I'm not trying to be doom and gloom about this section, but I have to say it: Budgeting without a regular paycheck or source of income is difficult. You can do it, but it's gonna take some work. I lay out some guidelines in the following sections.

Calculate bare bones expenses and income

The first thing you need to do is create a list of what you use and rely on every day. These items can include both fixed and variable expenses. You can refer to Chapter 2 for specifics or write down the following with the amount of each expense:

>> **Essential:** An *essential expense* is imperative to your survival. Shelter, food, transportation, and access to prescriptions are necessary for you to function every day, so any expense related to any of these four things is essential.

>> **Flexible (nonessential):** Anything you're paying for that you want to keep in your budget but can cut down on is *flexible*. A flexible expense may include costs like beauty services, new clothes, a membership to a gym you love, self-development activities, or entertainment.

>> **Not needed:** *Not needed* is pretty self-explanatory. If you can easily live without it, you don't need it.

An expense can be both flexible and not needed simultaneously. An example of this overlap may be how much you spend dining out. You don't need to go out, but you may want to include it in your budget because you enjoy it.

Next, make a list of your income. Every expense you've listed requires you to receive income to cover it, so knowing where that income is coming from is imperative. You also can use Figure 11-1 to note your expenses and income.

Having a record of where your irregular income is coming from, even if it's an estimate, can help you if you need to prove your income at some point. When you don't have regular paycheck stubs, institutions like rental companies and banks have a hard time assessing you as a customer.

Essential Expenses

- ☐ Rent/mortgage
- ☐ Property taxes and HOA fees
- ☐ Cellphone
- ☐ Necessary hygiene products
- ☐ Internet
- ☐ Utilities such as electricity, water, gas, trash pickup
- ☐ Car payment
- ☐ Car insurance
- ☐ Gas to get to and from work
- ☐ Groceries
- ☐ Prescriptions
- ☐ Health insurance
- ☐ Medical co-pays
- ☐ Items needed for school or work such as supplies, parking, certifications, and uniforms
- ☐ Food for pets and necessary medical care as well as needed supplies like litter or bedding

Income

- ☐ Freelance work
- ☐ Contractor work
- ☐ Side gig or part-time work
- ☐ Any payments you may receive like child support or Social Security
- ☐ Tips
- ☐ Commission
- ☐ Stuff you sell
- ☐ Rental income

Flexible/Nonessential Expenses

- ☐ Personal grooming services like eyebrows, waxing, or haircuts
- ☐ New clothes if not essential to work or everyday life
- ☐ Gym membership
- ☐ Personal trainers
- ☐ Streaming service
- ☐ Dining out
- ☐ Takeout coffee
- ☐ Alcohol
- ☐ Admission to fun events
- ☐ Subscription boxes
- ☐ Self-development classes
- ☐ Specialty cleaning products

- ☐ Stuff for hobbies
- ☐ Services such as landscaping, cleaning service, or food prep
- ☐ Traveling
- ☐ Alcohol
- ☐ Household décor
- ☐ Candles
- ☐ Self-development classes
- ☐ Specialty products

FIGURE 11-1:
A checklist of expenses and income.

Now, compare your income to your current expenses. If you find you can't cover your current expenses on a bare bones budget, it's time to go over to see what you can cut back or trim from the nonessential or "not needed" categories. It's important to ensure you can cover your expenses the best you can if needed.

Stick with cash envelopes

If you have irregular income, I highly suggest using the cash envelope budgeting method. This method is discussed in depth in Chapter 5.

Budgeting with irregular income means you need to keep your spending in check because the cash flow you have today isn't the same you'll have tomorrow. By putting cash into envelopes for dedicated spending, you'll be aware at all times how much you can comfortably afford without dipping into your income set aside for bills.

Use community resources

If you're struggling, I highly recommend looking into bill assistance, food banks, and other community resources you may qualify for. The following list offers a few options for national community resources you can try:

>> **211:** This national hotline can connect you directly to national and local community resources in your area. You can find it at www.211.org or by phone by dialing 211.

>> **Findhelp:** Findhelp is a national online database that connects you to food pantries, financial assistance, and free or reduced-cost services. Find out more information at www.findhelp.org.

>> **Benefits.gov:** Benefits.gov is the official benefits database for the U.S. government. This website gives more information and lets you know whether you qualify for services like Temporary Assistance for Needy Families (TANF), Supplement Nutrition Assistance Program (SNAP), Medicaid, and housing assistance. Visit www.benefits.gov.

>> **Healthcare.gov:** Determine whether you qualify for Medicaid, Medicare, or the Children's Health Insurance Program by visiting www.healthcare.gov/medicaid-chip/getting-medicaid-chip. If you don't qualify now, you may qualify for other subsidies to help with healthcare.

>> **RX Assist:** This website provides access to coupon codes and vouchers for your medical prescriptions. It also has a national patient assistance program directory to help you find additional prescription coverage in your local area. Check it out at www.rxassit.org/patients/resources.

>> **Health Center Program by Health Resources and Services Administration:** Health centers help provide affordable access to those who come from low economic backgrounds, veterans, and those experiencing homelessness. Services include pharmacy, general health, substance abuse, and mental health care. Find your local center by going to findahealthcenter.hrsa.gov.

REMEMBER

Asking for help may be very humbling and difficult for various reasons. But community centers exist for the good of the community. You shouldn't have to pick between getting the antibiotic you need or trying to survive with cold medicines. Take advantage of resources when you can, and please be kind to yourself. Everyone has needed help at one time or another, and that includes me.

I'm allergic to every antibiotic known to humanity, except a Z-Pack (Zithromax). During a hospital visit, I was diagnosed with pneumonia and needed an antibiotic. The generic for a Z-Pack was $50, and at the time I had only $10 in my bank account. I was so ashamed because I couldn't even afford an antibiotic, and I was supposed to be an adult already.

Trying not to cry in public, I told the ER doctor that I couldn't afford the prescription and asked whether I could buy anything over the counter instead. He said that if I could go to a specific pharmacy, it could waive the fee due to its partnership with the hospital. I dropped off my prescription and spent the whole time waiting, disappointed in myself. I wish so badly now that I'd had someone in my life to tell me not to feel bad or ashamed that I needed help. That's why removing the perceived shame from these situations for others is so important to me.

IN THIS CHAPTER

» **Practicing how to budget while in college**

» **Figuring out money management for couples**

» **Handling childcare expenses as a couple or a single parent**

» **Making the most out of your retirement funds**

Chapter **12**

Budgeting during Different Life Stages

Your budgeting method can change over time, especially as the stages in your life change. Going to college, getting married, having a child, and retiring are milestones you'll most likely face at one point in your lifetime. Each milestone is a major financial commitment that requires a unique money strategy. While your money may look different when paying off your student loan debt versus starting a family, you can absolutely utilize a budget to help you make the most of it. In this chapter, I provide information that can help you navigate financial decisions you will make as a college student, parent, couple or retiree.

Taking Responsibility for Your Money as a Student

When you combine the lack of personal finance knowledge most young college students have with the rising costs of education, it's no wonder paying off student loan debt is a common expense in many people's budgets. As I write this, the Federal Reserve estimates that U.S. consumers collectively owe $1.75 trillion dollars in student loan debt. Tuition for one year at a private school can be more than attending a public school for four years. For example, attending the 2022–2023 school year at the University of Southern California costs $63,468 for tuition alone. The tuition at the University of California, which is a public university, is $13,804. That's a drastic difference of $49,664.

The average amount of student loan debt is $30,000, which is too much money to owe when you're starting your career. For $30,000, you could buy a brand-new vehicle, make a significant down payment on a house, or even pay for the wedding of your dreams.

You don't need a job to learn basic personal finance principles. If you know them straight out of the gate, you're less likely to waste money instead of taking care of your financial priorities.

As a college student, you can use the following sections to help you determine the type of financial aid you may need and find other options for funding your education to set you up for a positive money future. To find out whether you are eligible for financial aid, you should submit the Free Application for Federal Student Aid (FAFSA) available online at studentaid.gov.

Understand your financial aid package

After you complete your FAFSA, the U.S. Department of Education (DOE) goes over your submission to see whether you're eligible to receive federal student aid. After you've been approved, it sends your information over to the colleges you're applying to or have already been accepted at. The college's financial aid office reviews your FAFSA and sends you a financial aid award letter.

How much assistance you receive depends on three factors:

>> **Cost of attendance (COA):** How much attending school for the year will cost you. Along with tuition and fees, each school factors in how much you'll need for room and board, books, supplies, and transportation.

>> **Your expected family contribution (EFC):** How much the DOE determines your household is able to help you pay for your education, based on your household's annual income and financial assets.

>> **Financial need:** How much federal financial aid you can receive after the college subtracts your EFC from your COA.

Table 12-1 provides some examples of how financial need is determined.

TABLE 12-1

Financial Need Examples

COA	EFC	Financial Need
$10,000	$0	$10,000
$25,000	$10,000	$15,000
$30,000	$15,000	$15,000
$40,000	$4,000	$36,000

Source: U.S. Department of Education (https://studentaid.gov/complete-aid-process/how-calculated#need-based / last accessed March 08, 2023)

Need-based financial aid

Not all need-based financial aid is the same, so understanding the different types is important:

>> **Federal Pell grant:** *Federal Pell grants* are typically for students with low EFCs. Unlike with loans, you don't have to pay Pell grants back to the government except for in certain circumstances.

>> **Federal Supplemental Educational Opportunity Grant (FSEOG):** If your college participates in the FSEOG program, it receives additional funding to help students who demonstrate the most financial need. Like federal Pell grants, you don't have to pay these grants back if your school determines you qualify. Unlike Pell grants, the school's financial aid office (not the government) decides your eligibility. These funds are limited, and after the school awards them, it's out of FSEOGs until the next year.

>> **Direct subsidized loans:** The government offers two types of direct loans you can receive to help with your higher education expenses, direct subsidized loans and direct unsubsidized loans. *Subsidized loans* are available to undergraduate students and offer better financial incentives than unsubsidized loans (which you can read about in the following section). The government pays your interest on subsidized loans while you're in school and for the first six months after you graduate.

>> **Federal work-study:** Your college's financial aid office offers work-study placements as financial aid. *Work-study placements* are part-time jobs that you can do on or off campus around your class schedule. I provide more information on work-study in the "Utilize your school's work-study program" section later in this chapter.

Non-need-based financial aid

If the amount of need-based financial aid you're eligible for doesn't cover everything (see the preceding section), you may need to consider non-need-based financial aid. This type of aid is based on the amount of financial aid you've already received, your college, and your enrollment status rather than your EFC. Table 12-2 provides some examples of non-need-based financial aid.

WARNING

This type of aid can come with additional costs that need-based aid doesn't have, so make sure to exhaust all your need-based options first.

TABLE 12-2

Financial Aid Examples for Non-Need-Based Aid

COA	Financial Award	Non-Need-Based Aid
$10,000	$10,000	$0
$25,000	$15,000	$10,000
$30,000	$15,000	$15,000
$40,000	$36,000	$4,000

*Source: U.S. Department of Education (https://studentaid.gov/complete-aid-process/how-calculated#need-based / last accessed March 08, 2023)

There are several types of non-need-based aid you can apply for. The factors that are used to determine how much aid you'll receive include tuition if you're living on campus and what your college decides is the total amount you'd need to attend school. Non-need-based aid can be direct unsubsidized student loans, federal PLUS loans, and grants.

>> **Direct unsubsidized loan:** Just like the subsidized loans in the preceding section, these types of loans are backed by the government. You don't need to be an undergraduate student, nor do you need to demonstrate financial need. Unsubsidized loans have fewer restrictions than subsidized loans, but you're 100 percent responsible for paying the interest from the moment you take out the loan.

>> **Federal PLUS loan:** Two different types of PLUS loans exist — Parent PLUS loans, and Graduate PLUS loans.

• *Parent PLUS loans* are loans made to the parents of a dependent undergraduate student. Parents applying for this loan must also have outstanding credit and not currently be in default with any other educational loans.

• *Graduate PLUS loans* are loans that graduate or professional students can apply for to help cover their education costs. If you're applying as a graduate or professional student, you must still have outstanding credit and be eligible for financial aid.

» **Teacher Education Access for College and Higher Education (TEACH) grant:** Unlike other grants, this grant is based on your agreeing to serve as a teacher for a specified period of time. To receive this type of funding, you must be currently enrolled in a school that offers the TEACH grant along with the other requirements of the program.

For more information on these financial aid assistance programs, please visit studentaid.gov.

If you're planning on taking classes during the summer or studying abroad, check out your school's financial aid office; you may be eligible for more financial aid. Schools sometimes offer additional assistance into the summer if you update your FAFSA with your educational goals. I received an additional grant the summer I completed my summer abroad program. This grant allowed me to take additional time off work without worrying about how I'd pay for the roof over my cat's head. Head to the earlier section "Understand your financial aid package" for more on financial aid.

WARNING

Student loans can also come in the form of private loans not offered through the U.S. Department of Education. These types of loans are funded by a third party with different terms and conditions. It's important to note the terms and conditions when looking into these types of loans. Also be aware that these loans are not eligible for payment plans such as income-based repayment through the U.S. Department of Education.

Apply for internships

An *internship* is a limited opportunity to gain work experience in your field of study, usually offered by a business or an organization. Through an internship, you assist with more general tasks that keep the organization running or with a special project to help you get the hands-on experience you need. Either way, you can list the work experience you gain through an internship on your resume. Internships typically last for a semester or the length of a school break, but some organizations offer the ability to intern year-round.

Understanding the different types of internships

Internships can be paid or unpaid.

» **Paid:** An internship that's *paid* provides you not only with work experience in the field but also with a stipend or salary you can use for your living expenses. Students with paid internships commonly work part-time during the school semester or full-time during summer break.

>> **Unpaid:** Internships that offer no financial compensation are considered *unpaid*. These types of internships give you an opportunity to work in your field of study and other perks, such as a recommendation from a well-known and respected organization that you can later use in launching your career. Unpaid internships do not always mean they stay that way, either. The organization where you've interned at can decide to hire you after your internship ends.

Additionally, internships may or may not come with college credit.

>> **For college credit:** Internships may take the place of a college class or add to your program of study to help you learn additional skills.

>> **No college credit:** Some internships don't provide college credit. You just get the work experience to use on your resume.

Internships can fall under more than one of these categories. For example, you can have an internship that's both paid and for college credit.

Finding a paid internship

One of the best ways to reduce the student loan debt you need to take on is to find ways to earn money that you can use toward your tuition and living expenses. If you find managing a traditional job while attending school difficult, you can research and apply for a paid internship.

You can find a paid internship a few different ways. The first resource you should be using is your school. Most program departments have a list of work opportunities students are eligible for based on where they are with their degrees. A lot of these opportunities aren't publicly offered or known, which is why speaking to someone in the career development center to find out more is important.

Another way to find a paid internship is to do your own research. If you have a company or organization you'd love to work for, check their career opportunities page on their website or call to ask to speak to Human Resources about internship opportunities. The organization may already have an internship program that you can apply for.

The professional networking platform LinkedIn (www.linkedin.com) can also be a way to look for paid internships. Make sure your profile is up to date and then click on the job tab at the top of your dashboard. You can search for internships related to your field or location and set job alerts that help you stay on top of your internship search.

In addition to LinkedIn, check out the following websites when hunting for a paid internship:

» Chegg Internships (www.internships.com)

» Youtern (www.youtern.com)

» CoolWorks (www.coolworks.com)

» Idealist (www.idealist.org/en)

» Internjobs (www.internjobs.com)

» Intern Abroad (https://www.internhq.com/)

» Intern Queen (www.internqueen.com)

» Media Bistro (www.mediabistro.com)

Utilize your school's work-study program

Many schools offer part-time jobs, otherwise known as *work-study placement*, to students. Work-study placements can be in any area of the school that needs assistance, but most positions are ones students can work into their class schedules. Common work-study placements may involve helping other students in common areas, such as the library; working the front desk for a department; or serving as a resident advisor/assistant (RA) in a residence hall.

REMEMBER

Schools may have more work-study applicants than positions available. If you're chosen for work-study, securing your job as soon as possible is important. Follow up with your financial aid office to make sure you know your next steps.

If you'd rather not leave campus but still want to make money, remember to note your interest in work-study opportunities on your FAFSA. Your school can match you for a job based on whether you are attending school full or part-time. Your school can also advise you to apply for an organization it partners with, such as a nonprofit, to help provide services as your work-study assignment.

Work-study placements are supposed to provide cash for your day-to-day living expenses. As a result, your income while working goes directly to you as a paycheck from your school. Some schools allow you to apply your work-study funds to your student account to help pay for your tuition or room and board.

Maximize student discounts

One of the best things about being a college student is the student discounts. Your favorite retailers know that as a college student, you aren't rolling in the dough. A cheap way for them to keep you as a customer is to offer you a discount. You should look for discounts while budgeting for any stage in your life but especially when you're not earning a full-time income.

I recommend you always check any business you're patronizing for student discounts, but here's a list of some that exist as of this writing to get you started:

- » Amazon (Prime membership at a discounted rate): www.amazon.com; click the Prime tab and scroll down to find the student plan

- » Apple (education pricing): www.apple.com/us-edu/store

- » AMC (discounted movie admission): www.amctheatres.com/discounts; scroll down to student discount

- » Allstate (student driver rate): www.allstate.com/auto-insurance/student-discounts

- » DoorDash (percentage off DashPass): help.doordash.com/consumers/s/article/DashPass-for-Students?language=en_US

- » Geico (student driver rate): www.geico.com/save/discounts/student-discounts

- » Goodwill (percentage off your entire purchase on designated day): goodwillscwi.org/stop/discounts

- » Hulu (discounted student plan): www.hulu.com/student

- » Lenovo (automatic discount on all products on top of sales): www.lenovo.com/us/en/d/deals/student-discount

- » Microsoft (student discount on Office 365): www.microsoft.com/en-us/store/b/education

- » Spotify (discounted rate): support.spotify.com/us/article/premium-student

- » State Farm (rate discounts for good students): www.statefarm.com/insurance/auto/car-insurance-for-teens

- » Verizon (discounted service): www.verizon.com/featured/students

Account for major and ongoing college expenses

Part of budgeting is going over your living expenses so you know where your money is going and can make sure you're adequately putting money aside for everyday expenses, like gas and groceries.

Sit down and make a plan for all your expenses. Tuition is probably the main expense that comes to mind, but other expenses involved when going to school can include things like these:

>> **Fees:** Many colleges have fees you must pay on top of your tuition. They can include registration, computer lab or library costs, access to certain student services, and fees related to classwork, like a science lab.

>> **Textbooks and other supplies:** Before class starts, your instructor usually provides a syllabus that indicates what textbooks and other supplies you need for their class. Even used textbooks can be expensive, so budget accordingly. Also think about equipment you need for school in general, like a computer.

>> **Room and board:** You always need a roof over your head, and college is no exception. Though some students live on campus, others choose to get an apartment nearby with roommates or continue to live with their families to help cut costs. If you're living on your own for the first time, you need to plan for household items you may not be used to buying for yourself. Don't forget your groceries, meal plans, and eating on the go in between classes.

>> **Transportation:** Whether you're driving yourself to school, riding your bike, or using public transportation, you gotta put money aside to help you get there. If you're taking your own car, you need to figure out whether your school requires a parking pass.

>> **Personal:** A cellphone plan, fun with friends, personal hygiene products, clothing, medicine, and other miscellaneous expenses can go under personal. You also need to factor in how you're cleaning your clothes if you're living on campus.

Sharing and Agreeing on Money Management as a Couple

One of the leading reasons couples cite when filing for divorce is money. How often have you and your partner disagreed about your finances, even if it's something small? And don't get me started on debt. Fifty-four percent of people surveyed by SunTrust Bank said debt is a reason to get divorced. Three out of five Americans even put off marriage so they don't inherit their partner's debt!

To avoid a headache and probably heartache, you must talk money with your partner ASAP. The following sections offer some things to consider when you budget as a couple.

TIP

Check out budgeting apps for couples. For example, Honeydue (www.honeydue.com) is an app that allows you to sync both your and your partner's financial accounts so you can easily see the funds you have available at any given time. It also helps you coordinate your bills and discuss spending as a team.

Get on the same page as your partner

The number one way to get your money management on the right path is to get on the same page as your partner regarding your finances. I don't mean that you need to agree on everything, but you do need to see where the other is coming from to meet in the middle.

Discover your money personality

One of the best ways to understand where your partner is coming from is to learn their money personality. A *money personality* is how you see money. Two of the most popular money personalities are spenders and savers:

>> **Savers:** A *saver* likes to think more about the future and ensures they live below their means. Typically goal-oriented, a saver doesn't spend money on things that don't matter to them. Most savers also forgo most luxuries to save more, which means they're sometimes perceived as cheap. They can also be anxious about money, wondering whether they're ever doing enough to save.

>> **Spenders:** *Spenders* tend to live in the here and now regarding their finances. They can still be goal-oriented, but they have an easier time focusing on what's fun in the current moment than savers do. Although spenders can be fun, they can also suffer from money anxiety when they have to be accountable for their spending. A spender can also have a hard time sticking to a budget.

Your money personality is a huge factor in how you see and interact with money. Knowing your and your partner's personalities is an important piece of understanding each other's habits and expectations. If you're a saver in a relationship with a spender, you may wonder when your partner will take their goals seriously. On the other hand, if you're a spender attached to a saver, you may accuse your partner of never letting you have any fun.

Partners can also have the same money personality. One of my best friends who is a saver is married to another saver. That's probably why they buy their cars in cash, but I digress.

By acknowledging the type of money personalities in your relationship, you can more easily find a compromise when goal setting and figure out a budgeting method that works for your relationship and how your household handles money. For example, in a relationship with differing money personalities, the partner who's a saver may ensure the bills are paid on time and money put away for retirement. The spender may be the one who keeps a list of items needed for the household and finds the best deals before shopping so that they can make the budget stretch.

TIP

You can find a ton of online quizzes to help you determine your and your partner's money personalities. My favorite is the money personality quiz by Fidelity. Along with discovering your money style, Fidelity lets you know your strengths and the areas that may need a little coaching. You can find out more at www.fidelity.com/learning-center/personal-finance/money-personality.

Don't be afraid to try out different budgeting methods

Getting used to using a budgeting method is hard enough for one person, let alone two people in a relationship. This challenge is why trying different budgeting methods when the current way of spending money isn't working is important. Using the wrong budgeting method for your family's finances can cause frustration and resentment. Those are both ingredients in a recipe for a budgeting disaster. You can read about a variety of budgeting methods in Part 2.

Use joint accounts in a way that works for you

REMEMBER

A common misconception when managing money as a couple is that you must share a checking account with your partner. As a personal finance expert, I'm here to tell you that this information is not only false but also seriously outdated. If having your money in a joint account works for you, then go for it. But you don't need to combine your finances with your partner's to be happy or have a successful relationship.

The joint checking account approach does have its merits. A joint checking account can make handling your household expenses easier for you and your partner. You can pay all your bills out of one account and easily go over your expenses as a family. You're not wondering who's paying what or where the money is coming from or going because you have it all in front of you.

But if a joint checking account doesn't work for your everyday household expenses, you can still share a joint account for sinking funds. *Sinking funds* are a separate amount of money you routinely save for expenses you know are coming up, such as regular car maintenance, holidays, and home repairs. I discuss the power of sinking funds in more depth in Chapter 3.

As a couple, having a sinking-funds account can help you and your partner pay for expenses that aren't everyday items but that you still share, such as gifts for other people or putting money aside for your pets. You can even have a sinking fund for goals, vacations, and other projects you decide to take on as a couple. Starting a sinking-funds account can help you learn each other's money styles in a fun and less stressful way than a joint checking account.

Identify financial abuse and financial infidelity

If you do decide to open a joint checking account (see the preceding section), make sure you always have your own separate checking or savings account. Even if you aren't the breadwinner in your relationship, having your own money set aside in case of an emergency is always important. This point is especially true if you need to leave your partner because of financial abuse.

Financial abuse is a form of domestic violence that involves one person cutting off the other's access to financial resources so they can't leave the relationship. Financial abuse can look like a variety of things, including (but *not* limited to) the following:

>> Forbidding the other person to work or ruining their career so they have no income

>> Cutting off the other person's access to financial accounts

>> Insisting all debt is in the other person's name

>> Coaxing the other person into committing financial fraud to reap the rewards.

Note: Although I'm talking about couples in this section, financial abuse can occur in any kind of relationship.

Financial infidelity is when one person in a relationship withholds information about their finances from their partner. Common examples include hiding the amount of debt they may owe, lying about their income or shopping habits, keeping secret accounts, or exhibiting any other type of behavior that affects their finances.

Make sure you're in regular communication with your partner to ensure you're on the same page about making major purchases or lending money to family members. If you suspect your partner is having financial issues, ask questions. An uncomfortable money conversation now can avoid a financial setback later.

If you or a loved one is experiencing financial or any other type of domestic abuse, please get in touch with the National Domestic Violence Hotline by calling 1-800-799-SAFE (7233) or by visiting www.thehotline.org.

Planning for Child-Related Costs

Babies are expensive. At the time of this writing, the U.S. Department of Agriculture estimates that raising a child from infancy to age 18 will cost you at least $17,000 per year on average. With thoughtful budgeting, however, you can navigate the costs for less.

Please keep in mind that planning needs are different for couples and single parents who are raising their kids. Single parents may not be receiving child support, which should be considered when creating their budgets.

Factor in housing costs

Housing is expensive. Housing costs usually depend on two factors:

>> Location (think a large metropolitan city versus a rural area)

>> Size of living space (for example, 900 square feet versus 1,600)

No matter where you live, though, you can find ways to cut housing costs.

First, consider space. Ask yourself how much house you really need — you may be able to get creative. If it's your first child, consider doubling your primary bedroom as a place where you both can sleep until they get older. If you have more than one child, can you get creative with room sharing? The Internet has tons of ideas you can use for inspiration.

Next, think about getting rid of extra stuff you don't need. Excess stuff can take up space in your home, which is problematic for both budgeting and housing. One of my tips for decluttering regularly is to keep an ongoing box for donation. Whatever I don't need goes into the box, and after it's full, I drop it off at my local donation center.

TIP

Everyone has stuff they don't regularly use but that still needs to be stored somewhere, such as extra furniture or holiday decorations. If you have things that need storage but don't have room to spare, consider a storage unit nearby. You can get the same space as an extra bedroom yet only have to pay one-fourth the cost.

Buy used

You may get the heebie-jeebies when thinking about buying something used, but buying items used is one of the biggest ways to save money, especially when raising kids. Entire consignment stores are dedicated to selling kids' clothing, toys, and furniture. You can also check consignment stores for equipment like pack and plays, high chairs, bassinets, cribs, and dressing tables. Another great thing about consignment? Once your baby has outgrown their items, you can sell them back.

WARNING

A couple of caveats on buying used:

>> You should always buy a new car seat, not used. Verifying the safety and age of the seat is different, so your best bet is to go with a new model.

>> Check for recalls on any baby furniture or toys before purchasing by going to www.cpsc.gov/Recalls. Even outside of recalls, many older models of baby furniture such as cribs and high chairs don't meet current safety standards.

Create an ongoing sinking fund for school expenses

There's an unspoken law of the universe that your kid will ask you randomly for money for different activities at school. With a sinking-fund account, you can easily withdraw cash when your child needs it. Or, to prevent pulling your hair out, put some cash aside in an envelope at the beginning of the semester to cover things like book fairs. This way, you're not caught off guard, and your child can participate in activities that "pop up."

Research daycare opportunities

According to Care.com, an estimated 51 percent of families in the United States spend more than 20 percent of their income on childcare expenses. The average family spends at least $10,000 on childcare for one child, which is more than the average cost of in-state college tuition ($9,349 as of this writing). Yes, you're most likely spending more on your kid as a baby than you will when they're getting their bachelor's degree.

Know the different types of childcare options to find the right fit for your child first and your budget second. The following are some of the most common ones:

>> **Traditional daycare:** Daycare centers are the most common type of childcare for parents. Daycare centers operate within a set schedule and help your child prepare for school by structuring activities in age-appropriate group settings. Some centers can be inside community buildings like churches or schools, while others are stand-alone businesses.

>> **Home daycare:** Some daycare providers operate out of a home to provide a smaller and more intimate environment. These providers also offer age-appropriate opportunities with fewer children so your child may receive more one-on-one care.

>> **In-home caregiver such as a nanny:** If in-home care is more comfortable, you can look to find a nanny or a babysitter. In-home caregivers can cost more than daycare, but this approach allows you to have more control over the activities your child takes part in and the environment. Another popular option many families turn to is asking a relative. You can make an arrangement to trade time for money, or they may even volunteer for free.

REMEMBER

Make sure to always look for licensed and experienced childcare providers. Both in and out of home daycares should have proof of their state license. Also check to see whether they are certified in CPR and have fingerprint clearance cards.

Look into a dependent care account through your employer

Another way to maximize your budget for child-rearing is to ask your employer whether your company currently allows *Dependent Care FSAs* (DCFSAs). A DCFSA is a savings account you're allowed to fund with pretax dollars. You can use this account for daycare and other childcare opportunities, such as after-school care or day camp during the summer.

A DCFSA is a great way to stretch your income farther because you can fund it with your gross income before taxes instead of your net (tax-deducted) income. Setting this money aside also means you also have less taxable income, which means you pay less in taxes. Check out www.fsafeds.com/explore/dcfsa for more information on how you can utilize this program.

TECHNICAL STUFF

Speaking of taxes, don't forget to take advantage of all tax credits you can, such as the Child and Dependent Care Credit. You can find out more about this specific tax credit at www.irs.gov/taxtopics/tc602.

Living off the Money You've Saved for Retirement

Often called the "golden years," retirement is the time in your life when you finally get to stop drinking that stale coffee your co-worker always makes. Even if you aren't a traditional office worker, chances are you're still ready to lounge around the house in your pajamas before filling your calendar with the next big thing. Plans you've had for years may come to fruition, along with those items on your bucket list.

As with any life stage, you may now have unique challenges regarding your budget. For example, most retirees are working with a fixed income. But you can still care for yourself and your finances.

TIP

AARP is a 501(c)(4) nonprofit that advocates for people ages 50 and up. AARP programs include tax assistance, legal counsel, and supportive services like food and living assistance, among many others. You can also get a committed advocate for issues like Social Security and navigating your Medicare. AARP members can receive discounts for healthcare, prescriptions, shopping, travel, and more. Check out www.aarp.org for more about becoming a member.

Examine your saving ten years before retirement

The ten years before retirement can be crucial. They're the time to check in to see the progress you've made when saving for retirement. Pull up all your retirement accounts and enter the amount you've invested into a retirement calculator you can find for free online. These types of calculators use the info you provide to tell you what your income will be when you're able to access the accounts. Charles Schwab offers a great one: www.schwab.com/retirement-planning-tools/retirement-calculator.

If you realize you haven't been saving adequately for retirement, it's not too late to utilize the time you have left. Open a 401(k) or IRA with your employer if you haven't already. Some employers offer a contribution match if you invest through them, which may help you catch up faster with your retirement savings.

You can also take advantage of catch-up contributions. As of 2023, you can make retirement contributions of up to $7,500 to 401(k)s, 403(b)s, SARSEPs, and government-issued 457(b)s. You can add an additional $1,000 to your traditional or Roth IRAs. These amounts are subject to change, so check the IRS website www.irs.gov/retirement-plans/plan-participant-employee/retirement-topics-catch-up-contributions for more information. Chapter 9 provides more information about different types of retirement accounts.

Understand your retirement budget

Different retirement saving vehicles have different rules regarding when you're eligible to make withdrawals. Benefits you may receive from the government, such as Social Security and Medicare also have different rules and circumstances, so you need to understand your circumstances and eligibility.

There are other ways you can cut costs before retirement to help your income stretch farther once you hit your golden years.

Trim your expenses and take care of lingering debt

With a limited income, retirement is a more important time than ever to cut expenses so that you can have more financial freedom. You can cut your expenses in various ways before and during retirement for less stress. Head to Chapter 2 for more on ways to cut back.

TIP

Clearing excess debt is a great first step if you're trimming your expenses. Being debt-free helps your budget after you're retired. You don't have to close any credit lines you have, but do make sure to pay off your credit card debt and address other debt like student and auto loans. Refer back to Chapter 10 for tips to help you eliminate your debt.

Another way to take care of debt is by paying off your mortgage. Housing is one of the biggest expenses, and a paid-off mortgage means one fewer expense to worry about. Other options for your housing can include downsizing to a smaller home to help save money on additional expenses like utilities and home maintenance.

Make sure you're signed up for senior discounts

I'm always envious of anyone who can use a discount, including senior citizens. Not only is it okay to eat dinner early, but you also get rewarded for it at restaurants! Discounts aren't only for restaurants, however. Many retailers, like grocery stores, have special days where they offer an additional discount to those 55 and older. You can also snag discounts by calling your service providers.

Prioritize your needs over others'

This suggestion may be one of the hardest to follow in retirement, especially if you have a huge family. But making sure you put on your own oxygen mask first, as they say, is imperative.

After you have your financial house together (thanks to your budget, of course), people will notice. They'll ask you for help, and it'll be up to you to determine what type of assistance you can provide. I receive letters frequently for my advice column from readers who are stuck between a rock (their finances) and a hard place (their families). Often, readers can't save for retirement because their adult children have needed financial assistance in various ways (although children aren't the only family members who can take advantage of you). I've seen everything from people draining their accounts to pay for their child's legal expenses to people letting their children move back home only to find those children now won't leave.

REMEMBER

Everyone needs help from time to time, me included. But it's a fine line between your helping someone and their taking advantage of you.

Don't let someone put your finances at risk because they can't get it together. Refer them to your local community resource center or help them find a hotline to call. If you agree to help financially, make sure it's an amount you can afford to *give*, not just loan. (Because if you've ever watched a small-claims-court show, you know how these kinds of "loans" tend to disappear into the ether.) Make boundaries clear so that you don't sacrifice your own retirement for the sake of another.

Chapter 13

Budgeting for a Major Purchase or Life Event

have certain feelings about spending a lot of money at once; chances are you do, too. Personally, I think having feelings, such as anxiety, is human nature. Money provides security, and spending a lot at once can seem scary. So can committing to financing a major purchase.

But isn't that why you started your budgeting journey? You wanted to be more in control of your finances, which means following through with some scary stuff — like making a big purchase without letting it break the bank. I show you how in this chapter.

Purchasing a Home

Thanks to network TV, buying a home looks easy. Whole channels are dedicated to finding a new home or remodeling the one you have. These shows can make the process look easy by cramming work that took weeks, and sometimes months, into a one-hour show.

Owning a home is most likely one of the biggest financial commitments you'll ever make. (I cover the remodeling bit later in the chapter.) Along with coming up with a significant down payment, you also have to make sure you can afford the monthly expenses such as a mortgage payment, property taxes, and maintenance. You can see how lots of people can get financially behind after purchasing a home.

I firmly believe that homeownership is a great dream and that anyone who wants to own a home should put it on their financial bucket list. I also firmly believe it's not for everyone (and not as great a financial investment as many want you to believe; historically, the stock market has outperformed real estate as an investment strategy).

You see a ton of "rules" about buying a home. Consider the ones in the following sections as financial suggestions to make your budget work for you when buying your next home. You can do anything on a budget, but you have to do as much research as possible. Planning can make or break a budget.

When you know your credit score and the down payment you want to make, you should research as much as you can on your own before you negotiate with lenders. Visit your local credit union or bank branch to learn more about mortgage interest rates without making a commitment. Since they want a crack at your business before others do, they may be more willing to offer you a competitive offer than anyone else.

Use the 28/36 rule

One of the first steps in buying a home is to figure out how much house you can afford. A home you like may turn out to have monthly mortgage payments that are twice your rent. That's where the 28/36 rule comes into play.

The *28/36 rule* is a guideline that can help you figure out what you can afford so that you're ready when it's time to apply for a mortgage. It breaks down like this:

>> **28 percent:** Your monthly mortgage payment shouldn't exceed 28 percent of your monthly income before taxes. For example, if you bring home $6,000 monthly, your mortgage should be $1,680 at most.

>> **36 percent:** Your total debt-to-income ratio (DTI) shouldn't exceed 36 percent of your monthly income before taxes, and that percentage should include your mortgage payment. For a $6,000 monthly income, 36 percent works out to $2,160. Subtracting the $1,680 mortgage payment from the $2,160 DTI means you can't have any other current debt payments that exceed $480 per month under this rule.

This standard is set in place by reputable lenders to ensure you can reasonably afford your home. Giving you a mortgage payment that takes up the majority of your income is setting you up for failure by making you *house poor*. A person who is house poor spends most of their income on housing costs, such as mortgage payments, property taxes, and other expenses that come with owning a home. The more your income is tied up in housing, the less you have to take care of your other expenses.

If your current DTI is keeping you away from owning a home, think of ways you can pay your debt off faster to create space for a mortgage. You can use one of the debt payoff methods I describe in Chapter 10 to figure out a game plan that works for you and your budget. In that chapter, I also share additional tips on how to negotiate with your creditors as well as how to refinance your loans.

If you're wondering what the mortgage may be on a home you're considering, check out Rocket Mortgage's online calculator at `www.rocketmortgage.com/learn/mortgage-calculator`. This tool factors in the home price, your down payment, and other factors like interest rate to help you understand how much your mortgage may be and whether it fits in the 28/36 ratio.

Determine your down payment

Another hurdle that may stand between you and homeownership is the time saving for a down payment takes. A *down payment* is the cash you put down upfront when making a large purchase, such as a home or car. The amount you can produce for a down payment can affect the type of loan you qualify for and the interest rate. When you can offer a down payment toward a home, it shows the lender you're financially responsible, which can help lower your rate.

The size of your down payment can also affect your monthly payment by lowering the amount of money you need to borrow to purchase your home. Borrowing less money means a lower overall payment, which means you're more likely to fit your mortgage within the 36 percent DTI I discuss in the preceding section.

In a dream world, you'd be able to put 20 percent of the asking price down when purchasing your home to reap the most benefits, such as a smaller payment. If your down payment is less than 20 percent of your home's purchase price, your lender may ask you to purchase *private mortgage insurance* (PMI), which protects your lender if you can no longer afford your mortgage payment. But depending on how much your home costs, 20 percent may take years to save, especially if you live in a high-cost-of-living area. My advice is to do what feels right for you. If you can put down less and still get a smokin' mortgage payment, go for it. Your dreams are worth chasing because life is too short. As long as it's in the budget, of course.

Certain types of loans, like FHA or VA (which I discuss in the following section), don't require you to purchase PMI. Depending on the lender, PMI may be factored into your mortgage payment for one lump payment. After you've built up 22 percent of the equity in your home, you no longer need to carry PMI.

Research your financing options

To make a mortgage work within your budget, you need to find the best financing option you can. The sheer number of loan types out there can be overwhelming when you try to do your research as a consumer. To help narrow it down, I suggest you consider these five types of loans when buying a

>> **Conventional mortgage:** The most common type of mortgage people take out is a conventional mortgage. A *conventional mortgage* is a loan through a private lender. It often has a lower interest rate but can also require a higher credit score to qualify for.

>> **Fixed-rate mortgage:** A *fixed-rate mortgage* is a loan that carries the same interest rate and payment toward the principal during the loan's lifetime. A fixed-rate monthly mortgage payment can be much easier to budget for.

>> **Adjustable-rate mortgage (ARM):** An *adjustable-rate mortgage* is a 30-year loan with an interest rate that fluctuates depending on the economy. You usually have fixed interest that's much lower than traditional loans for the first five years of your mortgage, but your interest rate can fluctuate. A fluctuating interest rate can balloon your payment up to something you can't afford, leaving you (and your budget) in hot water.

>> **Government-backed loan:** FHA, USDA, and VA loans are all United States government-backed. These loans also offer different requirements than others, such as having served in the U.S. military. Some benefits of a VA loan include: no PMI requirement; no restrictions on the amount you can borrow; and in some cases, no down payment is required.

>> **A jumbo loan:** A *jumbo loan* is required for purchasing a property that's a higher price than a traditional home. You need a high credit score and an extremely low DTI to be considered. (Head to the earlier section "Use the 28/36 rule" for more on DTI.)

One way to ensure you get the best deal when shopping for a mortgage is to work on your credit score (see Chapter 15). A higher credit score means lenders see you as more financially responsible. If your credit score is lacking, or you have no idea what it even is, try a free tool like Credit Karma (www.creditkarma.com). Credit

Karma lets you know your credit score (without a hard credit check) and what areas need work. It gives you recommendations on how to use your credit more wisely and advice from top financial experts.

Consider other homeownership costs

Owning a home comes with more expenses than just a mortgage payment. Besides your mortgage, you may also have expenses such as the following:

>> Property taxes

>> Insurance

>> Repairs and general maintenance

>> Landscaping

>> PMI, depending on where you purchase your property

>> A homeowners association (HOA) fee

Not all of these costs will necessarily pertain to a home you buy, but they're still something to keep in the back of your mind.

HOMEOWNERS ASSOCIATION FEES

Proceed with caution when homeowners association (HOA) fees are attached to a property. *Homeowners associations* are organizations that consist of residents of a given condo, planned community, or subdivision who enforce the rules. If you move into an area governed by an HOA, you pay it a monthly or annual fee that goes toward maintaining neighborhood or building amenities (such as a pool, landscaping, parks, or tennis courts) and sometimes services like snowplowing.

When choosing to live in an area with an HOA, do your due diligence: Research where your fees go and what rules and regulations you must abide by regarding your property. You may have to keep on top of your landscaping and keep clutter out of your front yard (even patio furniture). Some more extreme associations even require you to keep your home painted a specific color. One of my best friends was forced to paint her home because the HOA in her subdivision had voted on it. She had to pay $4,000 to paint in a color she couldn't choose within four months or get fined. (As a side note, overzealous HOA boards are another reason to make sure you're clear on what the community's rules are; sometimes the rules don't actually give the board the authority to dictate a certain change.)

Even if your house is brand new, having a *sinking fund* (money you save for expenses you know are coming up; see Chapter 3) to help cover your eventual homeowner expenses is important. How much you decide to save for homeownership expenses is up to you and your situation. If you have a newer home, you may not be as worried about something breaking and decide to save less than you would if your home were older. Remember that things break, and having money aside helps keep you and your budget strong.

The following sections offer a few approaches to saving for homeowner expenses so you don't panic when you need a new water heater or your kid accidentally puts a hole in the wall. You know, whichever comes first.

The 1 percent rule

Experts say that when purchasing a home, you should expect to spend 1 percent of the purchase price on maintenance. So, for example, if I purchase a home for $400,000, I need to put aside $400 a month for home repairs and property taxes. This math works out to $4,800 a year I should put aside on top of paying my mortgage payment.

The square foot rule

Another way to consider the amount needed for repairs is the square foot rule. Every year, you put one dollar aside for each square foot of your home. So if my home is 1,800 square feet, I put aside $1,800 annually for home repairs and maintenance. It's not saving quite as much as I would for the 1 percent rule in the preceding section, but it's still a reasonable amount that will come in handy if something breaks. This approach is probably the most reasonable rule to follow if you're buying a newer home.

The 10 percent rule

The last suggestion for saving up for a home repair fund is to consider putting aside 10 percent of your monthly home expenses (mortgage payment plus taxes and fees). This method includes more math than the two rules in the preceding sections, so if you're serious about your budgeting skills, this rule is for you.

Let's practice the 10 percent rule in a hypothetical scenario. Say I purchase a house for $400,000, with $40,000 — 10 percent — down (oof). If I secure a 30-year fixed-rate loan at a 5 percent interest rate, my monthly mortgage payment is $2,365.89. Add another $200 for taxes and $83.33 for home insurance, for total monthly home expenses of $2,649.22. If I put 10 percent of $2,649.22 aside per month, I save $264.92 per month or $3,179.06 per year.

Remodeling or Renovating Your Home

At the time of this writing, the average price to remodel a space like your kitchen is $25,000, and the process isn't as effortless as home improvement TV shows can make it look. (Especially if you don't have connections at a countertop supplier.) That's why I'm including renovation as a life event alongside buying a house and paying for a wedding. But you can remodel your home on a budget.

Before taking on a significant home renovation, check with your city to see whether you need a building permit. Adding additions to your home, converting a garage, building a fence over a certain height, installing a water heater, adding a fireplace, and making any changes to your main sewer line are all projects that may require a permit. Know what you're getting into if you decide to move forward without a permit. You may be on the hook for a fine, and an unauthorized home renovation can keep you from selling your home if the records don't match a home inspection.

Decide what amount you're comfortable spending

Home renovations can add up fast. Before dropping your credit card from shock, decide how much money you can allocate for this project. Create a sinking fund (which I cover in Chapter 3), to make home renovations a new line item in your budget, or allocate part of your next tax refund. By giving yourself an amount to stick to, you start to realize what's doable and can plan appropriately going forward. For example, if you only have $2,000 to set aside, you may not be able to cover a kitchen remodel, but a more budget-friendly bathroom remodel may be possible.

Keep an eye out for sales

Appliances and other big home purchases go on sale at different times of the year. If you're not in a hurry to replace everything all at once, watch the ads and purchase when you see a great deal. You can also keep an eye out for financing promotions, such as no interest for a certain time frame. If you have a plan to pay it off, go for it!

Be realistic about what you can DIY and what needs a professional

Unless you went to trade school, you probably don't have the skills to DIY an entire renovation. However, you may be able to tackle some projects yourself to cut costs. Painting, installing hardware, switching out light fixtures, taking your own debris to the landfill, and taking out old carpets and installing new wood flooring are all things you may be able to do all on your own.

Call a professional for the things you have no business trying to learn on the Internet. You can do unnecessary damage to your home or yourself when you try to take on skilled work such as plumbing or electric wiring. Hiring a professional to take care of a project can be expensive, but you spend less doing the project correctly than you do trying to fix something you broke.

The following list will help you get the most bang for your buck when you need to hire a contractor.

>> **Decide what you can comfortably afford.** Going into any home remodel requires you to know what budget you're working with. Knowing your budget ahead of time can keep you focused and prevent you from having a contractor crush your dreams with the costs.

>> **Get clear on what you want.** Just like other professions, some contractors specialize in one area, like a bathroom. Others only work with certain materials. When you know what you want, you know who you're looking for. For example, if you want an art deco bathroom with tiling, you probably shouldn't hire someone who specializes in rebuilding closets.

>> **Compete a mock-up of project costs.** Overpaying is easy when you're unaware of what the pricing should look like. Start researching pricing on the items you want to require with your remodel, such as specific faucets, countertops, and so on. Though a lot of contractors prefer you buy the material yourself, some will do all the legwork for you. You also want to research how much contractors in your area charge.

>> **Don't be afraid to ask the hard questions.** After you've found a contractor you like, get down to the nitty-gritty. How long have they been doing this work? Will the subcontractors they work with have unsupervised access to your home? Be sure to also ask about their pricing structure, what additional services they offer (like taking care of waste removal), and whether they offer a warranty for their work. Don't forget to ask for three references!

>> **Review the contract in depth.** Ensure you review your contract with whichever professional you choose so that you understand what each party is responsible for. Make sure the timeline is reasonable and that you're clear on how the contractor will receive payments and how to communicate during the project from start to finish.

Finally, if you won't have access to a specific area of your home while work is going on there, have a plan in place as to how you'll navigate the situation until the remodel is finished.

Buy used

When I first moved into my own place, I had no furniture except a bed, a bookshelf, and my childhood desk. Besides my first month's deposit, the additional $1,000 I had saved went to start-up costs like kitchen supplies and a couch I splurged on. I was never home, which made up for lack of furniture and having all my belongings in plastic totes. When I realized my cat had decided to reorganize the stuff in said totes, however, I started to look for furniture.

New furniture is expensive, so used furniture can be a great option. Thanks to websites like OfferUp and Facebook Marketplace, you can check out listings for furniture within your budget. I've seen people sell new furniture for a fraction of the price simply because they're moving or need to make room. I was able to score a $300 chair for $25! Sometimes people list items for free that you can pick up.

Besides online, you can check out furniture in places like your local thrift store and consignment shops. I've been able to negotiate almost $2,000 off of quality vintage pieces for my home at my favorite consignment shop in Phoenix (which is conveniently next to my fiancé's hang-out spot).

Inspect used items before you bring them into your home. Check for damage, like compromised legs or unraveling wicker. Don't forget to also check for bedbugs. Bedbugs are the evilest thing on the planet, and they aren't just for hotels anymore. Even if you don't spot a bug, look for past evidence of an issue, such as brown spots under cushions. Doing so can save you a ton of money, not to mention future grief.

Buying a Car

Another financial commitment many people make in their lifetimes is buying a car. I purchased my first car when I was 19 years old. It was a 2001 Ford Focus ZX2, and I loved it so much. Until it started to break. First it was a $600 transmission. Then it was something else, and so on. I couldn't afford a car payment plus the upkeep, and I needed to drive it to get to work. That's when I started to skip my car payments. My dad caught one of the red notices in the mail and bailed me out, but after that, I was on my own. The payment was only around $165, and I still couldn't figure it out. But Baby Athena had no budget and wasn't ready for car ownership.

Owning a car is expensive, especially when you factor in both purchase price and repairs/upkeep, but it's also a financial decision that's individual to you and your budget. Whether you're currently on the hunt or considering it for the future, buying a car doesn't have to be hard. Like anything with your budget, you have to do the research so you can make an informed decision. The following sections help get you started.

Choosing between buying new and buying used

If you've ever owned an older car and then gotten to drive a newer one, you can admit that sometimes — okay, a lot of the time — new cars are nice. They have that fresh new smell *and* upgraded features that you probably didn't even know about. The first time I found out car seats have air conditioners, I spent the rest of that evening in amazement.

New and used cars each have their advantages. Here are some of the benefits of buying a new car:

>> **The newest technology:** New cars have the latest features on the market. They have radios that automatically connect to your smartphone, sync to your phone's interface, and allow you to access everything on a screen built into your dashboard. Newer cars also offer safe driving features, such as letting you know when you're too close to another car and providing crash assistance, such as OnStar. Even built-in software can alert you if someone is driving your car recklessly while you're not even there. Did I mention the temperature-controlled seats?

>> **Extensive warranty coverage:** One of my favorite things about purchasing a new car is the included warranties. New cars offer two warranties:

- A *comprehensive warranty* (also known as *bumper-to-bumper*) covers your car if anything happens to it mechanically. For example, say your fuel tank needs to be replaced — the comprehensive warranty would cover this repair. Most new cars offer the bumper-to-bumper warranty for the first three years or 36,000 miles you drive.

- The *powertrain warranty* covers your engine, transmission, and drivetrain. The powertrain warranty is up to five years or 60,000 miles.

>> **Less maintenance:** Newer cars require fewer oil changes than older models. Traditionally, mechanics recommend that you go no more than 3,000 miles per oil change, but newer cars can go anywhere between 7,000 and 9,000 miles. You're also able to keep better track of other issues, such as alerts, because your car specifically tells you what's going on with no guesswork required. Another feature that I love is being able to monitor your tire pressure. Everyone needs new tires eventually, but keeping your tire pressure safe can help prevent costly mishaps such as a blown-out tire.

>> **Better financing options:** Purchasing a new car through a dealership can come with perks like better financing options. Dealerships commonly offer 0 percent interest during a sales promotion, if you have great credit. They may also offer cash back and free upgrades, depending on what vehicles are in stock.

>> **You will be the original owner:** When buying a used car, it's hard to know where it's been. Even with a CARFAX report, you might not get the whole picture. When you buy a new car, you know you're the first and only owner and you don't have to wonder what might have happened to it.

The following are the benefits of buying a used car:

>> **Pricing:** Buying a used vehicle rather than a new one can be much cheaper. Cars lose value the minute you drive them off the car lot, sometimes as much as 10 to 20 percent. So a $30,000 car could lose up to $6,000 the minute you wave goodbye to the salesman who sold your vehicle.

>> **Cheaper upgrades:** You can get newer technology when purchasing a used car. A 2018 model may not have the same features as the one released this year, but it still has upgrades that much older models don't have.

>> **Luxury brand accessibility:** You may not be able to afford a brand-new prestige car, but a previous model that's a few years old may be in your price range.

>> **Money saved over time:** Buying used cars saves you money over time. The car payments are typically less because of the amount financed and the term length. You can also save money on car insurance and registration fees.

If a deal is too good to be true, it probably is. When you're purchasing a used car, make sure you get a vehicle history report, like CARFAX (www.carfax.com). Vehicle history reports can alert you to service records, accidents involving the car, and how many owners the car had before being sold. Knowing what accidents the car was involved in can inform you of any structural damage and airbag deployment. (Airbags can't be used more than once.)

Thinking through insurance

When you're looking to purchase a vehicle (and even when you already have one at home), car insurance is an important consideration. The following is a list of six types of car insurance:

>> **Liability:** This coverage protects you when you're found to be at fault for another vehicle's damage during an accident. Liability covers car repair/replacement and any medical costs incurred from the accident.

» **Uninsured and underinsured motorists:** If you're in an accident and another driver is at fault, covering your damage is their responsibility. But if they don't have a current insurance policy, or their policy isn't up to par, this type of coverage can cover the damages and medical expenses.

» **Collision:** This type of insurance covers damages to your car if an accident is your fault. So if you drive into a pole, this coverage takes care of it.

» **Comprehensive:** If your car is damaged outside of an accident, comprehensive coverage pays for repairs or replacement. This damage is usually caused by weather or vandalism, but sometimes can happen if a house the car is parked at catches fire.

Note: Comprehensive insurance purchased with collision insurance is known as *full coverage,* which lenders require you to maintain if you're financing a vehicle. I carry full coverage even when I'm not financing a vehicle because I can rest easy knowing that a simple deductible can cover any damage to my car.

» **Personal injury protection (PIP):** This type of insurance can help you cover other expenses that may occur because of an accident, such as loss of wages from needing time off and childcare.

» **Gap insurance:** *Gap insurance* covers any difference between what you receive for a totaled car and what you still owe on that car's loan. If your car is totaled out, you receive only what your car is worth according to Kelley Blue Book (an amount referred to as *actual cash value*). So if you get $8,000 for a totaled car you still owe $10,000 on, you're on the hook for $2,000. If you have gap insurance, the insurance company cuts your lender a check for the remaining amount so you can fully walk away. *Tip:* I highly recommend gap insurance. Although it's an additional $10 to $30, you can have peace of mind knowing you're covered in an emergency.

If you're financing a car, check with your lender about what type of coverage you need to purchase regarding car insurance. Most lenders require you to have both comprehensive and collision coverage. They may also ask you to purchase gap insurance.

Insurance coverage varies from state to state, so always check with your insurance provider to make sure you're covered. When I moved from Nevada to Arizona, I discovered that windshield coverage is an entirely different add-on, even if you have full coverage. I'm happy I picked the coverage, because three days after I moved to Arizona, my car windshield was damaged on the freeway!

Purchasing a car in cash versus financing

Car dealerships roll their eyes when they hear someone is looking to purchase a car in cash. I can't blame them; dealerships make commissions off auto loans secured through their lenders as well as off any upgrades you add to your vehicle. Whether you choose to purchase your car in cash or finance it, ask yourself the questions in the following sections to help keep you and your budget on track.

What can I realistically afford?

If you have a sinking fund already established (see Chapter 3), you may know that you have money you can already use as a down payment. Depending on the price of the vehicle, you may be able to purchase a car outright. If you don't have the cash, you need to ask yourself how much your budget will allow you to put toward a car payment.

Sit down with your budget and review your current expenses. If you don't have the space for a car payment, see whether you can cut anything back or do away with something completely. You also need to remember to create space for the additional expenses of car insurance and registration, too.

Don't tell yourself you'll find the money later. Spoiler alert: You will not find the money later. When you use this mindset, you're setting yourself up for a repossession that can ruin your credit. Find the money now and then purchase your next vehicle accordingly.

Will I be approved for financing?

If you decide to finance your next vehicle, make sure you know what financing you qualify for. When reviewing your loan application, lenders look at your credit score, income, and what you can provide for a down payment. You save in interest and other financing fees over time with a better credit score and down payment. If your credit isn't the greatest, you may not even be able to finance a used car. Or you may be approved to finance a new car but at a much higher interest rate.

If you can only afford a $300 car payment but the lender wants $400 a month, you may have to reassess your budget again or look for a car with a lower price tag.

Don't take the car dealership's word regarding what you qualify for with financing options. Different dealerships have relationships with different lenders. So chances are that if you can get financed at one dealership, you can get financed at another, possibly with a better deal. This is why it's so important to do your own research when it comes to major purchases. Your personal bank or local credit union can also help you finance at a lower interest rate and payment.

Does taking out a loan rather than paying cash have any benefits?

Financing a vehicle at the right time can come in handy. If you can secure 0 percent financing, you only have to pay the principal of the loan, and no added interest. You can also utilize a car loan as a way to build or even build back your credit.

Planning for recurring costs

Buying a car is an exciting time, until you have to pay for recurring costs. That's why you need to make sure you're budgeting for them. Dedicating a sinking fund (see Chapter 3) for transportation costs is one way to access the cash you need when the time comes. It's also an easy way to budget for these types of expenses. Don't forget to save for oil changes, tires, batteries, and regular services such as a transmission flush.

You can save on recurring costs by educating yourself on your vehicle. Get on the Internet and read up on common issues your car may experience so that you can be prepared in case it happens to you. If you don't have a reputable mechanic, ask a friend or family member whom they recommend. If you need a specific part, check to see whether it's something you can purchase cheaper from an auto parts store and then have someone else install.

Downloading a free vehicle maintenance app such as Simply Auto (simplyauto.app) can help you save even more money on these types of costs. You can record service reminders so you don't miss out on regular oil changes. You can also track fuel and mileage efficiency and how much you spend on repairs and other costs. This kind of tool helps you plan how much to budget in your transportation category.

Sign up for loyalty programs. A lot of places send you coupons and service reminders if you join their email list. Some local mechanics even offer loyalty programs. Always make sure to ask so that you can be rewarded for money spent anyway and get coupons!

Paying for Life Events

Major life events can get you into debt if you aren't careful. Although you may not be able to afford everything you want, with budgeting, you can afford what's most important to you. The following sections help get you started budgeting for two kinds of major life events — weddings and starting a family — that can set your finances back.

Throwing a wedding

The popular wedding website The Knot publishes a study every year to determine the average cost of a wedding in the United States. As I write this, the average cost among 15,000 couples surveyed is $28,000 ($34,000 if you include the ring). That's a whole lot of money to drop on one day.

Although a major life event is a cause for celebration, it's not worth getting into debt over (and I know people who have done just that for the wedding of their dreams). You can put together a celebration you can remember for years on a budget, as I explain in the following sections. *Note:* I focus on weddings in this section, but much of this information applies to any major celebration.

Pick three things that are important and skimp on the rest

One of my favorite budgeting tips applies when you're planning your big day: Pick three things you absolutely must have that are important to you and then cut costs on the rest. Prioritizing the three most important things clarifies what you can get creative with. It may be difficult, and the list may end up being five things, which is okay, too. But brainstorming now can put you on the right path when you start to look for your venue and your flower and catering vendors, for example.

Think outside the box

I've recently learned the hard way that the most expensive time to party at a venue is on a Saturday night. This popularity is why you should consider having your wedding during the week. The venue will be at the cheapest rate, and you can also score discounts with vendors. If your heart is set on the weekend, have an early ceremony and serve brunch.

Another way to shave costs is to get married in the off-season. Demand for events spikes in the spring and summer and then tapers down during the fall and winter. You can save thousands just by being flexible with the date of your big day.

Keep the guest list small

Inviting everyone you know to what will surely be an epic celebration is tempting. But if your budget is limited, keep the guest list small. According to The Knot, the average catering cost per person is $75 at the time of this writing. Cutting your list from 150 to 100 can save you up to $3,750 just on the food. Start your list with close friends and family and go from there.

Research your venue

Do your due diligence if you need a venue for your big day. Be careful about considering places at the top of a web search. Yes, they can be popular, but many companies get higher search ranking because they pay for ad space. A *curated list* from an outside party like a local news reporter is a better place to start because these lists often have already done the basic legwork on the venue's name, location, and price range.

After you've identified a few venues to research, read the reviews and ask the venue for the price of packages offered if you can't easily find that info on their website.

Sorting through online reviews and evaluating what makes sense is up to you. People usually leave reviews only when they've had a bad experience or an extremely good one, so getting a feel for the average experience can be tricky. And sometimes reviews blame the venue for things it has no control over. I read a review for my venue that complained about the DJ, whom I later found out the venue had nothing to do with; the couple had selected the DJ themselves.

Who says you need a fancy setting or location for your wedding? Take advantage of the beautiful public spaces around you. Many cities allow you to get married at your local park if you pay for a permit. You can also consider museums and national parks to consider!

One more important point to research about potential venues: whether they allow outside vendors. Most venues have a list of preferred vendors. Sometimes using that list is optional, but some venues actually require you to use their preferred vendors for big-ticket items such as food, photography, and alcohol (and often receive a kickback from such vendors). Find a venue that allows you to source outside options to get the best deal.

Try to DIY as much as possible

If you or someone else in your circle is crafty, think about what you can do yourself instead of buying. You can easily find inspiration online and create items for the fraction of the price. (Just ask me what amazing things you can do with a vinyl-cutting machine and some glasses from the dollar store.) Other things you can DIY ahead of time include the following:

>> Stationery, including your save-the-dates, invitations, RSVP cards, and wedding programs

>> Flowers for your wedding party, ceremony decorations, and centerpieces

>> The veil

>> Accessories for the wedding party

>> Decor for the ceremony, including the aisle and a backdrop for the couple (don't forget about wedding signage)

>> The flower girl basket and ring pillow

>> A seating chart, numbers for tables, and favors

>> A photo booth for guests to help you remember the day

>> A music playlist (in place of a DJ)

>> Items for the bride and groom send-off

Starting a family

Adding a new member to the family is definitely a reason to celebrate! Raising a child is rewarding, but it can also be expensive. Because those expenses can add up quickly, planning your budget accordingly is important.

Review your health insurance plan

The biggest expense when starting a family arrives after your new loved one does. It's the hospital bill. The average cost of giving birth ranges anywhere from $13,000 to $23,000 without health insurance coverage, and pricing fluctuates based on procedure and hospital.

Here are some of the coverage-related costs you may incur during a pregnancy:

>> Your *deductible* is the amount of money you must spend out of pocket before your insurance will pay a portion of your medical treatment.

>> *Co-insurance* is the portion of your medical treatment insurance pays after you've met your deductible.

>> *Co-payments (co-pays)* are fees you pay when visiting a doctor or picking up medication. Co-pays are usually a flat fee, which means you pay the same price per visit or prescription refill.

Most health insurance plans must cover pregnancy and childbirth thanks to the Affordable Care Act (ACA), but each healthcare plan can provide different coverage. Understanding how much you'll be liable for when having a baby is crucial to your financial planning. For example, make sure you know whether your health insurance provider covers alternative birthing options so you can make the right choice for you and your baby.

Health insurance policies purchased on or before March 23, 2010, are considered *grandfathered* insurance policies and don't include some of the rights and protections the ACA provides. If you have a grandfathered plan, make sure you call your insurance company immediately to make the necessary changes to cover you and your baby during pregnancy.

Navigating your parental leave

When budgeting to start a family, review your employer's family leave policies and benefits to evaluate whether you'll have any loss of or gaps in regular income.

Family leave (also called *parental leave*) is the time parents take off to care for a child after birth or in the process of adopting or fostering a child. Twelve weeks is the standard length of time for parental leave and can be covered by the Family Medical Leave Act (FMLA). Before taking the time, check with your employer to see whether you meet all the criteria, or whether your employer is even required to provide leave.

You may be able to extend FMLA-backed family leave by going on short-term disability, although companies may ask that you use your paid time off and holiday time toward your leave or take unpaid time off before they'll pay you this benefit.

Though many parents can benefit from the FMLA, not all employers must provide it. Some loopholes deny FMLA coverage, such as working for an employer for less than a year or for a company that has fewer than 50 employees. To find out whether FMLA is an option for you, consult your human resources department or check directly with the U.S. Department of Labor at www.dol.gov/agencies/whd/fmla.

Some states legally require your employer to pay for all, or part, of your parental leave. Find out how to get in touch with your local DOL office about your rights at www.dol.gov/agencies/whd/contact/local-offices.

Be prepared to budget for new expenses

Starting a family can be costly, but it doesn't have to break you financially. Here are some expenses all new parents should plan for:

>> The labor and delivery co-pay after insurance

>> Supplies needed to feed your child (bottles, breast pumps, nursing pads, and cleaning solutions)

>> Items needed for traveling like car seats and strollers

>> Childcare expenses

>> Furniture such a as a crib, changing table, bassinet, high chair, and a comfortable place to feed them

>> Doctor co-pays for first-year wellness visits

>> A new dedicated place in your budget for ongoing expenses such as clothing, diapers, and food.

Also be sure to account for any changes in income that may come with parental leave (see the preceding section).

If you're unable to afford formula or diapers, reach out to a local organization that can help you get back on track. 211.org and nationaldiaperbanknetwork.org/ get-help-now/ would be a great place to start.

The time to practice having a lower income is before it goes into effect. Take a few months before family leave to factor your new addition into your budget.

5
Using Your Budget for Money Management

IN THIS PART . . .

Discover what to do if you lose your job or deal with a chronic illness; prepare an estate plan.

Stay on top of your credit score, build your credit, and review ways to use credit cards to your advantage.

Explore how to invest on a budget, handle your kid's college fund, figure out how to set both short-and long-term financial goals, and add some fun into your life.

Chapter 14

Budgeting for Major Life Changes

I had several teachers obsessed with telling me to "prepare for the worst and hope for the best" in high school. I wasn't always ready for a test, but when I was, the joke was on them. Can you imagine how I acted when I got an A?

The truth is, you may not always be ready for the worst. That's how debt happens. That's why you save an emergency fund and then save additional money in a sinking fund for ongoing expenses, like car maintenance. No one wakes up one day saying, "I think I'll blow a tire out on the freeway," but you still put money aside for it. (You can read more about emergency and sinking funds in Chapter 8.)

You can use your budget to prepare for the worst while hoping for the best. Losing a job, losing your health, and losing a loved one are some of the worst scenarios I can think of. In this chapter, I walk you through how to handle some difficult life-changing events that can affect your and your loved ones' financial stability. I hope you never need to use this info, but I want you to have it just in case.

Losing Your Job

A loss of income stream can hit you hard, especially when you weren't expecting it. The loss of your job? Now that can seem downright unimaginable and depressing.

In Chapter 11, I discuss how to keep your head above inflation and all the challenging costs it can have to you as a consumer. Another challenge that goes with inflation is that companies lay off their employees.

TECHNICAL STUFF

Decreased consumer spending can create a lack of revenue for a company. Think about it: If inflation is high, you adjust your budget to compensate for things you may be paying more for, such as groceries and gas. Because you're putting more money aside on essentials, you're allocating less to entertainment or shopping for fun. When you shop less, a company earns less, and profits go down. If a company isn't bringing in enough profit to justify the number of employees, it'll cut its workforce.

People who use their budgets to fulfill their financial responsibilities, dreams, and goals need to be ready for a significant hit in their finances at any time. This includes losing the main source of their income. In the following sections, I give you some tips for dealing with this situation.

Note: Although other personal finance experts deem some jobs recession-proof, your new, blunt best friend isn't one of them. (In case you're wondering, that's me.) I entered the workforce in 2008 during the Great Recession, and as someone who wanted to go into the public sector, it wasn't good. Nonprofits couldn't keep funding, and local and state agencies didn't care that I had a shiny new degree with experience. They were just desperately trying to keep the employees they had.

File for unemployment and other state benefits

After the initial shock of being laid off, your first step is to stop the financial bleeding that is a loss of income. If you're eligible, you can apply for unemployment insurance programs. The U.S. Department of Labor (DOL), in partnership with your state office, provides cash benefits to laid-off workers. Every state has an unemployment insurance program with different criteria and eligibility, but every state must still follow the national guidelines. The following sections address some concepts you may have questions about when filing for unemployment.

TIP

Employers might offer additional assistance during mass layoffs, like a meeting with HR reps, to discuss how to apply for unemployment or access COBRA (the continuation of health insurance through a former employer). They may also offer outplacement benefits from sources that provide career counseling and/or resume writing. Contact to your HR rep to ensure you're taking advantage of all the resources you're eligible for.

Eligibility requirements

Unemployment benefits eligibility means you qualify to receive assistance from your state office. The main requirement for unemployment benefits is that you're unemployed by no fault of your own (that is, you haven't been fired for wrongdoing or voluntarily quit your job). Most states need additional proof from your employer that you were laid off because it didn't have enough work to keep you on as an employee. Your state will also require that you worked a *base period*, which means you either worked a certain amount of time or that your earnings meet certain criteria. You may encounter other requirements on a state-by-state basis as well.

Apply for unemployment

Contact your local state benefits office to inquire about how to apply for unemployment insurance. You can find your local unemployment office directly on the DOL website at `www.dol.gov/general/topic/unemployment-insurance`. Some states may require you to come in and meet with a case worker, but thanks to the COVID-19 pandemic, most states have streamlined the process so that it can be done online or via phone.

To apply, you need to have the information about your layoff in front of you so that you can share it promptly when asked. The information can include the following:

» Your name, birthdate, and Social Security Number (SSN) or Employee Identification Number (EIN)

» Your address, phone number, and email

» Employer name, address, and phone number

» Name and email of your direct manager or HR department contact

» Your job title and the dates you were employed

» Your weekly schedule, including how many hours you worked

» Your wages and whether you were paid hourly or salary

After you've filed a claim, your local department will notify you of the status or if any additional details are needed to process your claim. The amount of money you receive in unemployment benefits varies from state to state.

TIP

The Workforce Innovation and Opportunity Act (WIOA) is a federally funded program that can assist you by paying for you to learn a new trade or go to school; providing cash assistance to help you with utilities, childcare, transportation, and clothing to help get you back on your feet; and helping you gain on-the-job training through paid internships. For more information, visit www.dol.gov/agencies/eta/wioa or find your local CareerOneStop at www.careeronestop.org/.

Additional state benefits you may qualify for

Although unemployment insurance benefits help you financially, they most likely don't cover all your living expenses. (Flip to the earlier section "File for unemployment and other state benefits" to read about these options.) That's why applying for additional benefits through the Family and Social Services Administration is important, even if you end up being denied for additional assistance. You can find out about these benefits and if you qualify at www.usa.gov. These are four main programs states offer that you may qualify for during your time of need:

» **Supplemental Nutrition Food Assistance Program (SNAP):** SNAP, previously known as food stamps, is state assistance that can help put food on the table. Funds are loaded onto an electronic benefits transfer (EBT) card that you can use like a debit or credit card at authorized grocery stores. The funds you receive are based on your income and how many people currently reside in your household. At the time of this writing, there are no restrictions on the type of food that can be purchased using SNAP benefits other than funds cannot be used to purchase hot or cold prepared food.

» **Special Supplemental Nutrition Program for Women, Infants, and Children (WIC):** Women who are pregnant or have recently given birth, infants, and children up to age 5 are eligible for this food assistance based on income guidelines similar to SNAP. Please note that WIC has a different income requirement than SNAP. In order to qualify, you must meet 100 percent of poverty based on net income whereas in most cases, with SNAP is 100 percent of poverty net *and* 130 percent of poverty gross. WIC has stricter requirements on what food you can purchase with the funds, but it does allow you to buy formula and other special-needs foods with a medical prescription.

» **Temporary Assistance for Needy Families (TANF):** TANF is cash assistance you can use to help pay for necessities such as rent, utilities, and childcare. Different states provide different types of cash assistance per income level.

» **National Medicaid and CHIP Program:** *Medicaid* is basic health insurance that provides state coverage insurance to low-income residents. State insurance can allow you to continue to seek medical assistance for annual wellness visits, management of chronic health conditions, and coverage for other serious health complications that may require a hospital stay.

CHIP (Children's Health Insurance Program): *CHIP* offers low-cost health insurance to children in families who don't qualify for Medicaid, although the eligibility criteria may be different based on the state you live in. Check with your state Medicaid office to find out more about eligibility requirements or go to the Healthcare Insurance Marketplace website at www.healthcare.gov. See the section "Make sure you have health insurance" later in this chapter for more information.

Assess your overall financial situation

After you've applied for benefits, sit down to assess where your finances are. You need to know what assets you have that can help get you through this tough time. Your assets can include information about checking and savings accounts (your everyday ones put aside for goals and your emergency fund) and how much you currently have in investments unrelated to your retirement, such as brokerage accounts, certificates of deposit (CDs), and money market accounts.

This is the money you have to see you through the upcoming storm you may face. You should always start with your emergency fund to help supplement any income and benefits you may have coming in. After your emergency fund, I recommend tapping into your savings accounts dedicated to your goals and dreams. Then turn to your non-retirement investments next. Depending on the investment type, you may incur certain fees or penalties. It's not ideal, but it can keep you above water until your next job opportunity presents itself.

WARNING

Only withdraw money from your retirement savings as a last resort. You can withdraw from your 401(k) or 403(b) without facing penalties if you're unemployed. Known as *substantially equal periodic payments* (SEPP), this move allows you to receive payments over five years if you're under 55. If this approach isn't an option financially, you can also consider a 401(k) or 403(b) hardship withdrawal. A hardship withdrawal is subject to a 10 percent penalty and taxes, but it can give you immediate relief when you need it the most.

Focus on essentials

In Chapter 4, I cover extensively the difference between your *needs* (things you absolutely must have to survive, like groceries and a roof over your head) and *wants* (things that are nice to have, like nights out with friends). At this time in your budgeting journey, you must follow a strict needs-only budget to help ensure your income and cash reserves can last as long as you need them to.

Financial expert Dave Ramsey advises focusing on your *four walls* (shelter, utilities, transportation, and food) when you've been laid off:

>> **Shelter:** Your rent and mortgage.

>> **Utilities:** Electricity, water and sewer, natural gas or heating oil, trash pickup, basic cellphone service, and Internet. Some people may disagree with me about the last item, and that's completely fine. But I'm telling you, in this day and age, the Internet is most likely necessary for your job hunt and your child's education.

>> **Transportation:** Gas or a commuter pass to run errands or go to job interviews; necessary insurance and car repairs.

>> **Food:** Food bought at a grocery store to make filling meals for your family without extra items such as chips or other nutrient-dense snacks.

I think the previous list may cover most people, but I'd add other items that also need to be covered:

>> **Essential pet supplies:** Your furry friends need food, cat litter, and preventative medicine. Spending $5 on a tick collar can prevent a huge vet bill later.

>> **Prescriptions and other medical co-pays:** You must take your medication as prescribed and seek medical care when needed.

>> **Basic clothing, hygiene products, and household supplies:** If your shirt tears, try to find a cheap off-label replacement. Same thing if you run out of shampoo or dish soap. For the latter two, you can find a great selection of items at the dollar store that work just as well as the name brands you find at major box retailers.

If any expense isn't included in one of these seven categories, cut it out of your budget for the time being. I'm the first to admit that that's tough and frustrating, especially when you're used to being able to get anything delivered to your doorstep on a whim and fall asleep to a streaming service after you've grabbed a meal with friends. But when you're laid off, the extras are done for the time being.

TIP

If you need more money to cover the essential expenses that you have coming in, consider grabbing a side gig. ridesharing, personal shopping, or pet sitting. For more ideas, refer to Chapter 8. I love the website Side Hustle Nation. It shares not only ideas but also resources and tools to help you get started on the right foot. Find out more at www.sidehustlenation.com.

Communicate with financial providers if paying down debt

Because focusing only on necessities is vital, as I explain in the preceding section, you need to hold off on any advanced debt repayment strategy that is, making additional payments to pay off your debt. Get in touch with your creditors to tell them what's going on and find out what type of relief they can grant you during your time of need, including postponing any payments.

Many creditors and service lenders have options if you're experiencing financial hardship. Some may offer to lower your interest rate or lower your minimum payments to something more manageable. Creditors and loan providers may also offer what's known as *forbearance*, letting you take a temporary payment break until you get back on your feet. These programs can last three to six months of no or lower payment to help you stay current with your account.

To work with your creditors in this situation, follow these steps:

1. **List each creditor, the type of credit line, and how much you owe.**

2. **Call a creditor.**

3. **When you have a customer service agent on the line, explain what's going on and ask whether you qualify for a hardship program.**

   You can easily use the following script after they've gathered your information to access your account:

   "Hello! How are you doing today? I'm sorry to say that I'm currently unemployed. Because of the loss of income, I can no longer pay this debt at this time. I understand that despite my loss of income, I'm still responsible for payment. Do you have any hardship programs I can apply for, or any other ideas of how I can stay current on my account while I look for employment?"

4. **Repeat Steps 2 and 3 for any subsequent creditors.**

Letting someone know your current financial situation may be stressful, or even embarrassing, but keeping others informed is important. The last thing you want is to have creditors turn your accounts over to collections and have a financial mess to clean up afterward.

Look into community resources

Even if you're prepped with your emergency fund, you never know what expenses you may incur between now and finding your next job. You can find the nearest community resources in your city by calling 211, doing an Internet search for "[your city's name] + community resource center," or taking a quick trip to your local library. You can also look to online databases for additional guidance and access to assistance. Here are a few online community resources you can access:

>> **AARP's Community Resource Finder (www.communityresourcefinder.org):** Made possible by a partnership with the Alzheimer's Association, the website helps you find care at home, community service, and housing options in your neighborhood.

>> **Findhelp.org (www.findhelp.org):** This website is a national database of food pantries and financial and housing assistance in your state. It also has additional resources to help with cost associated with utilities, clothing, employment, and medical hardships.

>> **St. Vincent De Paul (ssvpusa.org/assistance-services):** This charity is located throughout the United States to help with food scarcity and financial assistance for living expenses to prevent homelessness.

>> **Volunteers of America (VOA) Correctional Re-Entry Services (www.voa.org/correctional-re-entry-services):** VOA offers services like drug treatment, therapy, housing, and financial literacy and helps maintain employment and education for people recently released from incarceration.

>> **National Resource Directory (NRD; nrd.gov):** This website assists service-members, veterans, and their families and caregivers with resources providing support for rehabilitation and reintegration.

The following are a list of questions to ask each agency about the services they provide:

>> What population do you serve?

>> What are the eligibility requirements for services?

>> Is there an income limit for those who apply?

>> Do I need to provide certain types of documentation?

>> Where can I fill out an application?

>> Would I be assigned a case manager?

>> Is there a limit to how much aid I can receive?

>> Can I reapply after a certain period of time?

>> Does receiving this service require me to volunteer?

>> How will I know whether I've been approved?

>> Is there a wait list?

>> Do you recommend anywhere else I should apply for additional service?

Take care of your mental health

Losing your job can cause a blow not only financially but also mentally. You may face many emotions, especially if you had no say in your sudden change of employment status. It can be even harder to navigate if you're financially unprepared or have people relying on you as a provider. During times like these, you may need support but wonder how you can even afford it.

REMEMBER

Seeing a skilled professional isn't impossible, even when facing unemployment:

>> If you currently have some type of health insurance coverage, see what your plan covers for mental health services. You can also check out organizations like Open Path Psychotherapy Collective (openpathcollective.org). It's a nonprofit network that can help match you to a local therapist who offers services on a sliding pay scale.

>> You can also reach out to someone at the National Alliance on Mental Health (NAMI; www.nami.org) by calling 1-800-950-6264 or texting "HelpLine" to 62640. This free service connects you to a peer resource specialist who can support you by listening and providing additional resources that can be a good next step. They're also trained and knowledgeable in mental health and other relevant topics.

WARNING

If you're in mental distress, visit 988lifeline.org/talk-to-someone-now or dial or text 988 to be connected to a skilled crisis mediator who can help you. They can also advise you of services that are free or low-cost in your area.

Having a Chronic Illness or Short-Term Disability

According to the Centers for Disease Control, 60 percent of all adults in the United States have a *chronic illness*, which it defines as a condition that lasts at least a year and necessitates ongoing medical care and/or affects daily living. Diabetes, heart disease, and cancer are just a few of the common chronic illnesses. My mom faced multiple chronic illnesses that she battled every day despite having a smile on her face. She loved field trips and sending me off to school with cookies she'd decorated the night before, but I noticed that she wasn't around as much toward the spring. I wasn't neglected by any means. I just realized she slept during the day, and I'd have to visit her in the hospital sometimes.

My mom died a few days before Christmas in 2000. I didn't realize how hard it was to have chronic health issues until I started my journey in my late 20s, including cancer. Gratefully, I'm still here, but my health has greatly impacted my finances.

The average person in the United States spends $1,363 outside of health insurance premiums. But you can also be proactive with budgeting your money to prepare yourself for the future, whatever it may be.

Assess your resources and income

Being chronically ill can affect your income, most specifically your earning potential. Depending on your health condition and current treatment plan, you may require more rest than those with a clean bill of health. In my experience, needing additional rest can keep you from working full-time, which can affect your access to the employer-sponsored insurance that you need to help manage your illness properly.

The first step in managing your money with chronic health issues is to assess your resources and income. As I explain in Chapter 2, *income* can include any money received from an employer, a side gig you do from time to time, or disability payments you receive. In terms of dealing with illness, *resources* are benefits you may be eligible for, such as coupons that lower your prescription costs or a housing voucher because you're below a certain income level. If it's anything crucial or helpful to your overall living situation, make sure to include it.

Knowing how much income you have coming in means you can pick a budgeting method that works for you based on an actual dollar amount. Check out Part 2 for details on some common budgeting methods.

Look into ways to cut healthcare costs

At one time, I was paying over $600 of my take-home pay on costs associated with treating my chronic illnesses. I was financially strapped between prescriptions, chiropractor visits, regular doctor co-pays, and supplements. This amount didn't even include the medical debt I was paying off from my cancer treatment. Knowing that it wasn't sustainable didn't take being a financial expert. I knew it by simply checking my bank account balance.

Desperate not to let my medical costs keep me down, I got creative and resourceful. In the following sections, I offer some tips that may work for you, too.

Make sure you have health insurance

WARNING

Everyone needs health insurance. I've seen way too many financial influencers telling people on social media that they can cut costs by declining healthcare coverage. They insist you can cover your medical bills by negotiating the price so you're only paying for when you're sick. I'm here to tell you that this advice is utterly false, not to mention completely stupid.

I don't deny that health insurance premiums seem unaffordable, especially after you factor in co-pays and deductibles. But you know what's definitely unafford-able? Getting a medical bill for hundreds of thousands of dollars because you were in an accident or had a life-threatening illness. Or because that autoimmune disorder was really a symptom of almost-stage-3 thyroid cancer (oh, hello, it's me), which you now need numerous medical tests for. Many doctors in private practice won't even see you without insurance coverage. Yes, you can absolutely negotiate a medical bill (and I talk about how to do so in Chapter 10), but it's not a replacement for health insurance.

TIP

If you need affordable healthcare coverage or want to see what type of coverage is available, the Health Insurance Marketplace can help. The website walks you through individual plans you qualify for and explains terminology you may need to become more familiar with, like the difference between HMP and PPO. You can find a plan that not only is within your budget but also fits your needs. Find out more at www.healthcare.gov.

Take advantage of tax-free accounts

You can fund two types of accounts with pre-tax income to use toward your medical spending: a flexible spending account (FSA) and a health savings account (HSA). I highly encourage you to utilize these accounts if you have access to them. Using money you don't pay taxes on allows you to stretch your income farther than using your take-home (already taxed) pay.

FSAs and HSAs are set up differently and have different annual contribution limits, deadlines or grace periods, and stipulations about ownership and using rolled-over funds. An HSA also requires you to have a plan with a high deductible. Depending on your medical costs, high-deductible plans may cancel out the money in your HSA, so choose wisely.

For more information on HSAs and FSAs, check out the U.S. Department Office of Personal Management website (www.opm.gov/healthcare-insurance/healthcare/health-savings-accounts/comparison-chart), for a comparison chart outlining what's covered under each plan and the eligibility requirements, how to access these accounts, and what to do with the money you have left over from the year.

Cut costs on prescriptions

Ask your healthcare provider about coupons if your prescription costs seem high. Pharmaceutical reps regularly provide doctors with coupons, vouchers, and samples to share with their patients. Your medical provider wants you to be healthy, so they'll gladly share the wealth if you ask. If they don't have anything for your particular medication, chances are they can prescribe a generic or something similar instead.

Another way to save costs on your prescriptions is to look online for coupons. Always check with your medication manufacturer to see whether it offers payment assistance. If not, websites such as GoodRx (www.goodrx.com) can lower your prescription costs with coupons you can use at any participating pharmacy. Simply enter the medication you need into its search engine to find a list of nearby pharmacies that accept the coupon. You may have to go to a different pharmacy than your usual one, but the savings can add up if you need the medication regularly.

You can also ask your pharmacy. A good pharmacist wants you to make sure you can access your medication. They can't wave a magic wand and make it free, but they can offer suggestions such as trading your name-brand prescription for a generic version. When I was first prescribed one of my medications for my ADHD, my insurance didn't cover it, and I couldn't afford it at $120 per refill. My pharmacist did research, and by making a few adjustments, she was able to call in for a new script, which made my co-pay $40 instead.

Ask in advance for package deals

If you're visiting a doctor on a routine basis for medical treatment, ask whether they offer a package deal. Weekly visits to my chiropractor to adjust my back used to cost me $40 every time I went. After I joked about getting a punch card to earn a free visit, the person at the front desk got excited and told me they had package deals instead. Paying in advance for a package of adjustments brought my visits down to $24 each.

Anticipate the future

You know the importance of planning for your future. But facing a chronic illness may require an additional level of planning. What if one day your chronic illness or a temporary disability prevents you from working? Would you be able to cover yourself financially? What if you eventually need long-term care?

Ask your HR department whether your employer offers a chance to opt in to short- and long-term disability insurance plans. Many employers offer this as a benefit, and you can elect to enroll during open enrollment period. If your employer doesn't offer disability insurance, you can purchase your own plan through a reputable insurance company, such as State Farm (www.statefarm.com/insurance/disability) or Haven Life (home.disability.havenlife.com), which I highly recommend. Purchasing a plan can be done in just a few minutes online and their plans are reasonable for people of all income levels.

REMEMBER

Thinking about scenarios that may never happen can be emotionally exhausting. It's time spent on something you may not end up needing. But by walking yourself through the what-ifs, you can plan and budget better. You'll know what to do if the situation does arrive, and you won't be as caught off guard. You can't control everything that happens to you, but you can prepare for how you may react to it.

Figuring Out Your Estate Planning

One of the things I never expected to learn while becoming a personal finance expert was the power of grief. Elisabeth Kübler-Ross explains in her book *On Death and Dying* that people experience five different stages of loss: denial, anger, bargaining, depression, and acceptance. You can experience these stages at any time, and it's rarely linear. I've found that grief can bring out the worst in people, and no one is exempt, including family members.

That's why ensuring your loved ones are prepared for your death is important. Having an estate plan with clear instructions is one of the best things you can do for your family. You may not be able to wipe their tears when the time comes, but by getting your affairs in order now, you can give them more time to grieve later and perhaps prevent them from fighting over their inheritance, which can break a family bond.

Protect your assets

Planning for who receives what assets is referred to as *estate planning*. You should always know what assets you have as part of your overall financial plan, including the following:

>> Accounts and investments

>> Retirement benefits

>> Real estate

>> Anything of significant value, such as artwork, collectibles, and vehicles

You also need to know what you want your loved ones to do with these assets after you pass them on.

Two of the most common ways to plan for your estate are trusts and wills:

>> **Trusts:** A *trust* holds your financial assets so they're divided according to your instructions. For example, you can put stipulations on inheritance with a trust, such as designating that your beneficiaries receive money at certain life stages. If you have significant assets to leave your loved ones, a trust may be a better option. A trust is effective after you've signed it (that is, while you're still alive).

>> **Wills:** *Wills* are known as "simple" documents because the directions are easier to follow. A will doesn't stipulate or limit how much you can cover. It can also help you assign a guardian if you have children or pets who still need a caregiver. It may be a better choice if you divide limited assets only or have a lower net worth. A will doesn't go into effect until you're no longer living.

REMEMBER

You can have both trust and a will. In fact, many estate planning attorneys recommend this route because both documents limit any questions or doubts your family may have.

In some states, assets can automatically enter *probate* for years if they aren't covered by a will or trust. This situation can be detrimental to loved ones who depend on you financially.

Contact an estate attorney if necessary

Choosing between a trust and a will (see the preceding section), as well as handling all the work that goes into creating them, can be overwhelming. If you're undecided on how you should proceed regarding estate planning, or you're wondering how your assets may be affected at the time of your death, consult an estate attorney. Every state has different rules regarding the division of someone's assets.

An estate attorney can help you navigate these kinds of issues. Although hiring an attorney may seem pricey, your loved ones will be thankful you took care of your matters by using a professional. Just remember that your loved ones are worth it.

Use life insurance

Adding additional financial security on top of an estate plan can help you rest better at night. (You can read more about the kinds of estate plans in the earlier section "Protect your assets.") *Life insurance* is a contract between you and your insurance company that as long as you make the premium payments, the company will take care of your loved ones after your death. After you've passed and the company has received all proper documentation, it will award your family a lump sum.

The two primary types of life insurance are term and whole (permanent) insurance:

>> **Term:** *Term life insurance* provides your family with coverage for the length of time (known as a *term*) for which you purchase your policy. For example, if you purchase a term life insurance policy for ten years, your family will be covered for the next ten years, as long as you pay your premium. After your policy for those ten years is up, your family will no longer have coverage.

>> **Whole/permanent:** *Whole life insurance* provides you lifelong coverage, meaning it lasts indefinitely until you pass, as long as you pay the premium. It also can build substantial value over the course of your lifetime.

You and your family can choose from four types of whole life insurance policies:

- **Whole life insurance:** This type of insurance keeps your premiums and death benefits the same during the term of your policy. It also has guaranteed return payments from your insurance company.

- **Variable universal life insurance:** The coverage this policy provides allows you to invest the amount you've paid into the policy in different investment vehicles so your loved ones can have a chance at a larger payment. However, you can also lose all the money you invest.

- **Indexed universal life insurance:** This type of policy also allows regular premiums; it's tied to at least one stock market index and pays fluctuating interest based on the index's performance. Not all index universal life policies promise a return, but most do.

- **Universal life insurance:** This policy allows you to raise your death benefit and reduce your payments after you've collected enough money in your policy.

Review proper documentation

In addition to having your will and/or trust ready to go (see the earlier section "Protect your assets"), consider prepping an emergency binder for your loved ones. An *emergency binder* can help someone step into your life if something major happens to you, such as becoming incapacitated due to an illness or accident or passing away. With the right information, your loved one can run your household successfully and easily take care of your finances. A binder can also help provide stability for anyone who depends on you for care until further arrangements are made. Figure 14-1 is a checklist of important items you should include in your emergency binder, such as copies of medical cards, account numbers, and other related documents.

Emergency Binder

Personal

☐ Driver license or other government-issued identification

☐ Social Security or Certificate of Naturalization number

☐ Passport

☐ Birth certificate

☐ Marriage certificate

☐ List of emergency contacts (friends and family) and two numbers per person

☐ Instructions for dependent that rely on you for support, such as pets, children, and adults

☐ Employer information along with manager's contact information

☐ List of income sources and payments

Bank Information

☐ Financial institutions where checking, savings, and retirement accounts are located

☐ Account and routing numbers

☐ Name and beneficiary on accounts

☐ Answers to security questions

☐ Websites

☐ Phone numbers

☐ Copy of front and back of debit/credit cards

☐ Where the checkbook is located

Medical

☐ Insurance information such as provider, account number, and benefit amounts

☐ Health conditions or diagnoses

☐ Primary doctors, specialists, such as therapists with contact information

☐ Prescription medication and type of medicine, the prescribing doctor, and dosages

☐ Power of attorney and advance directives (for medical treatments, living will)

Estate

☐ Mortgage provider

☐ Title, deed, and loan paperwork

☐ Property tax information

☐ Utilities, other expenses, account information, and the amount owed

☐ Will and trust

☐ Estate attorney

☐ Vehicle information

☐ Insurance information

☐ Current debt and investments

☐ Login information to investment accounts

☐ Money owed by others

FIGURE 14-1:
Sample list of personal and financial records to be in an emergency binder.

IN THIS CHAPTER

» Discussing how to use credit cards when budgeting

» Building credit without taking on additional debt

» Finding out how to take advantage of credit card benefits.

Chapter **15**

Keeping Tabs on Credit Card Spending

A s I write this, the average American household has an estimated $8,942 of credit card debt. Using credit cards can help you when your bills are bigger than your paycheck (such as during times of inflation), but it can hurt you as well.

As I explain in Chapter 10, credit card debt is a *revolving debt*, which means you don't have to pay your balance (loan) every month. Instead, you can charge your maximum credit limit and have to worry about making only your minimum payment. Your credit card debt is also considered an *unsecured loan*, which means you don't have to put up collateral like a car or home to get the loan.

Only having to pay the minimum amount for a payment sounds dreamy, and it is. You can charge $1,000 and only have to worry about paying $25 back next month? Score! You can worry about paying the rest later, right?

REMEMBER

Your credit card company is counting on your having this mindset. When you're only paying the minimum payment, your debt continues to grow; the bigger the balance, the more you pay in interest. This cycle is how credit card companies make their money and why they're happy to give you the credit card in the first place. You can end up owing more than you had originally charged in the first place.

This isn't to say that credit cards are evil. When you use them responsibly, they can actually work to your advantage. Credit cards can help you establish and build your credit while maximizing the money in your budget. In this chapter, I discuss how to use credit cards to your advantage and avoid the pitfalls of excessive credit card debt.

Making a Plan to Use Your Credit Cards Wisely

You can honestly put nearly anything on a credit card these days, including your rent. But just because you can doesn't mean you should. Instead, you should charge only what you can afford to reasonably pay off within 30 days of receiving the bill.

REMEMBER

Sometimes, people just aren't in a place where they can use credit cards responsibly. That may be especially true if you're considering an envelope budget (see Chapter 5). Always ensure you don't charge more than you can pay back within the billing cycle. If you make a large purchase with your credit card, make sure you have a repayment plan ready so you can take care of it ASAP.

The following sections provide a few ways to ensure your credit cards are working for you and not against you.

Determine how much you can spend

One of the ways to determine how you use your credit cards is calculate 30 percent of your credit limit for the credit card you'll be using. As I note later in the chapter, to get a better credit score you should only be using a maximum of 30 percent of your available credit.

To find 30 percent of your limit, multiply the amount by 0.30. So, for example, say your credit limit is $10,000; $10,000 × 0.30 = $3,000. You should charge no more $3,000 on this card at any given time.

This guideline is harder to follow if your credit card has a lower limit. Thirty percent of a $500 limit is only $150. The trick is to match your expenses to your available limit and not any more money than that.

Be smart about which budget categories you charge

When you've calculated your 30 percent charge limit (see the preceding section), think about where you can best apply it to your monthly budget. First, look over all your monthly expenses to see what you buy regularly in one of your budget categories. For example, your food category most likely shows that you buy groceries each month.

Next, see how much of your grocery expenses you could put on a credit card while staying within the 30 percent limit. If your credit limit is $500, you could charge no more than $150 of groceries.

REMEMBER

Variable expenses, like groceries, may be easier to charge on a credit card because you have more control over how much you're spending than you do with fixed expenses like your rent. (Head to Chapter 2 for more on variable and fixed expenses.) However, don't go over budget — for example, don't use your credit card to buy concert tickets for $200 when your entertainment category budget is $50.

Pick a budgeting method for payoff

After you've decided what expenses you'll now be charging regularly, as I explain in the preceding section, you need to make sure you have a system in place to pay it off every month. The system in question is your budget, of course.

How you pay off the amount you charged looks different for every budget. For example, if you're following the 50/30/20 budget (Chapter 4), you're aiming for your credit card payment to fall under your 50 percent needs or 30 percent wants, or maybe even a mixture of both. If you're using the cash envelope system (Chapter 5), you subtract the amount spent from the appropriate envelope(s) and then deposit it into your bank account. The important thing is that you remember to account for your credit card spending in your original budget so that you can pay it off every month without incurring additional debt.

Avoid carrying a balance

When you don't pay your full credit card bill every month, you incur interest on the unpaid balance. In all reality, interest isn't something you should be paying when you can avoid it. Especially when it comes to credit cards.

Paying interest on your credit cards also means you spend more money on your items than the original purchase price. I'm all about buying things for the lowest price to make my money go farther, and a $100 purse isn't a steal when you end up paying $130 for it.

WARNING

I've received letters to my advice column from readers who've gotten themselves into a nasty cycle with their credit cards. Because they know they'll be paying their balance off the next month, they get stuck charging the equivalent of their next paycheck and don't have enough money on hand to pay their monthly expenses. Remember to only charge what you've planned, and not any more.

Set card accounts for fraud protection

The Fair Credit Billing Act (FCBA) protects consumers from fraudulent or unauthorized credit card charges. Under this law, the maximum amount of money you're ever out in a case of fraud is $50. That doesn't mean you necessarily have to pay for it; some credit cards offer $0 liability, and I've seen my bank refund me for fraudulent charges of less than $2.

Fraud protection can also come in the form of disputing a purchase on your credit card from a merchant who misrepresented their goods or services. After a popular subscription box company silently shut down, many customers filed disputes with their credit card companies to have their charges reversed. Some of these customers were out hundreds of dollars. I can't express enough how fraud protection saved them and their bank accounts.

TIP

A great way to be on top of monitoring your accounts is by signing up for transaction alerts. Every time I use my credit card for a purchase, I receive a text message from my bank letting me know the merchant and the amount spent. This setup gives you real-time information so that you can report fraud the minute it happens!

Improving Your Credit Score

Your credit score is one of the greatest financial tools available to you. Your *credit score* is a rating that can range anywhere from 300 to 850, with 300 being the worst and 850 being the best. A credit score can influence your ability to do the following:

>> Buy a house

>> Have a landlord accept you as a tenant

- » Pay for your utilities

- » Get cellphone service from a given provider

- » Get a job

- » Buy a car

- » Get good rates on a loan

- » Have enough credit available to you

In other words, I'm saying that your credit score can impact almost everything in your financial life. For example, the lowest credit score you can even have to buy a house is 620.

TIP

Not sure what your credit score is? I recommend going to Annual Credit Report (www.annualcreditreport.com). Authorized by federal law, this site helps you obtain free copies of your credit reports from all three major credit bureaus (Experian, Equifax, and TransUnion) during a 12-month period. After you enter your personal information, the site presents a detailed record of what you've applied for, accounts you've opened or closed, and anything currently in collections.

Figure 15-1 shows you how your credit score is calculated based on the following information.

- » **Payment history (35%):** When you pay your bills and debt on time, it reflects positively on your credit score. Paying your bills late or missing them altogether negatively affects your credit score. Late payments can make potential creditors assume you have cash flow issues and won't be able to make payments on time to them, either.

- » **Amount of money currently owed (30%):** *Credit utilization* is the percentage of your credit you currently borrow versus how much you have access to. Having a huge amount of debt, like student loans, isn't the worst thing in the world, especially if you're in good standing with all your payments. What hurts you is when you max out the credit limit available to you.

    Having an available credit limit of $10,000 can look impressive, until someone pulls your credit score and discovers you currently owe $9,800 to a creditor. Maxing out your available credit makes you look like you have a spending problem. No one wants to loan to someone who can't properly manage their money. That's why spending no more than 30 percent of your credit limit is a good idea.

>> **Length of credit history (15%):** Your credit score is also based on how long you've had available credit. Having had an account for a longer period of time typically indicates that your finances are more established. That's why the longer you have a line of credit, the better.

If you aren't using a line of credit, keep the account open by making the minimum effort. Many people close their credit cards that are their longest credit lines, which hurts their scores.

>> **Credit mix (10%):** The different types of credit and loans you have make up your *credit mix.* A credit mix includes credit cards, student and auto loans, and a mortgage. The more diverse the mix, the better, but you don't have to have one of each. Those looking at your credit want to know you can be responsible with different types of debt, but it's not worth taking out more than you can manage.

>> **New credit (10%):** Research by myFICO reveals that suddenly opening, or attempting to open, several new lines of credit at once most likely indicates some sort of financial difficulty. Even if you're not having financial hardships, lenders tend to err on the side of caution and assume this kind of activity is a red flag.

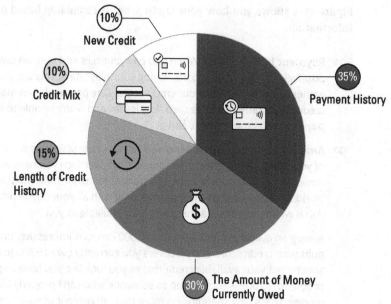

FIGURE 15-1:
Percentages used to determine your credit score.

TIP

Here are a couple of cool resources for working with your credit:

>> To see your credit score and get recommendations on improving it, check out the free tool Credit Karma (www.creditkarma.com). It offers weekly updates on your credit score and alerts you when any new accounts are opened, when you're late on payments, or when your credit utilization is high. I use Credit Karma as a way to keep my credit in check, especially as I build my score so that one day I can buy a house.

>> Experian Boost (www.experian.com) connects to your checking account and allows you to build your credit by paying your bills on time. As I write this, major retailers such as Netflix, AT&T, Spectrum, and more are connected to Experian Boost, so it's definitely worth looking into.

I advise finding out as much about your credit as possible and keeping it in a good place. So much more goes into building and maintaining your credit than I can cover here, so check out the latest edition of *Credit Repair Kit For Dummies* by Melyssa Barrett, Stephen R. Bucci, and Rod Griffin (Wiley) for more information.

Maintaining a good credit score can mean paying less in financing fees and interest and save you hundreds a month. The best example is a mortgage loan. If you took out $240,000 as a 30-year fixed mortgage with a 7 percent interest rate, your monthly payment would be $1,597 a month. If you could shave off 2 percent interest because a lender trusted your credit score, your payment would be $1,288. This decrease is without putting any additional money down. Over time, this lower rate means a difference of $111,240. I can immediately tell you that money would've been better off in a retirement or investment account.

Using Credit Cards to Your Advantage

My favorite part of using my credit cards responsibly (besides building my credit) is the ability to earn perks, or as they're usually called, rewards. Credit card companies commonly offer their customers one or more of these common reward programs:

>> **Cash back:** The most common credit reward you find is cash back. This type of rewards program allows you to receive a percentage of cash back for purchases. So if you spend $600 monthly on groceries and your credit card offers 5 percent cash back, you'd get back $30 monthly. Over a year, that adds up to $360. Often, the percentages are different for specific and overall purchases. For example, a credit card may offer 1 percent cash back on all purchases but 3 percent back when you purchase gas or groceries.

You can also earn cash back using your credit card at a certain retailer. Not too long ago, my Capital One card had the option to get cash back from Sephora. I used that 8 percent cash back to stock up on some makeup essentials.

>> **Miles:** The credit card company pairs with an airline, and you earn miles toward airfare when you make transactions. Every company has a different conversion of how many miles you earn per dollar you spend. (The mile exchange can be a bit weird; you may spend 20,000 miles for a flight that usually costs $200. But it's $200 you can now use toward something else.) You can also earn additional points when you spend on certain purchases or promotions.

>> **Points:** In this kind of program, every dollar you spend earns you points. After you have enough points, you can use them for gift cards, free travel, or your credit card balance.

Other credit card perks can include discounts, gift cards, and special access to certain places.

Utilize rewards like travel and cash back

I love earning rewards because I can use them to help stretch my budget farther. Here are some ways you can use credit cards to extend your budget and make your money work for you.

>> **Buy gift cards at a discounted rate.** Store-specific credit cards often have exclusions on what you can apply their discounts to, but you may be surprised to find that buying gift cards from other stores isn't necessarily one of them. I've been able to purchase gift cards at a discounted rate to use for Disneyland this way.

>> **Use exclusive store discounts.** Banks like Capital One often have a shopping portal where you can take an additional percentage off your purchases even if you don't have a cash back rewards card. Some retailers take off up to 11 percent when you shop through Capital One for purchases you'd make anyway.

>> **Use your rewards to help subsidize travel costs.** Saving your airline points can help you pay for flights to go home for the holidays or even toward helping you pay for a dream trip. I know people who have flown to Europe for free by using this method. You can also use points toward free hotel rooms, too!

- >> **Redeem points for gift cards toward everyday purchases.** You can use these gift cards to pay for items to help subsidize your budget. For example, if you redeem a $50 gift card to a gas station, that's $50 less that you'll need to allocate from your own paycheck toward your transportation category. You can then use that $50 to help pay off debt or put it into savings.

- >> **Put your cash back toward your bill.** Pay less on your credit card statement by putting your cash back toward it.

- >> **Enjoy member-only benefits.** Some credit cards offer additional benefits that you can only access if you have a card through them. For example, American Express cardholders can most likely access concert tickets before the general public. If you have a Disney Visa, you can go into secret locations at Disneyland and meet characters. Most airlines offer member-only lounges at major airports that allow you to eat for free and access free Wi-Fi. Some lounges even have showers or places to nap!

Use autopay for fixed expenses

Remembering every due date can be difficult, especially when you're making sure various bills are paid on time. This juggling act is why you should consider using your credit card to help autopay some of your fixed expenses. By signing up for autopay, you can sometimes receive discounts from your service provider. Plus, you'll never have to worry about paying a late fee again.

Depending on your credit card benefits, you could also earn points toward cash back or a free flight when you auto pay for fixed expenses rather than using your checking account. But be careful: in order for credit cards to work for you, you must pay them off in full every month. For a refresher, go back in this chapter to the "Avoid carrying a balance" section where you can find more information.

Chapter **16**

Using a Budget to Plan for the Future

B udgeting isn't just for day-to-day life. It includes accomplishing your future financial goals and dreams. Maybe you want to save more money for retirement in addition to your 401(k), or perhaps you have a kid who's obsessed with animals and wants to go to veterinary school.

Life is more than your responsibilities, too, so your budget should make sure your fun and happiness are also a financial priority. Budgeting is a marathon, not a sprint, and you need some fun along the way. In this chapter, I show you how to figure out your financial goals, and I provide some investment options and tips to help you plan for the future.

Setting Financial Goals

Your future is more than just preparing for when you grow old. You have other things to do with your time, which costs money. I discuss financial goals briefly in Chapter 2, but here I dive into how setting goals can help you have the future of your dreams and ensure you're taking care of your financial needs as well as your financial wants.

Identify reasons to set financial goals

Setting financial goals is important because your money needs to have a purpose in order to serve you. It's one of the greatest resources you have access to. When you set a financial goal, you take back control over your future. You're no longer letting the future control you instead.

Organizes your finances

Setting financial goals can help you keep your finances organized. When you're saving for a particular item or event, first you need to know how much money you already have saved. This step requires you to access your accounts so you can grab the information you need quickly. With an organized budget, that information is readily available to you at any time. See the budgeting methods discussed in Part 2 for more information.

Clarifies your values and priorities

Financial goal setting can also help you get clear on what your values and priorities are. Because you know where you want your money to go, spending on everything else doesn't seem as important. If you're saving for a vacation you're excited about, you're most likely cutting costs on things that aren't important, like dining out.

TIP

How do you know what's a priority versus what isn't? Think about your current lifestyle and write the three things you enjoy and look forward to the most. Next, write three things you literally couldn't care less about. The three items on your first list are your priorities, and the three items on the other list are the things you don't need to spend money on.

My current priorities are saving for my wedding, ensuring my pets are taken care of, and caring for myself. The things I don't need to spend money on are dining out, cocktails, and clothes. My friends even joke that eventually I'll die in a band T-shirt and jeans. I'm more than okay with it because I'd rather have healthy pets and consistent therapy than look fashionable!

Improves your money mindset

Working on financial goals can also help change your money mindset. Your *money mindset* is how you look at your finances and money in general — that is, your beliefs and attitude about money. It can be shaped at any time in your life, but for many people, their childhood upbringing establishes much of it.

Any time your brain picks up information, it processes it and then decides whether to store it in your memory or toss it. Sometimes you're aware of when your brain is processing information, and sometimes you aren't. This subconscious processing is where many money mindset beliefs can go wrong.

By watching how others around you act toward money, your brain is influenced to act oppositely or similarly. For example, say your upbringing was kind of chaotic. Your parents may not have paid the bills on time and thus gotten utilities turned off. Or maybe you frequently heard your parents cussing about bills. Your brain picked up on all this information and filed it as: "OMG, bills are dangerous. I don't want to experience this when I'm older. I'm scared."

You could've also witnessed someone battling a shopping addiction. Most people have had a relative who always had a ton of stuff in their house because they were stressed the other day and went to the mall for a pick-me-up. You may have looked around and seen unused stuff with price tags still attached. Your brain could've said either "These pick-me-ups aren't working if they still keep buying more" or "Okay, so if I get stressed, shopping can make me feel better."

REMEMBER

Your brain isn't wrong for processing the information either way, but the message you internalize may be harmful. Any harmful information can set you back without your even realizing it.

If you feel anxious, stressed, or overwhelmed when you think about money, setting a financial goal can help you overcome those feelings. When you set one financial goal and then work through the steps, you're retraining your brain to think about how you save money, which helps it have a more positive relationship with money. You're experiencing proof that you can manage your money to do great things.

Provides measurable progress

By setting financial goals, you know exactly what you're aiming for regarding your money. You can then put the right steps in motion to achieve your goal. If you're trying to save for a new car, you'll know to make it a line item in your budget so you can dedicate money toward it. You'll also start to look for used cars so that when the time is ready, you can get the best deal out there.

TIP

Visual learner alert! Breaking your goal down visually can help you feel that progress is more manageable. Don't be afraid to get creative when monitoring your progress. Draw one of those giant thermometers on a piece of dollar-store posterboard and write the total amount of money you need for your financial goal at the top. Then divide the rest of the thermometer into actionable amounts of money you can save. When you've saved any money toward that goal, color in the thermometer to the corresponding line. For example, if you want to save $1,000 in your emergency fund, draw lines on your thermometer for every $25. Then fill in a section of the thermometer every time you're able to dedicate $25 to that goal.

Builds confidence that extends to all areas of your life

Whenever you learn a new skill, you feel confident. Feeling confident that you can do something makes you feel accomplished and empowered, which makes you more likely to learn new skills and take on new challenges. Because you've mastered something before, your brain knows it can master something again.

Feeling confident in your ability to budget your money so you can hit your goals leads you to feel confident enough to take on other areas of your life. Knowing that you can do something difficult motivates you to do another difficult thing. Finding ways to feel confident can help you live a life filled with accomplishments and financial rewards.

Having confidence in your future isn't something a lot of people experience. I find this idea so sad because I want everyone to have something to look forward to. I want people to wake up and know that they can live life on their terms. I hope that after reading any of this book, you feel confident in your future, too.

Establish time frames

You can break financial goals up into short-term, mid-term, and long-term goals. Short-term goals are goals you can accomplish in a relatively short time frame. Mid- and long-term goals take — you guessed it — a longer amount of time to accomplish. Figuring out how to set financial goals and then breaking them down into a specific time frame helps you decide whether a goal is achievable or whether you're setting yourself up for doom.

Goals for six month to three years

Short-term financial goals are goals that you can usually complete in six months; *mid-term goals* may take up to three years. Three years probably seems like a long time to accomplish a goal, and depending on the goal, it may very well be. Everyone has different perceptions of time and how long something should take them. Circumstances also come up that can make you pause your progress or require you to revise the goal entirely.

Because everyone has different life milestones, your goals are completely up to you based on what you want to accomplish. The following are examples of short-term financial goals you can work on:

>> Build an emergency fund

>> Eliminate your debt

>> Take a self-development class

>> Contribute to a 529 college savings plan

>> Pay for a wedding

>> Save for a new or used car

>> Remodel or redecorate part of your home

>> Save for a down payment for a house

>> Pay for a semester or two of college

>> Get a job with better benefits

>> Max out your retirement account for one year

>> Have a no-spend year challenge

>> Go on that amazing trip you've always wanted to take

Goals beyond three years

Setting long-term goals is just as important as setting short-term ones. Thinking about what your future self will need in 5, 10, or 20 years can be overwhelming. Sometimes, I don't even know what I'll need in the next day or two!

You have to do a little more soul-searching when deciding what long-term goals you want to set for yourself. Here are some steps you can take to get you brainstorming:

1. **Plan a time in your schedule when you can have 30 uninterrupted minutes to yourself.**

   You want comfy clothes, a quiet space, a notebook, and a pen.

2. **Find a comfortable position to sit in, close your eyes, and breathe deeply for about two minutes so you can fully find your Zen.**

3. **Imagine you have a crystal ball from the coolest magic shop in the world that shows you where you are in five years.**

4. **Sit with this image for a minute; take note of the surroundings and how you feel.**

5. **Open your eyes and write all that information down in your notebook.**

6. **When you've finished writing, repeat Steps 3 through 5 for seeing yourself in 10 years and then 20 years.**

This exercise allows you to sit with your thoughts and feelings about your future. I hope you see something that's great and filled with love, but if not, that's okay too. Because right now, you have the power to change certain situations for the better.

Whatever you imagine for yourself is what you should consider basing your long-term goals on. Here are a few suggestions:

>> Invest as much as you can toward your retirement accounts

>> Build out a brokerage account with an investing strategy

>> Buy a home

>> Pay off your mortgage early

>> Buy a vacation property with rental-income potential

>> Start a business

>> Expand your family

>> Save for your child's college fund

>> Finish a college degree program

>> Pay off your student loans

>> Pay off a car loan

>> Donate a significant amount to a cause you care about

>> Max out your career earnings

>> Take a work sabbatical to recharge

>> Develop a plan for your estate or a trust

>> Make a plan for long-term care

Your long-term goals represent the life you want for yourself, and getting there is up to you. You can't control all outcomes of things you want, but you can most likely control your money.

Choose your savings accounts wisely

After you've decided what financial goals you're going to work on and figured out how much money you need to put aside to make them a reality, you have to ensure you're putting your money in an account that adequately matches your goals.

When you're saving for retirement, make sure you take an active role in any employer-sponsored plan you're enrolled in. See where and how the plan invests your money. Compare the different investment strategies offered and what risk tolerance they've identified. Make sure the risk tolerance matches the time frame in which you want to retire. You can always take more risks when you're younger, but as you get older, you should be more conservative.

When saving for personal goals on your own, check to see which bank can offer you the most competitive interest rate on your cash. Online banks usually offer the highest annual percentage yield (APY) through high-yield savings accounts, as I discuss in Chapter 8. But make sure you shop around and compare different incentives to help you get the most out of your money. Don't be afraid to use one account at one branch and another one at a different branch. Also, don't feel like you have to stick with the same financial institution for all your accounts, either.

TIP

A great way to pick the account for your financial goals is to have someone else do it for you. A Certified Financial Planner (CFP) can help you come up with a financial strategy to hit your goals in the fastest way possible. CFPs can also help you manage your financial investments. Even if you don't feel like you have sizeable assets, I recommend seeing a CFP; you can find a lot of free information online, but CFPs know things others don't to help you make the most of your finances. You can find a CFP by asking people you trust for a referral or checking out the Garrett Planning Network at www.garrettplanningnetwork.com.

Avoid early withdrawal from your savings accounts

Don't touch your retirement or personal savings accounts until the time is right. This guideline means no dipping into your house-down-payment fund to buy candles or transferring over money from your emergency fund because you spent too much on restaurant meals. No means no!

WARNING

This point especially goes for your retirement accounts and any money you're counting on using to help supplement your income in your golden years. Cashing in your 401(k) for something like a down payment on a home may be easy, but don't do it. You'll pay a penalty and taxes and be doing a disservice to your future self. Even if your partner has a retirement account they'll be happy to share, having something in your name for retirement too is always good.

Investing on a Budget

It is not necessary to do extraordinary things to get extraordinary results.

—WARREN BUFFETT

When you think of successful investors, Warren Buffett probably comes to mind. He's one of the most successful investors in the world, with a net worth of over $100 billion as I'm writing this. He became interested in investing at age 7 while reading F.C. Minaker's book *One Thousand Ways to Make $1000* (Dartnell Corporation). I was busy playing Barbies at age 7, so clearly Buffett and I are not the same.

You don't need thousands or even hundreds of dollars to start investing and succeed. Buffett started small, selling bubble gum to friends before eventually becoming the CEO of Berkshire Hathaway. As he said, sometimes the extraordinary results come from the most mundane things, as long as you have patience. The following sections show you how to invest on a budget.

TAKE ADVANTAGE OF RETIREMENT ACCOUNTS

I dedicate Chapter 9 to saving for your retirement, but I can't emphasize enough that you need to ensure that you're putting your pre-tax dollars to work in a retirement account. If you aren't already doing so, you need to get started now, even if it's just a few dollars per paycheck.

If investing in your retirement accounts sounds overwhelming to you, I get it. Sometimes, I need all the money I can possibly get. Life is expensive, and I often feel like I could be better spending that money somewhere else. So how about saving 1 percent of your income to get started?

If you make $50,000 a year and get paid every two weeks, put away $16 every pay period. By saving that small amount, you'll put away over $400 toward retirement over the course of a year without even realizing it. And if you can add pre-tax income to your employer's 401(k) or 403(b) plan, you can save even more — in addition to employer-matched funds (if offered). After a while, adjust your goal by another percent and then another when you feel comfortable.

Use a fee-based certified financial planner

Eventually, you get to the point where you've saved so much money with your budget (go you!) that you may need help making sure you're using the right investment accounts. This point is when you need to call in a *Certified Financial Planner* (CFP). A CFP provides assistance and information to help you plan your finances, such as advice to buy certain stocks or invest with one financial institution or help figuring out how to diversify your portfolio.

WARNING

What you don't need is biased advice. A lot of CFPs work for investment firms and therefore earn a commission on any products they sell or accounts they open on their clients' behalf. The more they can get you to buy, the more cash they have to line their pockets. So although that index fund may not be the best investment for you, a commission-based CFP may still encourage you to invest in it if it has a high commission for them.

A *fee-based financial planner* on the other hand, doesn't make a commission off you; you pay them a flat fee. That doesn't mean fee-based planners are cheap, only that they aren't making money based on what you do or don't purchase. I recommend a fee-based CFP who's also a *fiduciary*, meaning they accept legal responsibility to act in your best interests at all times.

Fiduciaries don't have a conflict of interest. They aren't opening up accounts for you that aren't the right fit because they're getting a kickback. They treat you with respect as a person, not as an ATM.

REMEMBER

I don't think CFPs who earn a commission are inherently evil. They genuinely care about their clients the majority of the time. But because their work is commission-based, you need to take their recommendations with a grain of salt and do your own due diligence.

TIP

To find a fee-based financial advisor in your area, try the Garrett Planning Network. It helps you decide what type of planner you should work with and locate one near you. I love this organization because it requires participating advisors to be fiduciaries *and* charge based only on time. Check out www.garrettplanning network.com for more information.

Think small with apps and robo-advisors

You may be wondering what you can do on a smaller scale until you get more comfortable with your cash flow. My answer: Help your money grow by using the smartphone in your pocket.

Investment apps are a great way to start investing on a small scale to help learn how the markets work. They're also a way to get help with managing your portfolio, because most apps work as a robo-advisor. A *robo-advisor* is an automated platform that invests your money on your behalf. After you answer an assessment based on your investment goals, a robo-advisor invests your money in a strategy to help you meet those goals. Most of these robo-advisors invest in exchange-traded funds (ETFs) or a mutual fund to help you make the most of your cash. Use the following list to begin your own research into finding a robo-advisor that works best for you:

>> Wealthfront: www.wealthfront.com

>> Fidelity Go: www.fidelity.com/managed-accounts/fidelity-go/overview

>> Bettermint: www.betterment.com

>> M1: m1.com

>> Empower (formerly Personal Capital): www.empower.com

>> Ally Invest: www.ally.com/invest

>> Marcus Invest: www.marcus.com/us/en/invest

Saving for College

College can be expensive. Every school's costs of attendance are different, and financial aid is never guaranteed. You can help limit student loan debt as much as possible with proper planning and saving, as I explain in the following sections.

TIP

One way to make sure your student does get any financial aid they qualify for is by having them fill out the Free Application for Federal Student Aid (FAFSA), a program through the U.S. Department of Education. You can read more about the FAFSA and financial aid in Chapter 12.

START SETTING COLLEGE EXPECTATIONS AND GOALS EARLY

The first step in college saving preparation is to make sure your child has the proper support in junior high (or middle school) to start on the right foot in high school.

Performing poorly in certain subjects in junior high can land students in remedial math and English classes during their freshman year of high school to help them get their skills up to the appropriate grade level. To attend most colleges, you must take a list of required classes throughout your high school career: certain math, history, and science classes, as well as fine art and foreign language. Always double check your state's department of education website for a list of what classes are needed to graduate. Then check college websites to see what classes are needed to apply for enrollment. You can then go from there to help your student pick their class schedule. Starting high school behind the ball can make finishing these prerequisite classes difficult, especially without some type of academic intervention such as summer school and tutoring.

Another option is to attend community college and then transfer to a four-year college. Tuition at community colleges is typically 50 percent less expensive than tuition at a state university. You can also earn an associate's degree that you can use to enter the workforce much earlier.

Tip: A trade school may be a better fit, depending on the type of career your child wants to pursue (see the accompanying figure). Trade schools focus more on vocational careers and certificate programs for all job fields. Some examples of programs available are automobile mechanics, radiology technicians, cosmetology, culinary arts, and legal services. Most trade programs take a year or less to complete. I highly recommend trade schools as an alternative to college, especially because many trades pay more than a career with a traditional four-year degree!

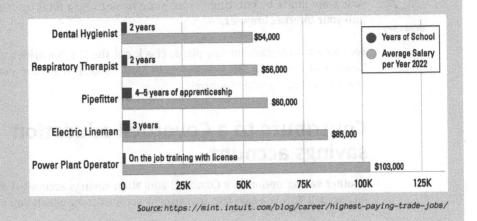

Source: https://mint.intuit.com/blog/career/highest-paying-trade-jobs/

Invest in a 529 plan

A popular way to invest in your child's future education is a 529 plan. A *529 plan* is a tax-advantaged saving account for a beneficiary's future education costs. You can choose from two types of plans:

>> **Prepaid tuition and education savings:** *Prepaid tuition accounts* allow you to open an account at a participating college or university for your child's tuition in advance. This account is a great way to pay ahead of time if you're confident your child will attend a specific school; you have one fewer thing to worry about in the future. The drawback, however, is that if your child doesn't attend the designated school, you'll most likely be reimbursed less than what you paid.

>> **Education savings plan:** This plan allows you to open an investment account specifically for qualified higher learning expenses your beneficiary may need in the future. Unlike prepaid tuition plans, you can use this account to pay for various things outside of tuition, such as fees and room and board, if you're over the age of 18. Although you can access 529 funds at a younger age, you can only use up to $10,000 toward tuition.

You can work your way around fees associated with 529s (such as additional broker fees) by choosing a direct-sold education savings plan through your state of residence. You can also avoid fees by paying online.

WARNING

A 529 plan has no yearly contribution limits, but you have to pay a gift tax on contributions over $16,000 according to the IRS. You can file lifetime exceptions to help alleviate paying taxes if you donate past the limit. As always, visit www.irs.gov/taxtopics/tc313 for more information.

REMEMBER

Every state also has a limit on the dollar amount that a 529 can hold. You can find your state limits by entering "[your state name] = 529 total contribution limit" into your Internet browser.

For more information on 529 plans, check out the U.S. Securities and Exchange Commission website at www.sec.gov/reportspubs/investor-publications/investorpubsintro529htm.html.

Contribute to a Coverdell education savings account

Another saving option is a Coverdell education savings account (Coverdell ESA). A Coverdell ESA is a tax-free investment account from which you can withdraw funds for educational expenses. Books, supplies, equipment, tutoring and other services are all things you can use the money in a Coverdell ESA for. These accounts also have income limits: no more than $95,000 to $110,000 for a single income and $190,000 to $220,000 income per year as combined income (as of this writing).

Contribution limits are much lower for a Coverdell ESA; you can contribute only up to $2,000 per year. Check out www.irs.gov/taxtopics/tc310 for more information.

Squirreling Away Funds for Future Fun

I'm the biggest advocate of ensuring you have a line item in your budget for fun, even if it's only $5 to start off (that's an ebook). But even while having fun, you still need to be somewhat responsible. Here are a few suggestions and tips to help you plan a budget for three types of fun activities: traveling, trying a new hobby, and enjoying a night out with friend.

Budgeting for travel

One of the biggest regrets I have is not traveling earlier in my life. In my head, traveling to New York City seemed impossible, but when I mentioned this dream on my blog, a fellow blogger said I could crash on their couch. It was the little step I needed to get things in motion.

In the following sections, I give you some tips for working travel saving into your budget. Maybe one of these nuggets is the little step *you* need.

Cut out budget excess to put toward travel

Go over your current budget and attempt to cut $25 out of it. Can you take $5 off groceries here or cancel this $10 subscription? Chances are that you can find the $25 if you really look for it. Don't go overboard — like a saltines-only diet — but do cut back the excess to afford something you'll appreciate more.

Set up an automatic savings account transfer

One of my favorite saving hacks is to set up automatic transfers to my savings account. Every time I swipe my debit card, $1 automatically transfers to my savings account. Almost every time I log into my account online, I'm shocked I randomly saved $70. Then I get giddy because I remember how it got there.

Start a small automatic transfer into a savings account you can tap into for traveling. Whether it's $1 or $25, those small amounts add up over time, and you'll be pleased when they do.

Sign up for flight alerts

One way you can save on airfare is to register for flight alerts. Google Flights (www.google.com/travel/flights) is a good resource. You can enter trip information, such as days to fly, the locations you're flying to and from, and the time you'd prefer to leave. (The cheapest days of the week to fly are Tuesday and Wednesday.) Google then sends you an email letting you know when the price changes. Another cool feature is that you can see whether the price you're considering is high or low based on price history.

TIP

If you're adventurous, try Scott's Cheap Flights (scottscheapflights.com). When you sign up for the email list, you receive a daily message with flights on sale worldwide for anywhere from 40 to 90 percent off. Some sales may be limited to certain airports, but they still have something for everybody — believe me. Can you imagine flying to Europe for $150? I've seen it happen.

Budgeting for a new hobby

One of the best things you can do is pick up a hobby. Not only does learning a new hobby help with cognitive function, it can help you relieve stress through a creative outlet. Hobbies can turn into an expensive pastime, but there's no reason you can't start that new banjo band on a budget.

Try a kit first

A lot of people go all in on a new hobby only to realize it's not for them. (It's a running joke among ADHD people that you become hyperfixated on something new, spend a bunch of money on it, and then never touch it again. I wish I didn't know from first-hand experience, but I do.) This approach can add not only to buyer's remorse but also to clutter.

Instead of jumping into the deep end on a new hobby, start small. Most hobbies have kits you can buy online to get you started with a few supplies for under $20. So instead of spending enough money to open your own candle store, you can just make one for yourself. This way, you can test the waters without spending a ton of cash.

Visit your local library

Community spaces like libraries are great ways to check out a new hobby for a free or reduced cost. They offer free classes like computer programming, upcycling, cross-stitching, and even Dungeons & Dragons clubs. A free class called "The Accidental Crafter" at my library encourages reluctant crafters to join, and it provides all the supplies — for free!

Shop at dollar stores

The dollar stores of today aren't ones your grandma made you go to when you were little. They sell name-brand products, including food, hygiene products, clothes, and everyday household items. They also have cool sections filled with all the craft supplies you can imagine — painting supplies, kits, googly eyes. Thanks to Dollar Tree, I made my Halloween costume out of fake flowers. I spent over $100 and endless hours hot-gluing, but my floral cap helped me be the May Queen of my dreams.

Budgeting for social activities

Expenses within your social-life budget — grabbing a coffee or drink with a friend or attending an event or a live show — will most likely increase over time. But you can make your money go farther by planning in advance and using the tips below.

Check out happy hours

I wish I didn't love dining out as much as I do. To me, nothing compares to celebrating someone over a meal or meeting up with friends at your favorite bar. But no matter where you live, that can get pricey. My favorite way to hang out with friends is during happy hour. I can get discounts on not only drinks but also on appetizers and sometimes meals. If I'm smart, I can get a drink and an appetizer, and then leave a tip for $10. I also get to hang out with people other than my cat.

Look for free things to do

My friends are always asking me how I know about the events I attend. Besides hanging out with a pretty diverse group of people, I type "Free things to do in [insert the city]" into my search bar regularly. You can find festivals, special exhibits at museums, and free movies if you just know where to look.

My favorite time to look for free things to do is around the winter holidays. When I was growing up, my parents would put me in the car with a blanket and cocoa while we drove around looking at Christmas lights. It's still a tradition I love to do to this day.

Use Groupon

Groupon is great for purchasing items on sale, and it's also great for finding discounted admission to things you want to try. My friends and I find concert tickets for a fraction of the price, which means we have more money for other concert items like drinks and souvenirs. You can also get discounted passes to check out fitness studios, sip and paint nights, and escape rooms.

6

The Part of Tens

IN THIS PART . . .

Use spending challenges and money mindset hacks to refresh your budgeting game.

Find ways to focus on your financial goals and explore fun approaches to saving and following your progress.

Chapter 17

Ten Creative Ways to Budget

O ne of the ways I've been able to stick to budgeting for as long as I have is by getting creative. I can only continue to pack the same lunch for so long before I want to chuck it in the trash before work. But I've made budgeting a game by doing different challenges and working on my money mindset. Not only do I love games, but I also love winning. In this chapter, I explain how I reset my budget when I need to so I can save money for my next adventure.

Make a No Spending Rule

One of the first budget challenges I ever participated in was a no-spend challenge. A *no-spend challenge* is almost exactly as it sounds: You don't spend any money for a set amount of time on certain predetermined items in your budget. (You can spend money on other things.) Some people stick to covering only their basics, but some people go even farther to save their cash.

TIP

I use no-spend challenges to use up what I have. As much as I try to be purposeful with my consumption, I still end up with more than I need or even have room for. I can relax by limiting my purchases and only spending cash on my needs and not my wants.

Avoid Buying New Clothing

Your closet may look like mine, with hangers missing and stuff ready to fall out. If clothing is your weakness, consider a no new clothing challenge. Decide for the next three months to not buy any clothing unless you absolutely need to. You don't realize how much you really have in your closet until you're forced to go through it.

Buy Secondhand Items

Cars aren't the only thing you can save on when you purchase secondhand; furniture, books, clothing, musical instruments, tools, appliances, toys, smartphones, and other electronics are all often less expensive used. This shopping method can save you hundreds of dollars. I saved a lot of money over the course of my college career by purchasing all my textbooks from their previous owners.

REMEMBER

Inspect the items you're buying secondhand before purchasing them. Used items are often still in great shape, but not always.

Shop Local

Shopping locally can save you money. Vendors who provide goods directly without going through a middleman or chain store can sell items for less. Selling locally means fewer costs in transportation to get items to you without the markup of a retail store. Check farmer markets to help reduce your grocery bill by purchasing locally sourced meat, produce, and dairy items. You can also shop for gifts and everyday items, such as candles, soap, and homemade cleaning products.

Reset Your Daily Habits

You'd be surprised at how much money you spend just out of habit. When I started working at home full-time, I noticed that my checks started to last longer. That's because I'd spent money out of habit every time I'd gone to work. Grabbing a latte, escaping the office for lunch, and spending $5 here and there really adds up. Working from home, I no longer had those habits.

Commit to tracking your schedule for one week and see exactly what habits cost you money. Then commit to changing them. If you dine out because you're exhausted by the end of your workday, try batch cooking on the weekends. Buying too many duplicate items because you lose track of them? Make a point to spend ten minutes a day organizing your supplies. By assessing your habits, you can reset them to better suit the stage of life you're in.

Allow for a 30-day Waiting Period

In the age of instant gratification, financial purchases are just a click or an app away. Major retailers make the shopping process seamless for a reason. When you can save your credit card information and get personalized recommendations for things you never even knew existed, spending money on items you don't need in the first place is easy.

If you want to make a purchase that isn't essential to your survival, wait 30 days before you hit "buy." By giving yourself 30 days to think about it, you may realize you no longer want the item in question, which frees up your money to put somewhere else.

Look into Sustainable Living

Sustainable living is a lifestyle that encourages you to improve your eco-footprint by using less of Earth's resources. By focusing on using fewer resources, you're creating less waste.

This benefit also applies to your finances. If you're using your bike or public transportation to reduce your carbon footprint, you're not putting money toward gas. Making sure you don't waste food can lead to a smaller grocery bill. Buying used where you can means less stuff goes toward the landfill. (It's also more cost-effective, as I explain in the earlier section "Buy Secondhand Items.")

Consider Minimalism

Joshua Fields Millburn and Ryan Nicodemus of The Minimalists define *minimalism* as a way to eliminate life's excess so you can concentrate on things that are important to you. Minimalism isn't just for physical possessions. You can apply it to any area of your life, such as your budget, to help you cut the crap out so you can spend more time and money on your values. By deciding what's important, you can put more money toward what you value instead.

Practice Gratitude

Saying "thank you" is one of the fastest ways to turn your mindset around. Focusing on what you *don't* have and losing sight of what you *do* have can be easy, at least for me. By taking the resources and opportunities you have available for granted, you can stall your growth and feed into the "I don't have" loop.

TIP

Every day, say "thank you" for three things. You may be surprised at what you take for granted and what you can improve.

Use Visualization When Goal Setting

Confession: Sitting next to me on my desk is a vision board featuring my book cover. Not the book cover you have now — I made one by printing off another *For Dummies* cover and replacing the book's subject with the word *Budgeting* because the real cover didn't exist when I set this goal. It will stay on my board as a reminder of how powerful visualizing your future can truly be.

REMEMBER

You're more likely to remember your goals when you're repeatedly reminded of them. If you can visualize it, you start to pick up on opportunities to make it a reality.

If you like making collages for a dream board, cut out photos and inspiring quotes that put a smile on your face. Of course, you don't have to do a full-on vision board, but you can find visual ways to remind yourself why you're starting your new money journey. Here are some examples:

>> Print a photo of your dream home and put it next to your keys so you see it every time you leave home.

>> Download a debt tracker and color in another section every time you pay $5 toward your debt.

>> Save a picture of your dream travel destination as your desktop background.

>> Write an affirmation on a slip of paper and stick it in your wallet.

Chapter **18**

Ten Ways to Stay Motivated When Following a Budget

Budgeting gets easier as you figure out how to make it work for you. But just because it's easier doesn't mean you don't lose motivation from time to time. Keep the tips in this chapter in mind when your eyes want to glaze over from looking at your budget.

Define Your Why

When you're changing your finances around, knowing why you're doing it in the first place is important. Old habits are familiar and comforting, which makes them easier to stick to than trying something new. Your brain likes comfort because it keeps you safe, so staying consistent in your budgeting can be more difficult when you don't have a convincing why.

TIP

Make your why clear and specific. Instead of saying, "I just want to be better with money," say, "I deserve to be comfortable in retirement." By being clear, you become powerful.

Document Your Journey

Keeping track of your budgeting progress in a way that you can look back on can help reignite your motivation when you're flagging. I started my first personal finance blog to keep me accountable for my finances; I never thought that it would change my life, but it did. Documenting my journey enabled me to see how far I'd come and then encouraged me to keep going. It also reminded me of the things I did to move the needle so I know what to do in the future if I get stuck.

Prepare to Deal with Burnout

You'll inevitably experience burnout at least once on your budgeting journey. When it happens, give yourself a month off.

REMEMBER

That advice sounds counterintuitive, but by allowing yourself space to breathe, you'll be more motivated to come back than if you hadn't taken a break. You wouldn't force yourself to run if all you could do was walk. Give yourself time to be yourself. Your budget will be ready when you come back. The important thing is that you do come back.

Tackle a 52-week Challenge

The 52-week challenge is one way to see big results by starting with small steps. It goes like this: Every week, challenge yourself to save a dollar more than you did the week before. So the first week of the challenge, you save $1. The second week, you save $2 and then keep going from there. By the end of the challenge, just consistently saving an additional dollar a week creates a savings of $1,378.

Put Away a Dollar a Day

If you're looking for extra money here and there, put aside a dollar bill daily (or transfer $7 into your savings account a week). You'll save $365 over the course of a year; that can cover your holiday shopping or maybe a weekend getaway.

Automatically Transfer $20 a Week

If you want an easy way to hit your goals, set up an automatic transfer of $20 to your savings. By putting aside $20 a week, you're saving almost $100 a month seamlessly without any effort. This strategy is an easy way to build an emergency fund of $1,000 by the end of the year.

Celebrate Paying Off Debt

Paying debt at an accelerated rate can be disheartening. Even though it's sped up, sometimes it feels like it'll never end (hello, student loans). So divide your debt payoff journey into milestones and then celebrate every time you hit one. Paid 10 percent off? Have a nice dinner. Stuck to your budget for a week? Get that coffee.

Never forget that you're worth celebrating. You deserve it.

REMEMBER

Visually Represent Progress toward Major Purchases

If you're a visual person, print off one of the hundreds of free trackers available online. These trackers assign amounts to different boxes or shapes that you can then color or mark off as you go. Seeing your progress all at once can help you assess your hard work so you keep going. Plus, it's fun.

Grab a pack of different colored sticky notes if coloring doesn't sound appealing. Assign a dollar amount to each note and then stick it up on the wall after you've saved that amount. Eventually, your sticky notes will start to accumulate, and you'll laugh.

TIP

Think about the outcome

If you're not a visual person, take time once a week to reflect on your financial goals and focus on the outcome. During this process, imagine how you'll feel once you've accomplished your goals. If saving for a vacation, think of the sights you'll see and the food you smell. If you want to pay off a credit card, imagine how you'll feel when you log into your credit card account and see a zero balance. By letting yourself feel your accomplishment momentarily, your brain will register that staying on track will get you to that goal.

Write a Recap of Your Accomplishments

If you're not a visual person, write yourself a recap. Sit down and think of everything you'd share with someone if they were sitting next to you and then write out all the things you've accomplished like you would a letter to a friend. Brag about your emergency fund and share how meaningful accomplishing it was to you. Describe the newfound cooking skills that helped you shed dollars off your restaurant budget. You'll be surprised by how excited you'll become (not to mention how kind you'll be) when you treat yourself like a good friend.

Index

About the Author

Athena Valentine Lent first learned the power of a budget in her early 20s. Once homeless when she was in high school, personal finance was not something her family taught or understood. After acing her own personal budget, she was able to go on to complete an associate's degree in criminal justice from the College of Southern Nevada. She then pursued a dual bachelor's degree in criminal justice and criminology from Arizona State University, as well as a counterterrorism certificate.

While serving the nonprofit sector for 20 years, Athena became passionate about financial representation for the Hispanic community after learning that other first- and second-generation Latinas lacked proper money management skills just like she once did. This passion led her to start the popular website Money Smart Latina and to advocate on issues such as the Latina wage gap and multigenerational housing.

Now Athena is an award-winning financial columnist for *Slate* magazine. Her work includes items for BuzzFeed, Prudential, Experian, T. Rowe Price, The College Investor, and Money Under 30, to name a few. She also serves as a community liaison for FinCon, an annual conference for content creators and brands in the financial industry.

When not working, you can find her reading a Stephen King novel with her main man, a polydactyl cat named Harrison George.

Dedication

"I want to thank me for believing in me. I want to thank me for doing all this hard work. I wanna thank me for having no days off. I wanna thank me for never quitting."

—Snoop Dogg, Walk of Fame acceptance speech

Author's Acknowledgments

First, I'd like to thank my dream team from Wiley: Tracy Boggier, Donna Wright, Megan Knoll, Vicki Adang, and Jana Lynch. Tracy sent an email that changed my life. Donna taught me about communication, Vicki helped me bring this book to you, Megan made me sound good, and Jana shared with me the Oxford comma.

Next, shout out to my editors Paola de Varona from *Slate* magazine and Megan Liscomb from BuzzFeed. I thank the team over at FinCon, Jessica Bufkin, Libby Gifford, and Tara Brown. I'd also like to shout out Phillip Taylor, who founded the conference that introduced me to the PF community. Moriah Chace held my hand the whole way, and J.D. Roth watched me grow.

I want to thank my support system, the Athena Hype Crew: Sandy Webb, Regina Alvarez, Gino Alvarez, Victoria Smith, Kandra Wiseman, Nicole Gorman, Jenny Spencer, Danielle McFarland, Shane Hand, John Carlson, Miranda Mexiner De-Wolf, Cody De-Wolf, Briana Ford, Trinetta Lipsey, and Ivon Castillo Galavan.

Thanks to my cat, Harrison George, for teaching me that I'm never alone and my dogs, Drifter and Annebelle Peaches. Shout out to my therapist for helping me gain the skills I needed to be where I am today.

Last but not least, I want to thank my fiancé, Josh Kalla. He didn't blink an eye when I quit my day job and put me on his health insurance. I love you, penguin.

Publisher's Acknowledgments

Senior Acquisitions Editor: Tracy Boggier
Project Editor: Donna Wright
Copy Editor: Megan Knoll
Technical Editor: Jana Lynch

Production Editor: Saikarthick Kumarasamy
Cover Image: © Africa Studio/Adobe Stock Photos

Take dummies with you everywhere you go!

Whether you are excited about e-books, want more from the web, must have your mobile apps, or are swept up in social media, dummies makes everything easier.

Find us online!

Leverage the power

Dummies is the global leader in the reference category and one of the most trusted and highly regarded brands in the world. No longer just focused on books, customers now have access to the dummies content they need in the format they want. Together we'll craft a solution that engages your customers, stands out from the competition, and helps you meet your goals.

Advertising & Sponsorships

Connect with an engaged audience on a powerful multimedia site, and position your message alongside expert how-to content. Dummies.com is a one-stop shop for free, online information and know-how curated by a team of experts.

- Targeted ads
- Video
- Email Marketing
- Microsites
- Sweepstakes sponsorship

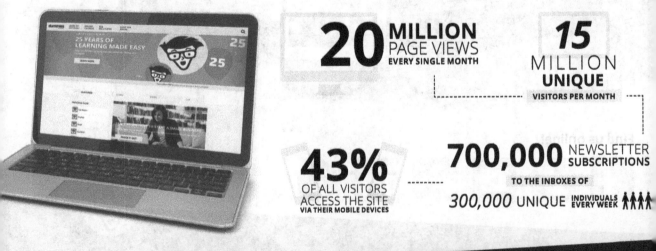

20 MILLION PAGE VIEWS EVERY SINGLE MONTH

15 MILLION UNIQUE VISITORS PER MONTH

43% OF ALL VISITORS ACCESS THE SITE VIA THEIR MOBILE DEVICES

700,000 NEWSLETTER SUBSCRIPTIONS TO THE INBOXES OF *300,000* UNIQUE INDIVIDUALS EVERY WEEK

PERSONAL ENRICHMENT

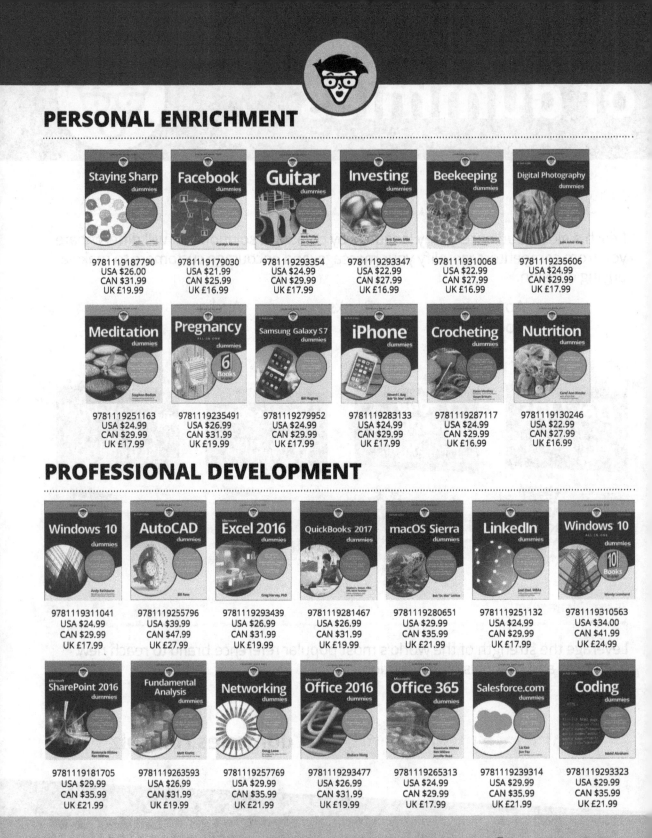

Staying Sharp dummies
9781119187790
USA $26.00
CAN $31.99
UK £19.99

Facebook dummies
Carolyn Abram
9781119179030
USA $21.99
CAN $25.99
UK £16.99

Guitar dummies
Mark Phillips, Jon Chappell
9781119293354
USA $24.99
CAN $29.99
UK £17.99

Investing dummies
Eric Tyson, MBA
9781119293347
USA $22.99
CAN $27.99
UK £16.99

Beekeeping dummies
Howland Blackiston
9781119310068
USA $22.99
CAN $27.99
UK £16.99

Digital Photography dummies
Julie Adair King
9781119235606
USA $24.99
CAN $29.99
UK £17.99

Meditation dummies
Stephan Bodian
9781119251163
USA $24.99
CAN $29.99
UK £17.99

Pregnancy All-in-One dummies
9781119235491
USA $26.99
CAN $31.99
UK £19.99

Samsung Galaxy S7 dummies
Bill Hughes
9781119279952
USA $24.99
CAN $29.99
UK £17.99

iPhone dummies
Edward C. Baig, Bob "Dr. Mac" LeVitus
9781119283133
USA $24.99
CAN $29.99
UK £17.99

Crocheting dummies
Karen Manthey, Susan Brittain
9781119287117
USA $24.99
CAN $29.99
UK £16.99

Nutrition dummies
Carol Ann Rinzler
9781119130246
USA $22.99
CAN $27.99
UK £16.99

PROFESSIONAL DEVELOPMENT

Windows 10 dummies
Andy Rathbone
9781119311041
USA $24.99
CAN $29.99
UK £17.99

AutoCAD dummies
Bill Fane
9781119255796
USA $39.99
CAN $47.99
UK £27.99

Excel 2016 dummies
Greg Harvey, PhD
9781119293439
USA $26.99
CAN $31.99
UK £19.99

QuickBooks 2017 dummies
Stephen L. Nelson, MBA, CPA, Aidan Nisbet
9781119281467
USA $26.99
CAN $31.99
UK £19.99

macOS Sierra dummies
Bob "Dr. Mac" LeVitus
9781119280651
USA $29.99
CAN $35.99
UK £21.99

LinkedIn dummies
Joel Elad, MBAs
9781119251132
USA $24.99
CAN $29.99
UK £17.99

Windows 10 All-in-One dummies
Woody Leonhard
9781119310563
USA $34.00
CAN $41.99
UK £24.99

SharePoint 2016 dummies
Rosemarie Withee, Ken Withee
9781119181705
USA $29.99
CAN $35.99
UK £21.99

Fundamental Analysis dummies
Matt Krantz
9781119263593
USA $26.99
CAN $31.99
UK £19.99

Networking dummies
Doug Lowe
9781119257769
USA $29.99
CAN $35.99
UK £21.99

Office 2016 dummies
Wallace Wang
9781119293477
USA $26.99
CAN $31.99
UK £19.99

Office 365 dummies
Rosemarie Withee, Ken Withee, Jennifer Reed
9781119265313
USA $24.99
CAN $29.99
UK £17.99

Salesforce.com dummies
Liz Kao, Jon Paz
9781119239314
USA $29.99
CAN $35.99
UK £21.99

Coding dummies
Nikhil Abraham
9781119293323
USA $29.99
CAN $35.99
UK £21.99

dummies.com

dummies®
A Wiley Brand